TRANSDIMENSIONAL MIND

"Chris H. Hardy offers us a creative and imaginative synthesis of how multilevel superconscious psi works. By integrating hyperdimensional and quantum theories, she articulates how the higher Self integrates psi perceptions with collective consciousness through a synchrony of minds and souls linked by telepathic harmony and world soul development. She also provides many examples of her own paranormal encounters and integrates a diverse range of psychic research, afterlife theory, and the roles of dreams and altered states. A rare and gifted ensemble! A remarkable tour de force!"

Lee Irwin, author of *Divine Feminine Gnosis*

"Chris H. Hardy is a long-standing intrepid trailblazer in the study of consciousness, and her *Transdimensional Mind* is no exception. Part memoir, part field report, and part new physics, this remarkable book provides readers with a road map to help them protect themselves from danger, dream about future events, develop their intuition, and attune themselves with animal allies and the Earth. Each chapter tells its own story, elevating readers' awareness and alerting them to capacities they barely knew existed."

Stanley Krippner, PhD, Emeritus Professor at Saybrook University, California, and author of *A Chaotic Life* and *The Voice of Rolling Thunder*

"As a researcher, I have been deeply engaged in the intersection of physics and consciousness for more than two decades. In Chris H. Hardy's *Transdimensional Mind*, I discovered a bold and intellectually stimulating contribution to the field. Hardy brings a rare combination of scientific literacy and experiential depth to her exploration of the higher Self as a hyperdimensional presence. Drawing on principles of nonlocality, energy fields, and quantum coherence, she presents a framework in which psi phenomena are not anomalies, but coherent expressions of an expanded model of mind. Her discussion of superposed landscapes, faster-than-light information transfer, and mind–matter interactions is both provocative and firmly rooted in rigorous research. This book challenges many reductionist assumptions and invites us to reconsider the very architecture of consciousness. It deserves thoughtful attention from scientists, scholars, and seekers alike."

Shelli Renée Joye, PhD, author of *The Metaverse of Consciousness* and *The Electromagnetic Brain*

TRANSDIMENSIONAL MIND

The Higher Self's Potential for Protection, Precognition, and Guidance

CHRIS H. HARDY, PhD

Bear & Company
Rochester, Vermont

Bear & Company
One Park Street
Rochester, Vermont 05767
www.BearandCompanyBooks.com

Bear & Company is a division of Inner Traditions International

Cataloging-in-Publication Data for this title is available from the Library of Congress

ISBN 978-1-59143-552-5 (print)
ISBN 978-1-59143-553-2 (ebook)

Printed and bound in the United States by Lake Book Manufacturing, LLC

10 9 8 7 6 5 4 3 2 1

Text design and layout by Debbie Glogover
This book was typeset in Garamond Premier Pro with Abolition, Agenda, Gill Sans MT Pro, and ITC Legacy Sans used as display typefaces

To send correspondence to the author of this book, mail a first-class letter to the author c/o Inner Traditions, One Park Street, Rochester, VT 05767, and we will forward the communication.

CONTENTS

List of Illustrations vii

Acknowledgments xi

✻

Introduction: Mulling Over Collective Intelligence and the Rise of Psi Talents 1

1 In Tune with Gaia and Our Deep Self 13

2 Self-Defense 31

3 Animal Allies 78

4 Anomalous Body 100

5 Fields of Synchronicities 118

6 The Power of Intent 149

7 Energy and Frequency Anomalies 177

8 Chakras Vibrating with Our HD Self 206

9 The "Superposed Landscape" Phenomenon 219

10 Hyperdimension, Sacred Volumes, and Earth's Grids 245

Conclusion: Intending a Soul-Harmonized and Eco-Friendly Planet 273

❋

Bibliography 275

Index 280

About the Author 288

LIST OF ILLUSTRATIONS

I.1. Naga King, Dashavatara Temple

2.1. *a.* Koh Lan island facing Pattaya Thailand (detail);
b. Thai fishing boats

2.2. Shiva androgyne, with Ganga flowing down from his ascetic bun

2.3. Statue of Shiva as a yogi, with bun and snake

3.1. Shiva lingam and yoni temple at Lepakshi

3.2. A sort of Pi gate as a bell hanger. Shiva temple within the Pashupatinath Temple complex

3.3. (*top*): Shiva-Pashupati seal, Mohenjo Daro, Indus Valley;
(*bottom*): Cernunnos with animals on the Gundestrup cauldron (detail)

3.4. Sumerian sun god Shamash with Anunnaki horns

3.5. Sambar deer in Thailand, with V-shaped antlers

3.6. Mercury/Hermes with caduceus

3.7. Unicornfish-rider on the eighteen-hundred-year-old Gundestrup cauldron

3.8. (*top*): Narwhal shape and size;
(*bottom*): The orangespine unicornfish

3.9. Rock formation near the Queen's Bath, Hampi

4.1. Mural of Tlaloc paradise (Tlalocan), Palacia de Tepantitla, Teotihuacan, Mexico

4.2. Map of Ancient Egypt: the Nile up to the Fifth Cataract
4.3. Precinct of Mut, nested in its sacred lake, at Karnak temple
4.4. Hypostyle Hall at Karnak Temple in Luxor.
4.5. Sunset over the Nile from Sherari Island, Dar al-Manasir, Fourth Cataract
4.6. Calanque of Sormiou-Cassis, Côte d'Azur, France
4.7. Whirling Dervishes: Statue of Mevlana (Rumi) in Buca, İzmir, Turkey
5.1. A Pi gate: the Hindu torana at the Fort of Warangal, India
5.2. Pi gates on the façade of Angkor Wat, Cambodia
5.3. The Gate of the Gods: Kamiiṣo-no-Torii at Oarai Isosaki Jinja shrine, Japan
5.4. Spontaneous candle-wax sculptures during writing
5.5. Sun god Helios, stone relief
5.6. Archetype of the eternal youth Hermes/Mercury: *The Genius of Liberty*
5.7. Vaishnava sadhu in Kathmandu with locks falling to the ground and an Urdhva Pundra mark on his forehead.
5.8. The Hindu dholak drum
7.1. The electromagnetic spectrum
7.2. The higher chakras and their energy field
7.3. Chladni vibration patterns on a sand-covered plate
7.4. Chladni six-point-star pattern on a triangular plate
7.5. *a–c.* Chladni base-4 mandalas of increasing complexity with the frequency rising
7.6. Kekulé's daydream vision of the structure of benzene as an Ouroboros
7.7. A sixteenth-century woodcut of Archimedes's eureka moment
7.8. A Klein bottle
9.1. The subtle resonance of my altar stones in the hyperdimension's layers

9.2. *The Flight of the Pi*
9.3. *The Flight of the Pi.* Detail of Meteora
9.4. Eye of Ra, Egypt
9.5. Pauli's World Clock dream sculpted in wax in my candelabra and its ad hoc interpretation
10.1. The Great Pyramid of Giza in March 2005
10.2. The soul or *ba*, as the deceased-headed bird, exiting the dead mummified body
10.3. Platonic sacred volumes in Kepler's solar system model
10.4. Magnetic field lines around a bar magnet
10.5. *a–b.* Electric fields
10.6. Crossing of four cosmo-telluric lines undulating vertically
10.7. Pauli's Deep Reality dream
10.8. Two-center geodesic Roman mosaic floor, second century CE
10.9. Checkerboard representation of a field of particles with alternating focus

COLOR PLATES

1. *Princess Bari Holding the Flower of Resurrection*
2. Double aura of Padmasambhava, seated in his pure paradise
3. The Tuatha Dé Danann as depicted in John Duncan's *The Riders of the Sidhe*
4. (*top*): Vaishnava sadhu in Kathmandu;
   (*bottom*): Shaiva sadhu in Varanasi
5. Celtic god Cernunnos with stag horns and unicornfish-rider (Gundestrup cauldron)
6. Granite boulders of Matanga Hill, Hampi
7. (*top* and *bottom*): Temple of Amon in Luxor city, Egypt
8. Thoth-Hermes, god of knowledge and science, with an ibis head
9. Hypostyle Hall at Karnak Temple in Luxor

10. The Nile River near the Fourth Cataract: Dar al-Manasir
11. Calanques of Sugiton, Morgiou, and Riou Island
12. The Exotic Garden in Eze
13. *Whirling Dervishes* by Jean-Léon Gérôme
14. Japanese torii (Ryobu style) at Itsukushima Shrine
15. Torana at Sanchi stupa, Satavahana period
16. Singing pillars of Vittala Temple, Hampi
17. Teotihuacan, Pyramid of the Sun, Mexico
18. The Great Goddess of Teotihuacan
19. Kukai, "Child Grand Master," flying to heaven on a lotus
20. Meteora, Greece. Striking monasteries atop stone pillars

ACKNOWLEDGMENTS

I want to acknowledge with this book the two main sources of knowledge who have illuminated my path of exploration and have inspired and guided me toward discoveries and accomplishments that I hadn't even fathomed could happen in my life. Namely, Gaia, the alive flame of our collective consciousness breathing through the whole of Nature and our planet. And my own Self, with whom I had a direct communication since the very beginning of my quester's path and who acted as my true ally and inner guide.

My heartfelt gratitude to my publisher, Ehud Sperling, and to Jon Graham and Christian Schweiger for welcoming this book and for their support in launching it.

Finally, I want to express my thanks and deep appreciation to the whole team at Inner Traditions for their professional talent and great synergy, especially Jeanie Levitan, Kelly Bowen, Beth Wojiski, Aaron Davis, Kayla Toher, and the ubiquitous gate-opener Manzanita Carpenter-Sanz.

INTRODUCTION

MULLING OVER COLLECTIVE INTELLIGENCE AND THE RISE OF PSI TALENTS

When I first had the idea, a few years back, of gathering in a book the strangest psi experiences I had lived so far, I intended it to strengthen my spiritual focus and give me courage during a very stressful period for me at both the personal and geopolitical levels. My rationale was that, by remembering what my Self and my own conscious mind had been able to accomplish factually and in the real world, it would give me wings and boost my confidence not only in what I personally could strive for but also in what we could expect our collective consciousness to undertake. I was already coping with this tumultuous period by doing a lot of meditation and visualizations, as well as regular antistress laughing interludes with online stand-up comedians.

Moreover, I thought that writing such a book (or at least a first volume) would enhance and supercharge my own psychic energy and give me more Self-power and resilience; these were the very soul qualities that all decent and responsible persons drastically needed in order for us to thwart the constant attacks on our values and integrity, on international humanitarian and rights groups, and on democracy and the rule of law, and moreover to avoid being swept uncontrollably into whatever heart-wrenching catastrophe or crisis was the order of the day. And indeed, it is an exercise in collective intelligence that we all go through, while tightening our immaterial interpersonal bonding to fortify our resolve and inventive strategy.

In dire straits, the individual Self improvises . . . how much more the Selfs of all sensitive people concerned! Thus, a new awareness is kindled within the collective unconscious—the deep reality through which all our psyches are interconnected between them and with all the living.

This interconnectedness, at a basic level, prompts personal synchronicities—the meaningful coincidences we experience. But, working at a higher level, the collective intelligence adds a dose of synchrony between kindred minds, an accord and a rallying in shared values. With the collective fabric thus expanded and vibrating in sync, it confronts the problems and threats to our societies and the planet and creates solutions that are both incredibly innovative and mightily efficient.

What is at stake is the Earth's soul conquering and mastering the primitive dominator, despotic and sadistic instincts that are body-driven and egomaniacal. In brief, this is a mind-over-might challenge for humanity. No wonder then that, in this battle, women and minorities have been standing up magnificently, at all levels and positions. But make no mistake, the solution will be achieved by the collective intelligence of all humans who exemplify the soft power of spirit, benevolence, and protection of lives; they will be raising themselves at the forefront because humanity's life and spirit, and the Earth's soul, are at stake.

This mind over might has been a personal challenge for me since I awoke to meditation and my own Self at eighteen. For a dozen years, I read in earnest loads of ancient and modern treatises about spirituality, esoterica, Kabbalah, fringe science, and the like—this in between years of travels in India, the global East, and Africa, penniless, without luggage, and mostly barefoot. All these readings—especially the Indian and Tibetan treatises on meditation and the yogic path, and the biographies of yogis (such as Yogananda, Vivekananda, Milarepa, Padmasambhava)—infused in me the deep certitude that, as concerning yogis, great masters, and saints, *the awakened mind was immensely more powerful than all physical and instrumental powers.*

Let me point out that this is where the Eastern lore differs fundamentally from the Western lore: the Eastern philosophy deems that all humans can develop mind-powers of the highest order on the condition that they work on themselves relentlessly. In contrast, in the West, until quite recently, the skeptics (both the rationalists and the religious bigots) were claiming that psi powers were just fraud, and that they were the work of hubris and/or the devil and would lead one to wreck one's life or to hell no less—unless one was a recognized saint/master (within their own creed only). I've also witnessed that many spiritualists and members of esoteric fraternities were deeply averse to psi capacities and self-development, as they only clung to a rich transmitted tradition of craftsmanship, sacred architecture and geography, and, of course, symbolism; most had long lost, in my view, the capacity to experience such personal mind feats. Apart from notable exceptions (such as enthusiasts in the research sphere and the publishing and media worlds), many went on repeating a dire warning: "Humanity is not yet ready!"

However for those of us in our late teens or early twenties, psychic energy and psi were already part of our daily lives and a new dimension of reality was open for us—a definite rebuttal of their warnings by tangible and recurrent facts. We were already experiencing a range of anomalous phenomena; meditation and heightened states were enhancing our perception of another layer of reality. There was definitely a world, another dimension altogether, beyond what our materialist science and pundits had rationally mapped.

Yet at one point, in my late twenties, I faced a stark and troubling acknowledgment: I was absolutely convinced the sages of old were right and authentic when they described indomitable spiritual powers and psi capacities (or *siddhis*). Yet India, with its venerable and fecund religious lore (Hindu, Buddhist, Sikh, Jain, Islam, and more), as well as its awesome antique science (astronomy, medicine, and philosophy), was unable to avert being colonized by the British Empire for nearly a century (1858–1947). And I was seeing countries mostly populated by great monks and wise men, such as Tibet, Myanmar (ancient Burma), and Cambodia, falling prey to military and/or authoritarian regimes, at an immense human and spiritual cost. Among them, India was the only country to have gained its independence through mind-power, that of Mahatma Gandhi—who was an adept at meditation and often undertook hunger strikes as a political wedge; Gandhi led three nationwide protests, in 1920–22, 1930–34, and 1942, that finally achieved India's independence. As for the other spiritually focused countries, obviously, and despite age-old claims, their yogis, monks, and wise men (even collectively) hadn't had the mind-power necessary to resist the military and/or technological might of despots, colonialists, and terrorists of all types. That was a problem for me. Were the greatest psi and mind capacities no match for scheming dictators and hard metal armaments? Or were we not up to the task yet (or *again*)?

To be honest, I now remember that the Chinese Book of Changes—the I-Ching—has, as one of its 64 × 2 × 6 situations, one in which a "noble heart" (a sage quester) is constrained and without influence at the court of a despot, and he is advised patience in waiting for another cycle of time by the book. As if this greatly superior mind of the Taoist sage couldn't overwhelm, or at least rein in, the limited, egomaniacal, gaslighting, and greedy mind of the tyrant, and this for decades. Thus, the traditional idea of siddhis being outstanding derived mostly from the Indian lore!

As time went on, new countries were being subdued by force. My reaction to these dire geopolitical facts was "Yes, certainly the sages of great antiquity have displayed and observed in themselves such eminent mind-power. . . . Yet is that enough to protect a country? Clearly, many sages and whole peoples have also been subdued by tyrannical forces."

This was the case for Padmasambhava, an Indian yogic and tantric master (of the highest *mahasiddha* stature) who brought the Tantra

Buddhism to Tibet at the end of the eighth century. While some of his feats are inflated by legend, others, relating to the mastery of specific mind capacities, cannot be just imagined.

Padmasambhava, deemed a Buddha, had the gift of seeing and conversing with the local nature spirits (little devas); he rallied them to be the protectors of Buddhism—including the mysterious Naga Queen and King, a Royal Cobra lineage of wise and superconscious beings, with a human torso and the lower body of a serpent (see fig. I.1). The Nagas were revered as instructors of secret tantric, or mind-power, science and protectors of the sages. This tradition exists in several cultures, starting with Enki in Sumer (in some depictions), the cobra deities as allies in Khmer religion, and Typhon, son of Gaia, in ancient Greece.

Fig. I.1. Naga King, Dashavatara Temple; sixth century CE (Deogarh, Uttar Pradesh, India)
Photo by Bob King

At the time, the awakening of my whole generation to their inner Self gave me hope we would someday achieve such *mind-stronger-than-armament* and that we would manage to finally install a wise and soul-searching cooperation and synergy among nations and disarm the whole planet.

Were we not, since the mid-sixties, in a collective awakening cycle? Were we not (I and others I knew as well) able to perform psi feats that many traditions and lines of great masters had lost sight of for centuries? Were we not the living witnesses that some (at least) of these siddhis were real and efficient—able to change the stuff of material reality, even if minutely?

It was dire evidence that, unfortunately, the older generation of modern sages and initiates had lost the knowledge and mind-power to perform the age-old feats. Then it was up to new phoenix generations of gifted questers, bent on learning and reawakening ancient wisdom paths and psi abilities, to work intensely on ourselves to reach that aim, both personally and collectively. We should be the ones to strive to achieve a collective intelligence and shared intent that could stall and ultimately defeat the despotic and unchecked drives of leaders in our human societies! In fact, even when these principles were enshrined in laws and constitutions, the thrust for them to remain or to become a reality had to be mental first.

Meanwhile a magisterial effort was undertaken in all societal domains to infuse in our societies the defense of human rights and the international law-based order, accountability, oversight, and transparency, as well as the fight against climate disaster by numerous worldwide NGOs and organizations. It was also crucial for multinational organizations, especially the United Nations, to strive to become central actors and deciders, as well as lawmakers, in the geopolitical arena, provided they promoted the international rule of law.

By now and in the same vein, at top speed and yet sans fanfare, our societal paradigm is reinventing itself to be in accord with the necessity to save the planet and therefore to adjust and harmonize all our rules and business behaviors to the green revolution, just as it had for some years been prioritizing a large spectrum of human rights.

As for me, I settled on a middle path. I decided to trust the ancient and pervasive ways of wisdom, because they were a real practical and experiential learning path from which I had received amazing gifts, and because this path never fed me with fixed ideas and encysted beliefs, nor did it ever constrain my freedom. And simultaneously, I was going to find ways to prove to myself that it was indeed possible for the Spirit and the Selfs to be stronger than brute force.

I made it a challenge, an oath taken with myself, that I would labor ceaselessly for it. This is how I ardently explored the spiritual and psi capacities that emerged spontaneously on my path, inciting and pushing myself to further expand, diversify, or deepen them. I was also memorizing and analyzing all psi anomalies I was experiencing in order to better understand this dimension of the Self—a superconsciousness and psi potentials that are the inner treasure each person can tap into.

I was the seat of recurrent psi phenomena of a variety of types, to the point it was a continuous stream of anomalous events being superposed to my daily life. In fact, these psi perceptions, anomalous events, and spiritual states were so deeply and congenially entwined with my conscious experience, like a depth dimension, that no particular event ever plunged me into fear or confusion. To the contrary, any foreboding or perception of danger triggered a shift to a heightened state, in which my Self would take the reins. As a result, no anomaly drew more out of me, as a response, than a careful attention to details and to the unfolding situation, in order to learn more from them and to be able to compare them later.

All in all, it showed me that the Self and psi were real and could exhibit factual tangible strength, so much so that one could just envision them to be honed into becoming so powerful as to defeat or outmaneuver brute force. I made that my mantra.

Of course, I was aware that individual psi feats didn't in the least reach the strength needed to protect a whole country from being invaded in the first place, or to get back on its feet if it had been overtaken by an autocratic regime, either domestic or foreign. That would necessitate tapping into a harmonized collective intelligence field honed with a momentous strength in both intent and vision.

I believe that now the world clock is set on the ultimate test of a planetary-wide and synchronized collective intelligence, intent on pacifying Earth so that we may address the climate turmoil endangering the very future of our planet and thus humanity.

As I was turning thirty, my work was still focused on the exploration of consciousness within myself, but now I added the scientific research, and as soon as I had passed and digested my doctorate, I dove into theory building.

Driven by this keen intent to unravel the deep reality of consciousness, I was regularly experiencing new leaps—a threshold would be passed, a new capacity would suddenly blossom. These were often centered on either a spiritual state or a psi capacity; yet the most unexpected leaps for me were those happening in the intellectual and theoretical research sphere. For example, the writing of a sci-fi book on artificial intelligence, *Butterfly Logic*, triggered a leap in intellectual complexity, such that it forced me to upgrade my theory of mind—*Semantic Fields Theory*, SFT—which was still in its early pre-publication stages.

More precisely, as I turned thirty, I had gone through a life-turning change and had decided to devote myself to scientific research on consciousness and psi (and years after a master's degree in sociology, to pursue a doctorate in ethnology on the subject, which then led me to be a researcher at the Psychophysical Research Laboratories in Princeton, New Jersey). It was only a decade later that I endeavored to build SFT—a theory of mind, consciousness, and psi diverging from the obsolete cognitivist paradigm. I was using systems theory, chaos theory, and transpersonal and Jungian psychology to map the mind as dynamical and evolving networks (called *semantic fields* or, in short, *syg-fields*).

Let me note here that through my wide-spectrum interest in science, especially the cognitive and parapsychology frameworks, I was becoming acutely aware of two facts. The first one was that our current scientific concepts and theories were desperately unable to integrate and explain, or even address, the spiritual and psi phenomena we were experiencing. (And the worst part is that it is still that way, as only Jungian psychology has integrated psi to date.) The second was that our individual lives were severely constrained by the societal reality (with its various organizations and information technology sphere), which itself was deeply shaped and restrained by our scientific paradigm. As a case in point, most psi researchers were convinced that until a theory of psi gained wide scientific acceptance (and that meant beyond psychology), all our experimental and laboratory results would not be accepted as proofs.

In fact, the psi capacities of our mind and higher consciousness, the Self (soul, solar angel), as I had experienced them for years, reached well beyond our spacetime laws and limits. This was especially evident with the mental capacities to foresee the future and have precognitive dreams (precognition), to receive clear telepathic thoughts, or to get in sync with other minds in a telepathic-harmonic field (or *Telhar field*). (We'll see various examples of those psi feats in this book.) A cognitive theory had now to integrate these psi capacities as the new normal of people becoming sensitives all over the planet.

Psi capacities contradict thoroughly the electromagnetic and spacetime laws (hence the stubborn skepticism and denial of most scientists). Even more crucially, the psi and spiritual experiences I lived couldn't be explained without an *energy* of consciousness, one able to tinker with our material world, modify events and objects (as in psychokinesis or PK), reorganize subtle biological systems (as in healing), or even give a powerful blow to an aggressor (as we'll see). And this energy of consciousness had to be of a higher dimension (or manifold) than the matter and spacetime manifold. I called it *semantic energy* or, in short, *syg-energy*—the meaning-creative energy of our higher Self. Since both our Self and syg-energy operate in the *semantic dimension*—beyond space and time, unconstrained by the light-speed limit—they can organize synchronicities, the meaningful coincidences through which our own Self sends us signs and guidance.

Another such conceptual-logical leap happened to me when, in 2012, I elaborated a cosmology based on cosmic consciousness (the realm of all the Selfs) as a *hyperdimension* existing before the Big Bang (the inflation phase) and both surrounding and pervading our matter universe (the 4D spacetime). Syg-energy, the energy of the Self orchestrating psi feats, was now the hyperdimensional mode of communication and operation that could override the matter laws. (At the time I'm writing this, I'm now advancing, step by step, my modeling of the diverse psi and spiritual feats I was able to witness firsthand.)

Yet I know that the mind capacities I've discovered so far (and those I'm still discovering) are only tiny windows enabling me to glimpse into the vast unknown reaches of the hyperdimension of the Selfs—that is, cosmic consciousness—itself in continual evolution through the Selfs that constitute it.

Indeed, the most astounding aspect of both our individual and collective consciousness is the fact that they are not fixed. Consciousness is an experiment-in-the-making, forever evolving with the exploration endeavored by a whole people and by creative individuals as well. Consciousness is like the stuff of art: it is molded and arranged, experienced and expressed, over and over again; then it blossoms at a new level at very special moments, in great waves of change, such as the one humanity is going through right now, and especially when the better soul of humanity has to fight for its principles and values, for its very expression, freedom, and future evolution; and then it concocts, for achieving it, a new leap in collective intelligence, such as now. If we make it (and I don't doubt we will), we'll find ourselves on a totally new level, on a new path of humanity's mind and psi capacities, closer, each of us, to our own soul and to our collective Self, the One-field, the Earth's soul, Gaia.

With this book, I intend to give you a taste of what kind of feats our personal Self can achieve—in real time and in the real world—when we keep working on ourselves along whatever inner paths of self-development we have chosen. As soon as you take such a path, provided you avoid any indoctrination and fixated creed, you will see psi potentials emerge effortlessly in your life, some being quite stunning and surprisingly efficient.

It is the unrelenting contact and rapprochement between our ego (our physical and social persona) and our inner Self—during meditation, creation, altered states—that enables the Self to suddenly take the reins of our life to protect us from an accident, or an aggressor.

I now know that it was my own Self, or more precisely the fusion ego-Self, that steered and effected most of the weird events and psi feats that I'll recount in this book; but the way I ascertained this was by mulling on them and, especially, comparing them. However, gathering for this book the most perplexing feats I had lived, some from decades ago, turned out to be a unique opportunity. When I started to compare them anew—now with a solid foundation and a new paradigm in cosmology and hyperphysics—I was bursting with new insights about our Self's modus operandi and capacities, which I will share with you. And lastly, it led me to some new discoveries as to the nature of the hyperdimension and how our hyperdimensional Self can influence, and tinker with, our physical world. This will be particularly discussed in the last chapter.

Let me give you a quick overview of the book chapters.

The first chapter shows how we can penetrate the magic of the Earth-Soul, as an art of globe-trotting, and the soft influence of our own Self in concocting key events in our life.

In the second, we'll explore how, despite being a soft power, our

Self can deliver blows as hard as a boxer's punch and masterly ensure our self-defense.

The third recounts a shamanic connivance with animal allies and how they suddenly manifest themselves to help us.

In the fourth, we'll discover that when in a deep trance state, the body reacts differently to shock, without pain or bruise.

The fifth is devoted to the fascinating phenomenon of synchronicities or, precisely, fields of them; when a cluster of visions and dreams predicts a journey and a future momentous event, even to its precise date.

In the sixth, I'll show the real power of intent—accomplishing our conscious goal even if the Self has to manipulate reality in hard-to-believe ways.

The seventh will ponder anomalies in frequencies to understand the nature of our energy-body performing out-of-body experiences; we'll also explore the interaction between electromagnetic waves and the hyperdimensional syg-energy. And it will reveal a higher dimensionality to sound and music.

In the eighth, I'll recount mysterious, yet recurrent, experiences of vibrating chakras and explore the Self's role in them.

In the ninth, we'll zoom in on the "superposed landscape" phenomenon—a strange superposition of the immaterial realm with the spacetime one, during two social gatherings, one a spiritual rally and the other a burial service; we'll see the superposition of sacred objects as well, inviting us to mull on a layered hyperdimension.

The tenth focuses on sacred volumes and the "waves of form" that they produce—a property of hyperspace; I'll relate my repeated visions of a grid on the sky in sacred places, and discuss their relationship and similarity with other types of proposed Earth's grids. This in turn leads to some insight about a checkerboard structure of the hyperdimension pervading our matter world.

1
IN TUNE WITH GAIA AND OUR DEEP SELF

Psi capacities do not emerge out of the blue and they are not sustained or improved unless the individuals work on themselves with whatever array of self-development techniques they choose. Even a naturally gifted person can only extend and diversify these skills if they nurture a strong link to their higher Self—our inner guide and personal solar angel residing in the hyperdimension of souls (in short, the HD). The fact is, both spiritual and psi talents are rooted in our hyperdimensional Self, and the stronger and more resilient the connection between our ego and our own Self, the more capacities will emerge in our lives, in the safest and most beneficial way for us and for others.

This is a person who has managed many leaps into their own self-development who is talking to you. And the sudden awakening of my own psi talents was triggered by my enthusiastic practice of meditation and fervent reading of ancient yoga treatises at eighteen. But before that, I used to write poetry when immersed in a deep communion with nature, to the point where I could sense the living spirits of trees and flowers. And I loved this secret bonding and nurtured that fusion state however I could. This is surely why, when I started meditation, I immediately opened states of deep harmony with the soul dimension—and suddenly I was able to see the energy of consciousness, what I call the semantic or syg-energy. That of course rendered me conscious not only of the way it manifests and interacts with our energy-body and chakras but also how it influences our social persona.

While this soul-to-soul communion is not recognized as a spiritual or a psi talent, I regard it now as the fertile ground out of which many other talents may blossom. Indeed, I can spot it as the decisive factor operating at many levels; notably, between minds in telepathy and telepathic-harmonic (Telhar) fields; as a mind-molecular synchrony in healing; and in mind-over-matter or PK capacities.

The concept of Gaia, referring to the Earth seen as a whole ecological and synergic system, was developed in the late 1970s by James Lovelock in his book *Gaia: A New Look at Life on Earth.* It was itself rooted in a new paradigm introduced by Ludwig von Bertalanffy in 1968 that saw the world as complex interwoven systems and not individual mechanical objects anymore. For Lovelock, the Earth was an organic system, thus part of the living, and as such Gaia was able to self-organize and tune herself to sustain its own living conditions. However, this concept had its roots in the alchemic and Hermetic philosophy's assumption that our planet had a soul, called World-Soul, which they understood as belonging to the divine realm and infusing all matter systems and living organisms (see Hardy 2024). Their concept of World-Soul meets Jung's concept of *collective unconscious* (or "objective psyche"), which refers to our humanity's transpersonal and shared psychic and archetypal roots (and a reservoir of immense knowledge), which remains unconscious until the individual embarks on a path of ego-Self harmonization (Jung's *individuation process*).

In my life, this soul-to-soul communion triggered an astonishing new emergence when I started hitchhiking through sub-Sahel Africa, and I began to harmonize my spirit with the spirit of Gaia, our Earth-Soul.

PROTECTED BY GAIA: THE MAGIC OF THE EARTH AND THE ART OF GLOBE-TROTTING

I started hitchhiking around France when I was sixteen years old, and at seventeen, I pulled off a memorable escape from a mind-numbing, awfully boring stay in Hamburg, in the north of Germany, where I was supposed to attend German classes all day long and was set to endure in the evenings a narrow-minded old lady, for a whole month. After not even five days, I had had more than enough of it. I persuaded another student, a Swiss girl my age whom I had befriended, to cross Germany, hitchhiking all the way to Munich in the south. We took the decision to leave the next morning.

That same day, on arriving at the old lady's house in the evening, I told her I wanted to call my parents, who had planned to drive and meet me in Hamburg at the end of my stay, as part of their holidays, and together we would drive back to Paris. My parents being renowned caterers in Paris (among the kings of chefs), I knew how to put them on my side. Complaining about the boring and useless classes (no reaction so far), I added to my father and my mother listening, "And on top of that the only thing she gives me to eat, lunch and dinner alike, is the same dish of cold pork charcuterie. My parents were horror-struck: "Comment! Comment!" they both erupted. They agreed immediately to my plan. I told them that instead of meeting in Hamburg, we would meet that same day of our appointment, the thirtieth, in Munich instead, hmm . . . at noon in front of the central post office.

On the road we went, freewheeling and happy. We had a fantastic trip discovering Germany, with so little money we had to sleep in barns incognito along the way.

That morning of the thirtieth, in Munich, after more than three weeks of wandering together, I had said good-bye to my road pal, letting her go all the way back to Switzerland alone, without any qualms—

first because we both had become very daring and carefree, and second because I'd have done it myself without any problem.

Forward a dozen years, and a woman in her thirties approached the podium table at the end of a lecture I was giving in Paris and revealed she was my old road pal. We went to have a drink and as she confided to me, it didn't turn out that well for her. When she indeed reached her home in Geneva, she had the whole of Interpol looking for her and her father locked her up in her room for a couple of months after that. Unimaginably for me, not all parents were treating their adolescent children as responsible adults like mine were. (I wish I had at least asked her if she had called and told her parents as I had done, and of course my own parents wouldn't have objected to taking her back to Geneva on our way and dealing with her parents. I had been really stupid.)

Then, that same year, I started residing more and more often in the largely unused country house of my parents in Igny, a far-south suburb of Paris. As I wasn't the legal age to have a driving license yet, I used to hitch my way back and forth. It was in this house that I got involved in ancient Eastern treatises and shamanic lore and started teaching myself meditation. When I finally got my driving license at eighteen—as soon as it was legally feasible—it didn't change what had become a fixture in my way of life, since the old and defective car I inherited kept breaking down, leaving me stranded on the road regularly. The following three years, while studying at Sorbonne, then Vincennes University (Paris-VIII) for a bachelor's degree, I felt so free and eager to discover the world that every now and then around the full moon I would hit the road, alone or with some friends, sometimes driving my old car, more often than not on hitchhiking sprees.

The first thing I became aware of, in these hitchhiking journeys of two or three days, was that I was prone to meeting people harboring similar interests and a spiritual outlook. My conversations with the drivers who had given me a lift ranged from spiritism to physics to sacred places.

Among memorable cases were a driver who belonged to a spiritualist group and introduced me to one of their healing rituals in a church where he was heading, and in which I took part; and another driver who dropped me at St. Blandine Church in Lyon so that I could visit what he had described as a very esoteric place, while he managed an hour-long appointment with a client, and then fetched me there to take me a few hundred miles farther on his way south.

Furthermore, I acquired a knack and never waited more than five minutes for a lift, even when, in subsequent years, I roamed across the worst dirt roads in Africa or deserted roads in India. In the rare exceptions that saw me stuck on a road in France, there was absolutely no traffic at that hour.

I felt secure and protected by this attraction of similar minds, but at the core, my meditation practice gave me the utter confidence that my guide, my higher Self, was keeping me safe. This notwithstanding, I developed an acute sense of the psychology of the drivers—systematically male—who picked me up. In the rare glitches due to dire circumstances, like being stranded on a deserted road at night and given a lift by drunkards, I would devise ad hoc psychological tricks and successfully manage a graceful exit.

Hitchhiking with little or no money, especially in developing countries, is a great way to learn a range of skills. In the early times of globe-trotters, when only rare hippies would hit the wild roads, we were deemed outsiders to any social order, and thus social rules didn't apply to us. Even in this time of heavy tourism and worldwide backpackers, local people tend to project their own nature on the foreigners without any withholding, as if they were unconstrained by their usual social and moral bindings. The good man will be kind to strangers, the scholar will set up a learned exchange, the robber will try to take something even from the poorest backpacker, and the cruel and vicious men will try to corner and rape lonely women. The road is a teaching in crude and unchecked behaviors unrestrained by any fear of being caught. And so, as a globe-trotter, you quickly learn how to build up a permanent but relaxed alertness, that soon extends into a refined foresight of people's behaviors.

In a matter of a few weeks on the road, any hitchhiker has already reached an acute and constant sense of their surroundings—animals, humans, and the environment. This is akin to a 360-degree attention range, at any instant. Without ever looking left, right, or around, you know, when you are in a coffee shop, where everybody is, what their movements are, and each person's mindset.

One does that by extending one's "body of sensation" and psi listening to the whole room, or, if you are outdoors, to the space around in a large circle of a few hundred yards. This enlarged field of receptivity, beyond noting instantly any posture and movement, has also a hyperawareness state and a telepathic component. It catches any abnormal attention given to you even from a distance, any ulterior motives or schemes directed at you, thus giving you ample time to change your plans and get out of harm's way. To describe it more precisely, I would say that it's definitely an extended field of energy—constituted of the subtle energy of consciousness, semantic or syg-energy* (as I call it in my theoretical work). This extended syg-field opens itself like an umbrella, spontaneously, in any crowded or unsecure situation, about thirty to forty yards around oneself (or taking a whole hall). And on the road, I had ample proofs that it was deployed continuously around me, day and night, even while I slept, and that it encompassed a far greater distance (more on this soon).

After a few years of traveling, this extended field of awareness has become like an instinctive behavior. Even while drunk at a cozy social gathering, you'll have an excruciating awareness of each and every person's moves and their feelings. A funny but handy practical application is the detection of any movement of the tiniest bug. For example, one

*I coined the term *semantic energy* (in short, syg-energy) to designate the energy of consciousness (nonlocal and hyperdimensional); and the derived term *semantic field* (*syg-field*) as a field constituted of syg-energy and organized by the mind, whether consciously, as in psi phenomena, or unconsciously.

afternoon in India, I was sitting cross-legged on a cushion on the tile floor of the terrace of my rented house, fully absorbed in studying an ancient Vedanta text. Nevertheless, I detected the move of a one-inch small scorpion of a light color, normally undistinguishable from the large tile floor, that had just moved from the low wall on the other side of the terrace, about ten feet away. Strangely, it was scurrying along a diagonal line straight toward me, who knows why; but I got on my feet instantly and had ample time to brush it away.

IN TUNE WITH GAIA: A SERENDIPITY PATH

I don't remember ever deciding to practice this protective and extended syg-field, or ever consciously planning for it. If the situation feels even a tiny bit strange, the umbrella just opens and I find myself in a hyperaware and hypervigilant state.

In contrast, I remember clearly that on one or two occasions, I did some protective visualization before falling asleep in the wild on a simple Indian longyi, in sub-Sahel Africa. I projected the strong intent that I would wake up instantly if an individual or a beast were to trespass a circle of six feet around me. And indeed it worked perfectly and became such a fixture that it was still active a decade later, to my own embarrassment when it was triggered by my life companion.

On this first trip through Africa, in which I hitchhiked for nine months from the South of France, to Tangier in Morocco (in the Strait of Gibraltar), and all the way to Mombasa in Kenya, I willingly created another sort of widely extended syg-field. I did this in Mauritania when I left the desert and reached the savannah region in the far south, and then in Mali. Having decided that I was not going to hitchhike back through the Sahara desert to return to France, I then shifted my global aim to going back to India by crossing sub-Sahel Africa all the way to the Indian Ocean. At that point, I knew I would have to cross through wild regions of tropical savannahs and equatorial rainforests. I was cheerfully barefoot and without any money, with just a small bag across my shoulder. How was I to make things safe for me? I had a sudden insight.

I reflected that if I was maintaining a strong empathic connection with the Earth (as a conscious entity, Gaia), then she would protect me from any harm from animals or nature, and even from human beings—whom, I pondered, she could certainly control in such natural village settings. I couldn't fathom her to have this ability in cities, in which her presence is hardly felt through the thick layers of concrete. This is maybe why, during this whole trip, I resolutely kept out of cities, generally crossing them right away as quickly as possible, up to the two last ones, Nairobi and Mombasa, where I got stuck for quite a while before I could manage to cross the ocean.

I remember that, during this first musing, I was standing on a dirt road, a piste, ready to start hitchhiking that day. I started to invoke the Earth, and created an empathic link with her as a spirit residing in the landscape, within the very ground I was treading on. Around the dust road was a large expanse of trees and bushes, with occasional houses and huts. I expanded my consciousness over that landscape, and deep within the ground, all the while talking to Gaia, asking her total protection from any harm from nature or beings. And while doing so, I felt immediately confident that she would indeed protect me *for as long as I was keeping in touch with her.* This prayer I did only once, but in contrast I was very keen to keep expanding my consciousness to that of Gaia and to the whole landscape around me as well as the road ahead toward my next destination. It became a permanent state of attunement with the Earth that, as I was surrounded by natural settings unbroken by buildings and crowds, was just spread around me. As far as I could consciously feel it, it was in the range of one hundred miles. And indeed, this syg-field worked miracles, as I didn't encounter any obstacle nor any problem that I couldn't solve on the spot during this whole trip of about seven months in deep Africa (beyond the previous two months I took to cross North Africa's Sahel region).

Of course, the connection to the living Earth—as a state of consciousness rooted in empathy, as well as a flow and a synergy with nature forces and spirits—is the foundation of shamanism. An extremely touching and inspiring expression of this powerful magic arising from the deep connection with Gaia is the exquisite Korean painting *Princess Bari Holding the Flower of Resurrection* (see plate 1). Note that this goddess has the power of resurrecting the soul of the deceased (this power symbolized by the flower in her right hand), while significantly her left hand rests on her matrix, her innermost feminine power—thus expressing the deep intermingling of the living spirit (immortal Self or atman) with the feminine generative life-force. She was invoked by shamans conducting funerary rituals, using paintings such as this one, to assist the souls from the Beyond. In fact, Princess Bari was deemed a psychopomp—that is, a conductor of the souls of the dead toward the divine abode—and furthermore the patron goddess of shamans. Princess Bari is thus on a par with Hermes, who is guiding the souls of the departed but who is also the "messenger of the gods" to the humans, which means that he, like Princess Bari, was relaying sacred semantic energy from the Selfs dimension (the divine realm) to humanity, and especially to questers.

I soon realized that this "field of attunement" was not only very extended but also continuously activated and operating, especially during the night. There were just too many extraordinary encounters (people and places) and marvelous synchronicities while traveling. Synchronicities—or meaningful coincidences, as psychologist Carl Jung called them—were permanent and overabundant. Not only in the highly attuned spirits of the people giving me shelter at night (similar to the encounter with the spiritist I mentioned earlier), or the wonderful events happening that night in the villages where I would sleep, but also in systematic streams of synchronicities (what is called a serendipity), as I will describe them.

On reflection, the only way I could explain the continuous suite of synchronicities that I experienced during this crossing of Africa is to admit that during the nights my higher Self was preparing and organizing the next leg of my journey. That meant I was using the superconscious abilities of my Self to scan ahead both the terrain and the people, and to weave the future encounters and events. In other words, my Self, during my sleep, was selecting, among potential drivers in the region, which ones I would encounter to give me a lift, and who would offer me shelter at night in their home (generally a family), and in which place I would be staying for a specific event such as a full moon or a local sacred ritual.

As I was able to figure it out retrospectively while mulling over anomalous events and encounters during this whole trip, it was my extended syg-field that allowed my superconscious Self, during my sleep, to scan the territory I was going to hitchhike through the next day and even up to three days ahead, this amounting to a 150-mile (240-km) radius.

But before I made that conscious visualization in the south of Mauritania, I certainly had a long time of attunement and an extended field of perception while I crossed the Sahara desert from the south of Morocco down to the south of Mauritania, where I then followed the Senegal River toward Mali. In the desert, the merchant trucks take local people on to the next big town for a small fee. We were always sitting atop the load—generally huge canvas bags of dried fruits or vegetables, piled up well above the sides of the truck's body, thus giving us a 360-degree view of the desert rocks and dunes. There were between five and ten local travelers for each thirty-six-hour leg of the desert-crossing journey, and, save for one occurrence, I was always the only Westerner up there, immensely grateful to have been deemed worthy of an exceptional free lift from the imposing and fiery-eyed Tuaregs.

My constant contemplation of a grandiose desert landscape from high up, in a state of heightened consciousness for whole days and nights, must have created spontaneously such an empathic field with

Earth—but this connection was not yet directed at Gaia as the Earth's soul and at her global consciousness.

Two Streams of Synchronicities

Here are some of the hardest-to-explain recurrent events; namely, two streams of synchronicities (or serendipity) that happened during this whole African trip (including the Sahara crossing).

The first stream is already complex and double: (1) I never waited more than five minutes on a road for a vehicle to pick me up, even on the remotest pistes of the rainforest in Nigeria, Central Africa, or Zaire (Congo) or in the desert; (2) when expressing I had no money, the driver would accept to take me onboard for free, this despite all trucks systematically asking for fares from passengers. Indeed, on only two separate occasions had I walked on a road by myself for a good half hour, and it had been of my own volition: I had needed to let go of some steam after being unfairly treated, both times by young white people my age arrogantly cruising Africa in expensive vans for their holidays.

Typically, I would stay exclusively in villages and small towns, and would look for a family there to give me shelter for the night—which was easy given Africans' very hospitable nature. I would just stroll around the place and wait for a person—generally a woman doing chores in the street in front of her house—to initiate a conversation and offer me a stay at their home; then I would share the dinner with the family, often within the circle of women who are customarily eating next to the circle of men in the same room.

A second unexplainable suite of synchronicities was the fact that I crossed all borders (both on the way in and on the way out) of all English-speaking countries without any visa, not even a transit one, for the simple reason I had no money to buy them and anyway didn't want to linger in big cities. And systematically, without any planning on my part, something unusual, different each time, would happen at the borders and I would cross them unimpeded. Now, from Nigeria up to

Kenya, I went through Nigeria, Cameroon (French-speaking), Central African Republic (French-speaking), Zaire (Congo), Uganda, Rwanda, Tanzania, and Kenya—that's six English-speaking countries, but in the French-speaking enclaves, they started to also check French people at the borders.

Altogether, that's eight countries times two (entering/exiting them), thus sixteen checkpoints crossed without proper papers or proper money; and this, without having ever done—or even intending to do—anything but head straight for the customs office or officers on standby there.

The absolute constancy of these odds-beating events makes them outstanding anomalous phenomena reaching well beyond the types of psi events that are weighed and calculated by using statistics and probability laws. For example, in a standard "ganzfeld" telepathy experiment conducted in the Psychophysical Research Laboratories (PRL) where I worked as a predoctoral student, the subject (confined and isolated in a Faraday cage chamber) had to choose, between five possible results, what image (or target) was selected randomly and transmitted by the sender. The probability of the result being due to chance alone was thus one chance in five.* But in my precise real-life case, the probability for a person to be allowed by custom officers to pass a single border without proper credentials is extremely small in the first place (and very far from the fifty-fifty chances for one hundred cases used in yes/no or head/tail coin-flipping instances). So when you multiply these very slim odds by the unfailing constancy across sixteen borders, that's an astounding departure from the statistical mean altogether. In other words, it amounted to a highly anomalous and large-scale suite of psi occurrences.

In my opinion, these two interwoven streams of serendipity belonged to an order or dimension beyond normal events. They were

*On experimental psi research, see Radin 2006, 2009; Radin and Nelson 1989; Mishlove 1975; Ullman et al. 1973; McRae 1984.

springing forth and organized from within the dimension of my Self attuned to Gaia's immense collective-consciousness field.

OUR OWN SELF'S SOFT GUIDANCE THROUGHOUT OUR LIVES

As I pointed out earlier, psi and synchronicities are the daily stuff of all real solitary globe-trotters *because* these are the ways that their higher mind weaves their survival. Yet, the relentless synchronicities a traveler meets on the road stem not only from their own Self guiding and protecting them, but they are also made possible by a clear mind intending to keep pursuing its most essential soul path. This is maybe the crucial element, because when on the road, the globe-trotter's psyche quickly lets go of all mundane and emotional worries and thus clarifies itself. This mind-clearing process (and the synchronicities it allows) would not likely happen to most casual travelers but only to humble explorers of diverse countries, ethnicities, and cultures. The fact that their path is constantly opened and cleared of any obstacle is not something that is remarked or conceptualized by the traveler's conscious mind. The clear mind is like a flow of alive consciousness, and it welcomes any opportunity or affordance that seems to be moving along with this flow, as something self-evident, *allant de soi*, absolutely normal and expected within this clear mindset. It's only long afterward that the anomalous nature of a systematic bending of the odds—such as the two streams of synchronicities I just reported—can be sorted out and pondered as such, when the traveler is not in the efficient or exploring mindset anymore. However, globe-trotters will recount with awe the extraordinary chance they had to come across such and such event or person.

As for the times during which we're living in a city (which I've done a lot when I was not voyaging), these same life-changing events—the constant opening of one's path—are also happening in the usual social settings, but in a more subtle and convoluted way. As city-dwellers, our minds are clogged by an array of events, problems, tasks of all kinds, that arise from a dense social life; as a result, the workings of our deep Self are less recognizable, save from very strong anomalies, such as a precognitive dream. Yet the bending and weaving of events toward a definite path will also appear clearly if we look back at a whole period of our life and sort out the threads that led us to another essential cycle, life task, or encounter.

This is precisely what I was forced to realize in my own life regarding my now decades-long involvement in scientific research on consciousness: there had been a turning point at twenty-one! At that moment in my life, my ardent thirst for going to India to learn and tread a yogi path could have impeded that later major opus in my life—and yet, an invisible hand forced me to wait and secure my bachelor's degree.

An Invisible Hand Forces Me to Complete My Bachelor's Degree

How I got my doctoral degree was nothing less than a sinuous and outlandish affair. And yet, when I look retrospectively at the fact that most of my life has been devoted to my research on consciousness taking me through a series of scientific fields, I cannot fail to see a powerful invisible hand driving that meandering path and putting it back on track at some crucial moments. And, no, that invisible hand driving our destinies is not what people call fate or destiny, or else an invisible angel or guide. I came to fathom that it was, for the better part, our own higher Self.

The first totally anomalous event occurred when I passed my end-of-high-school degree, as we'll see in chapter 6.

The next interference by my Self as regards my studies and diplomas, in order to end up with a doctorate, happened during the third and final year of my bachelor of arts degree (in sociology). But let me explain that at the time in France there was a strong cultural presumption, in terms of intellectual capacities, that a person was either a literary/artistic mind or a (hard) "scientific" mind, and you couldn't be both—and that these trends were already showing in their teens. My older sister was intending to study medicine. As I was already writing poetry, I was thinking of myself as a writer, a literary mind, and my family understood me that way. So it was unthinkable for me to imagine that one day I would turn to science and do theoretical research for which I would need to have a doctorate; to the contrary, I was drawn to follow in the footsteps of my adored poets and musicians in their disdain and let go of the mainstream society and of course its institutions, including diplomas. Yet, I relished starting university because it was my door to total freedom-cum-honor. Yet, when I landed at Sorbonne's Modern Literature department for my first year in a three-year bachelor's degree, I became truly upset by the "stupidities" I deemed the professors were saying about my preferred writers, and by the system of quantitative notations; I resented having my intimate relationship with my poets and authors dissected and objectified. Thus, when, after our student revolution in May–June, we were offered an "experimental university" in Vincennes, north of Paris, I not only enlisted myself there but shifted from Modern Literature studies to the ethnology department, where my love of traditional cultures and my passion for Indian spiritual knowledge could express itself, until I would set out on my own *Journey to the East*, Hermann Hesse style.

Long before I reached this third year, given my in-depth dive into meditation, ancient treatises, and esoterica, I had become a sort of local guru, and my parents' country house bordering the woods in Igny, south of Paris, where I was living alone, was nevertheless an ebullient hub. It's as if my own self-driven spiritual transformation had spread around me, to not only my circle of friends but the older age group of my sister's medical student friends, and even the circle of my seven-years-older brother and his ex-art school buddies. Suddenly, we had all turned into hippies on a quest, avid for traveling, reading spiritual and esoteric lore from many cultures, and dressing in Indian shirts.

I don't remember why and when, during that final year, I became convinced that I had only two or three years of life ahead of me. But then it launched a whole new outlook on my life, a process of maturation that suddenly bloomed feverishly about three months before my bachelor's degree that late June. Since my awakening at eighteen, my sole aim had been to attain enlightenment. I was not sure I was going to achieve it in such a short time, but I decided I should strive toward it as intensely and as quickly as I could. So, how could I best use the little time I had? What could best propel me? It occurred to me that I would learn the most if I was willingly putting myself in the absolute opposite situation than the one I had been living in up to now. And that meant three things: being alone, living without money, and being in a faraway land. And of course this "faraway land" could only be India—the long-awaited Journey to the East.

At that moment, any other consideration, such as my bachelor's degree, faded into nothingness. I had to leave everything behind and hit the road toward India, hitchhiking my way there with no money (anyway, I had none at that point).

That March night, in the Igny house where I was living blissfully by myself, south of Paris, I took the decision to leave with just a tiny bag, not the next morning but the day after. I would have gone that very next morning, but for one problem: I had promised my greatest university friend, Danièle, to help her move her stuff from a flat in the 16th Passy quarter to her new flat in the south of the 14th with my car. So I was going to help her move in the afternoon, then come back to Igny for the night, leave my car in the garden, and hit the road the next morning. I didn't mean to even warn my parents or anybody in my family of my departure; although I was of course going to share my plan with Danièle, who knew all about my passion and would certainly envy me for taking such a radical step.

In the afternoon, I'm now entering Paris from the south and, on my way to her place, I have to cross the large Denfert Plaza, next to where my parents live. After we have moved her stuff, and while driving her back to her old flat and crossing this plaza again, I make a bad move and superficially collide with the door of another car, without hurting anyone. The driver and his wife howl at me and gesture crazily for us to go and park our cars on the side, so as to fill in an accident report form, and then they drive there ahead of me. But at that moment I think full speed that, if I do that, it will impede me from hitting the road, because I would have to deal with their insurance company, who, otherwise, would track down my own insurance to my parents and bother them. As it took me a second to figure this out, while the car I banged is moving past the intersection toward the bend, I swing my car and take a side street at a right angle, one that led precisely to where my parents live. Danièle understood what was at stake for me and went with it.

We reach her place late evening. We share a last tea and a bite, full of anticipated nostalgia and feverish dreams; finally, we bid good-bye to each other with a solemn and profound hug, and I get back swiftly in my car to keep moving forward with my own plan, and first, to get back to Igny for a last night before the great departure.

On the large and now deserted avenue leading south by Denfert Plaza, I see a guy with his thumb up to get a lift, a bit too late in the dark, and while swerving abruptly toward the pavement, I hit the curb with my front wheel. But not too badly, I thought. The guy gets in and sits down—there's only one straight avenue all the way to Paris's southern Porte d'Orléans, and that's where he is going of course. But while crossing Denfert Plaza, at about the exact same place I had the accident earlier, suddenly my tire is flat, I'm scratching the asphalt with my wheel, and my car stops. My car was very old, the tires secondhand reshaped ones, and, well, I must have banged it too hard on the pavement's side. The guy is nice and helps me push my car up to the curb, where I have to leave it, some few hundred yards from my parents' flat. And now we laugh as we stand together on the curb to hitchhike to our respective places. I know my plan is dead; I won't be able to depart and hit the road the next day. Worse, I'll have to come back to Paris and take care of my car the very next morning, because it's not an authorized parking place. And now it hits me in the face that it was not without reason that both accidents happened at one block from my parents' home. The sign was clear. The cosmos was signaling me that it was not the right time to leave.

I finished my bachelor's degree and, without even waiting for the formal document, started my travel the way I had envisioned it: whatever money I had (from an unexpected small heritage from my grandmother), I gave to my brother, save for the strict amount of money I thought I needed to reach India while learning my way in Middle Eastern countries and the Indian subcontinent—where I would then be alone, without money, and in an unknown land. But this time, my departure was under much more favorable auspices: not only was my future doctoral degree not jeopardized, but moreover momentous events on my way to India were set like the pieces of a puzzle.

2
SELF-DEFENSE

In no other domain is the Self power so evident and dramatically displayed as that of the defense and protection of one's own ego and body persona. And given that I spent years traveling alone and mostly penniless across two continents (Africa and Asia), my own Self had quite a number of occasions to warn me of danger great and small in unfamiliar places. And yet the instances that posed the greatest threat to my life or health happened in my birth town, Paris, and later in my family's backyard in Provence. Through the accounts that follow, we'll see a powerful entity, the Self, using an immaterial and definitely beyond-spacetime energy—which I termed syg-energy and which has been called *ki*, *chi*, or *kundalini* energy in Eastern lore—to repel, frighten, or even conciliate aggressors in the most potent way. However, the Self doesn't act solely on the psychic level, and we'll watch its full potency as a force able to strike blows propelling a male attacker two yards backward, or acting as a full-blown cuff thrusting me off an electrocution source. Some occurrences, revealing a quasi boxer's punch through a closed door and window, will ascertain the immaterial or, more precisely, the hyperdimensional nature of this syg-energy. And if an energy or a force that belongs to our spirit and Self definitely exists beyond spacetime laws, then it is of the highest import (for us in our lives, and for science) to analyze the way it acts and interferes in our lives and in our physical world. Because the events happened in widely different contexts and situations, we'll be able to assess the global strategy and the values driving the actions of the Self.

A PSYCHIC BLOW AS HARD AS A BOXER'S PUNCH

After a decade spent exploring the world and the unknown reaches of consciousness through diverse spiritual paths, I started my thirties and the next decade of my life with a renewed momentum and thrust for writing. True to myself, before and during my years of travel, I had always kept on writing—be it a journal, poems, a master's thesis in anthropology, and a few atypical short stories; in fact, I had, since my adolescence, identified with and thought of myself as a "writer," labeling it boldly on my passport even though I was still a high schooler.

After a long search, I met my first publisher, and wrote my first book in a few months. It focused on the anomalous events I had experienced up to that point; in a second part of the book, I embarked on explaining these, in terms of our higher Self intruding in our daily life, as well as the connection to immortal guides and nature spirits. As my publisher was just starting his own publishing house, my book was off to market in no time.

I had come back to Paris, my birth town, from a fourth trip in Africa and a long stay in Ivory Coast with Pat the guitarist, where I had eventually ended our relationship, being gripped by the realization that I had drifted away from my own soul path.

These first two years after my return were some of the most intensely packed in my life, that saw a drastic shift in focus from a wanderer's life toward living in a large social network in Paris while entering the publishing milieu and swiftly focusing on a doctoral thesis and scientific research.

Soon, I launched the work for my second book, consisting of interviews of leading scientists who were including consciousness in their scientific paradigm. I was thus getting to know some of the greatest French brains of the time. I would also host dinners for these scientists, presenting them to my publisher and journalists, together with my new boyfriend, Paul, a flutist and musician with the highest empathic talent and emotional quotient (or EQ) I have ever encountered in my life.

In parallel, I was looking for a university professor who would agree to be my director for a doctoral thesis tackling parapsychological phenomena (and nothing else)—a domain that was deemed a vast scam by the current materialist paradigm that I had taken to heart to topple. After a year and a half of facing only refusals, I finally interviewed for my book the renowned maverick professor Remy Chauvin, an ethologist and sociologist, who not only agreed to be my thesis director but furthermore opened the link with J. B. Rhine, who in the 1930s had launched the first ever parapsychology lab in the United States. Rhine developed protocols to test extrasensory perception and launched the new field of parapsychology within experimental psychology, in Durham, North Carolina. (The lab was at first affiliated to Duke University, then independent, and is now known as the Rhine Research Center).

On with my story. Between completing my first book and getting the opportunity to write the second one (that came to me in the most synchronistic way), there were three months during which I started practicing Aikido (I would persevere for years in this quite spiritual and soft-power fighting technique); I also engaged in a brief relationship with the sensei—a great martial art teacher.

All the while, I was living again in the family country house in Igny, at the edge of the Verrières forest, and that day I had driven to Paris to buy a new Aikido vest—the real Aikido one instead of the generic martial art vest I had. The martial art shop was on a tiny triangular plaza, near Châtelet Plaza, squeezed at the entrance of the Les Halles tunnel. In Paris in that epoch, it was still possible to park just about everywhere and, for such a short time, the odds of getting a parking ticket (still affordable) were greatly compensated for by the enormous time needed to find an authorized parking spot and then to walk back and forth. However, on arrival at the plaza, I found that the half dozen greatly coveted spots there were all already taken. The only way to park my wrecked secondhand car was in front of the entrance of a restaurant marked by two small pine trees planted in big cement boxes. I reflected that at this midafternoon time, there would not be any customers there, and that anyway there was more than a yard for people to pass on each side in between the restaurant doorway and the pine trees. More precisely, to leave enough space for other cars to move out of the plaza, I had to fit my front right tire (the passenger seat) practically against one tree box and the rear right tire against the other. Something that, being a deft driver, I did precisely to about an inch.

And of course, I thought I needed only fifteen minutes to get the right size of a vest made in only one design. Yet it was a good thirty minutes later that I emerged out of the shop and, happy with my purchase, walked round my car and got in the driver's seat, throwing the shop bag on the back seat.

At that moment, I saw a short and nervous man coming out of the restaurant porch in a fury, his twisted face and clenched fists showing all the symptoms of a Latin alpha male's temper tantrum, in somebody accustomed to be the unchallenged boss. And now he is dashing around my car toward my driver side, ready to hit me hard as far as I can sense. I'm taking it all in, mind in overdrive, when I remember my car doors don't lock from inside; the guy will open my door and land his fist on my face.

At that point, I become incredibly cool, devoid of any fear, poised in myself, hyperaware. I observe the guy rushing toward me, now half a yard from my closed window, aggressively throwing his left hand toward the doorknob, his right one raised in a clenched fist, ready to hit me in the face.

And I look at him starkly in the eyes. At this instant, the body of the man is violently yanked backward a good yard, so violently in fact that his arms jerk up and he is fumbling on his feet to regain his balance, lurching two or three steps backward. In the same movement, he turns on himself and staggers toward the back of my car and with an angry gesture, shouts for himself "(Quelle) connasse celle-la!"—his first word lost for me in his gesticulation . . . but easily recognizable as "(What a) jerk, this woman!" And in the same sweeping movement, he scurries to the porch and gets back in his restaurant.

At which point, I turn the contact key, put the transmission into reverse, and exit the plaza in the coolest manner.

I was totally stupefied by what had happened. In my good sense, I had only looked the guy in the eye, coldly, with full knowledge of his intended violence toward me. In my stream of consciousness, I had had no plan, not even a thought, about how to cope. I had watched, hyper-aware and in perfect self-control, and had tensed up for what I thought was an unavoidable blow hitting me. (But I hadn't moved at all, hadn't done a thing to either react in a martial art way or to protect my face.)

Yet, while looking the guy in the eye, something, a force, had been unleashed. A force that didn't belong to my conscious mind (which we call in psychology by the substantive "*the conscious,*" as differing from *the unconscious*, both making up the consciousness of a person). A force strong enough not only to stop a furious gesture but to invert a thrust forward into a powerful thrust backward, putting the guy off balance and having him strive to both regain his equilibrium and find a quick explanation for his rational mind. The angry shouting of "What a jerk, this woman!" making it as if "the woman" was such a poor jerk that he had decided to let go of the offense. And, if asked about it, I have no doubt that, in his own memory, this was now the story of what had happened.

Now, I was left to wonder what or who had acted; what was this force able to punch so hard at an enraged combatant launching a forward attack as to hurl him abruptly two or three steps backward?

Furthermore, the way the guy had been raising both of his arms as an effect of the shove, and then gesticulating with them to regain his balance, seemed to imply he was knocked on the chest.

The only conclusion I could muster was that this was a force stemming from my superconscious Self and its own subtle kundalini energy flowing through the chakras.

This unconscious feat revealed to me that the Self can do much more than just concocting and weaving events and encounters in our lives or being able to peer clairvoyantly and precognitively beyond space and time through the spiritual dimension. Obviously, the Self was also able to control precisely the force fields of an enigmatic energy pertaining to consciousness—something I called at the time psychic energy (following Jung's term), or kundalini energy (as the Indian yogic term goes), and that I came to label syg-energy in my theoretical work.

Now, here is an interesting element to ponder: that of the instant "rational" explanation emerging within the mind of the restaurant boss.

The first interpretation that comes to our mind is through the famous *cognitive dissonance* process. Most people cannot witness or watch an event that is totally at odds with their basic worldview or that contradicts the science of the day that deems reality to be only matter (and matter laws). The more their mind is fervently adhering to and blinkered by this materialist paradigm, the harsher will be their immediate reaction to this cognitive dissonance, so that they will instantly come up with a rationalization (an explaining away) that can assuage and reassure their own conscious. This is why it is so hard (and in fact quite impossible) to persuade a staunch skeptic of any psi phenomenon by showing him loads of experimental evidence. Any rationalization, however impossible by itself, will do for them—even one that is a hundred times more complicated than the simple telepathy or precognition phenomenon. Faced with receiving such a powerful and unfathomable blow by a woman sitting behind a closed window, the conscious mind of the manly boss instantly makes up the story that he controls himself and *decides* to turn around so as not to hurt a woman, even such a "connasse," a jerk!

But there is another possible explanation to his rationalization. It could be understood as a suggestion that my Self would have fed to the mind of the aggressor. In that case, my Self would have fed him the suggestion at the same instant it delivered the psychic blow. The suggestion that "seeing a woman at the wheel, he was deciding to let go of the offense" would blur his memory and erase in his mind the absolutely anomalous event that had taken place, replacing it with the rational explanation. That, indeed, would be, from the part of the Self, a very sophisticated move! Taken together with the blow, it would figure an extradimensional entity at work, able to counteract a physical body threat, yet deploying a supreme intelligence and benevolence to keep an immature psychological persona intact.

There's some ground to consider this latter explanation as plausible. If it had been only a protective move initiated by my Self and triggered by my helpless situation, my Self's interference would have aimed only at protecting me—by delivering the punch to throw the guy off. In contrast, if my Self was aware of a larger reality, namely that this necessary action would destabilize the aggressor's mind (as it contravened basic matter laws), then the Self would also influence his mind and provide the quick fix of a rationalization.

To keep the aggressor mentally sane was definitely not a consideration belonging to my ego consciousness at the moment I was being threatened. It had to be that of my Self!

A Hyperdimensional Energy of Consciousness—Syg-Energy

With much more experience, my take now is that our Self is definitely, as psychologist Carl Jung considered it, an entity of a higher order, endowed with superconscious and psi capacities and connected to the *collective unconscious;* the Self operates beyond space and time constraints so as to weave synchronicities, and is able to communicate and even interfere with our conscious ego's stream of thoughts and even behavioral choices. Yet Jung didn't address the capacity of the Self to influence matter systems and biological bodies (that is, psychokinesis or PK).

However, this is something I've been able to model in a complex systems and cosmology framework, as a hyperdimensional energy of consciousness: semantic (meaning creative) energy, in short, syg-energy. All humans possess syg-energy naturally, both as constituting their energy-body (chakras and astral body) and as the energy proper of their Self on its own hyperdimension (their syg-field).

In *Cosmic DNA at the Origin*, I have proposed a hyperdimensional cosmology positing a universe endowed with cosmic consciousness. This hyperdimension preexisted the Big Bang (the inflation phase) and birthed our matter universe; it exists before and below Planck scale (the first quantum), the scale at which space, time, and the first particles (bosons, electrons) are born, thus the electromagnetic spectrum is deployed and its laws start operating (for example, the speed-of-light limit). Then the atoms and molecules and all matter and bio systems will follow. The hyperdimension exists as hyperfrequencies, both at the origin and at the (sub-quantum) core of any particle, and as such it pervades our matter universe, any atom, cell, and organism.

In this framework, syg-energy is the very energy of this consciousness-hyperdimension. It belongs to another energy spectrum (the syg spectrum) than the electromagnetic (EM) energy, and as such it abides by widely different laws. Syg-energy is immensely faster than the speed of light, and unbound by spacetime and EM laws. Since our Self belongs to the hyperdimension (HD), syg-energy is also the energy of our Self consciousness; it is what constitutes our mind and energy-body—that is, our syg-field. All syg-fields create, all together, the semantic or syg-hyperdimension (*Syg-HD*) as cosmic consciousness (Tao, brahman, the collective unconscious) and thus each person's Self and syg-field is a participant and co-creator. I proposed that the universe's HD has two more components, with hyperspace and hypertime entwined with Syg-HD. (More on Syg-HD and energy anomalies in chapter 7.)

But let's ponder how an "energy" (delivering the blow) could pass through the metal and glass of a car door. We already know that neutrinos can traverse or tunnel through a mountain or pierce through the ground without any problem. Hyperdimensional waves/strings (as the *sygons* constituting the syg-energy that I postulate) can tunnel through matter without alteration by definition, because they don't belong to the matter and spacetime dimension (as they exist below Planck scale). The sygons can crisscross time and space at near instantaneous speed as well. Indeed, the fact that this psychic blow was sent through a layer of matter (glass and metal) does prove that it had to be a beyond-spacetime type of energy—that is, hyperdimensional by definition—such as syg-energy.

So then, how could a hyperdimensional energy target or affect a specific body or any matter or biomatter system? This is where our good old rationality (based on matter laws) fails completely. Syg-energy, as a hyperdimensional energy of consciousness, abides by the *intent* or spiritual aims of a person, and specifically their Self's intent and goals. And for all of us, a basic goal of our Self is first and foremost to protect us physically and psychologically, and then of course to guide us toward a higher spirituality and knowledge. (Whether we listen to and follow the prodding of our own Self, is our personal choice.)

Mind-over-Matter in Martial Arts

In several Asiatic martial arts, we find the mention and even the practice of psychic blows operated by the ki energy (Japan), or the chi (China), the subtle kundalini energy (India) of our chakras and energy-body (the syg-energy). Specifically, all martial arts teach us to develop the energy of the hara (the chakra about one inch below the navel), which is the most powerful chakra in terms of its effect on matter systems. How strong the evidence is in the rare video clips meant to present such feats (e.g., in Southeast Asian martial arts) is yet to be studied. However, the sole existence of such a concept (let alone its practice) within several martial arts speaks of its reality at the very least in the past, even if present-day masters may not attain its full mastery.

Our Selfs Also Use Humor to Teach Us

Of course, there was a subtle humor, I believe, from the part of my Self, that this precise martial art blow would be demonstrated as real and achievable to my conscious mind, precisely at the moment I was exiting a martial arts shop. It's as if my Self had concocted this situation for a learning episode and had primed my mind to react with the secret power of the ki, since I was powerless to move in my seat-constrained position. Let me express here that my conscious must have necessarily been fused with my Self in order to make the psychic blow work in a perfect way, and in order for me to watch it work. Furthermore, there would have been no learning if my conscious wasn't part of the agency, so that I would be able, come a similar dangerous situation, to again make this feat happen.

Needless to say, when, after our next Aikido session, we went as usual to a nearby café to relax and socialize, and I recounted my experience, I was met by very skeptical and annoyed glances. How a newbie in Aikido could ever imagine to rival the great masters of old was very badly received, especially by the sensei.

Yet I wasn't a newbie in terms of kundalini energy (the subtle energy filling the kundalini channel and awakening and connecting all the chakras). Having started meditation at eighteen, and having experienced my first kundalini awakening a few months later, I had learned to master and even direct this ki energy already, since nearly fifteen years ago, although using other chakras. This is a common but false assumption that a given mind-power or psi capacity can be achieved only within a given practice. And I had spent my whole conscious life thus far exploring and mastering the power of my own mind and Self. In fact, the question of which chakra the ki energy originated from in this Aikido shop instance remains open; as we will see in the electrocution case (further in this chapter), my Self appeared as a human silhouette hurtling from the outside to yank me off the source, thus implying no chakra whatsoever was involved.

I have had two clear-cut experiences that are a variation of this psychic blow phenomenon. However, both contain an added element—namely, a particular shriek—that blends the effect of the blow with that of the shriek and thus blurs its specific effect. Both anomalous events happened years before the Aikido shop one; the first in Manali when I was twenty-two and the second in Thailand in my mid-twenties. It's interesting to note, regarding what we just saw about my Self teaching me how to use my syg-energy for self-defense, that in these two previous occurrences, I was at a loss as to how I was so suddenly saved from harm and as to why my aggressors abruptly let go of me—apart from attributing it to my teacher in one case or to my own Self in general.

Only in the Aikido shop instance was my posture totally immobile, my mind and mouth silent, my stance poised, my car door and window closed, and nobody else around the plaza—thus leaving absolutely no other possible explanation than the powerful syg-energy blow delivered by my superconscious Self.

However, to talk about the other side of the coin, I myself twice received a psychic blow, one time delivered at a distance by the man who was my spiritual teacher in India (Karl), and the second by a goddess from whose altar I had taken and started eating a consecrated fruit. Both times, it was like a strong wind falling vertically on the top of my head, strong enough to push my head down, yet painless, despite nobody being around me at that moment.

I'm going to recount these two experiences of a psychic blow-cum-shriek phenomenon after we pore over the scientific research done on large-scale psychokinesis (PK), or mind-over-matter.

The Scientific Research on Large-Scale Psychokinesis

The most rigorous and astounding research on PK consists of the hundreds of laboratory experiments aimed at studying the effect of mind over bio-systems or healing—a capacity called bio-PK. Interestingly, these show also that it is our intent that singles out specific systems to be influenced (yet without deeming the Self the agency of this intent, as I do myself).

Bio-PK is one of the best proven psi capacities, with hundreds of controlled double-blind laboratory experiments. In many studies, the subjects were psychic healers, since healing is the most significant and useful type of bio-PK. Healers are asked to make plants C and G grow quicker. Yet C and G have been selected randomly among a group of plants (unknowingly for the experimenters) and the healers must avoid having any effect on the other nearby plants (called control plants). All plants are positioned in the same room with a controlled temperature, they are watered in the exact same way, and they receive the same light.

My own understanding of this selection feat is that the mind of the healer, in that case, works in sync with their Self to have a healing influence at great distances. In their conscious mind, the healers know only that they must affect plants C and G, and no other plant there. But their Self, as a hyperdimensional consciousness able to see and hear at a distance, knows how to target these experimental plants in a very specific way—something that is proven by the magnitude of the positive psi results, which are so high as to refute an effect due to chance alone.

Thus, a meta-analysis on healing (bio-PK) done by William Braud in 1985, and using the 149 experiments conducted up to that date, showed that 53 percent of them were statistically significant—a very impressive result when only 5 percent would show that something more than chance was involved. (On bio-PK, see also Schwartz and Dossey 2010; Dossey 1989; Schlitz et al. 2004; Krippner and Welch 1992.)

The first large body of experimental PK research was conducted using dice by J. B. Rhine from 1934 to 1941 and used ever more sophisticated devices to throw the dice. Psychologist Jeffrey Mishlove reported in his comprehensive book *The Roots of Consciousness* that they totaled

651,216 throws of the dice and gave "10115 to 1 odds against chance occurrence" (Mishlove 1975).

Then, experiments focused on micro-PK (PK at microscopic scale), using random number generators, also called random event generators (RNGs, REGs). In these, subjects were intending to affect the RNGs' output while seeing the results in real time over a computer graph. It was notably conducted for years in the Princeton Engineering Anomalies Research Laboratory (PEAR) lab in Princeton, New Jersey. A meta-analysis of all known RNG studies, or micro-PK (with 515 experiments by 91 researchers), gave the incredibly high probability of p < 10^−35 (Radin and Nelson 1989). (More on micro-PK in chapter 8.)

Prior to laboratory experiments, renowned scientists conducted studies of mediums with macro-PK abilities (the term used for human-scale PK). D. D. Home, the greatest such subject, was investigated in the early 1870s by chemist and physicist William Crookes, who devised devices to circumvent fraud (but was nevertheless tricked by some mediums). Home was able to make an accordion play and move seemingly by itself inside a cage. He was also repeatedly witnessed levitating.

Levitation is also a feat of macro-PK, in the sense that a body weight and/or gravity seems to be disturbed. There have been reports of individuals seen spontaneously levitating, their bodies rising into the air and remaining suspended. The phenomenon is especially associated with Catholic saints, notably St. Teresa of Avila and St. Joseph of Cupertino. (See Braude 1986; *Psi Encyclopedia*, Levitation.*) Let me clarify, however, that levitation of the full body has nothing to do with out-of-body experiences (OBEs) or astral travels. In astral travels, only the invisible energy body (with the I-consciousness) is traveling through space or repositioning itself in another location (and/or time frame). All my experiences are about the latter, and I've not to this day felt myself, or been witnessed, levitating or translocating with my body.

**Psi Encyclopedia*, a database on psi research spearheaded by and integrated in the website of the Society for Psychical Research (SPR) in the UK. All articles are written by the experts in the field; see the article by M. Potts on Religious Levitation at their website.

PSYCHIC BLOW WITH MARTIAL ART SHRIEK IN MANALI

In the first year that saw a group of Western spiritual questers in Manali (northern India), only about thirty of us were there, renting a handful of village houses or rooms in the surrounding mountain and valley. Manali stood in the foothills of the Himalayas, in the Beas River valley, on a road from Shimla to Sir Bhum and Leh in Ladakh. It was then a big village populated with mountain Indians and about two hundred Tibetan migrants. There were hardly a dozen shops outside the permanent market shacks—mostly vegetable, groceries, and bazaar; add to that a few Indian chai shops and a handful of restaurants and Tibetan food shacks. And of course there was nothing that looked like a guesthouse, even less so a hotel, and hence our need to rent rooms. As we were all mostly penniless, we would gather with some friends around the one person able to find the money for the monthly rent, which must have been extremely low given that we could (when we had that chance) eat a dessert-size dish of dal (the traditional lentil dish) and two chapatis for a single rupee at that time. In our house, this person was Karl.

High on the southern mountain, on the other side of the Beas River, were the sulfur hot springs at Vashisht, and farther up Vashishtha Temple, featuring bathing pools for both men and women. It was of course a delight to bathe in a huge stone pool filled with sulphurated hot water, and a change from our customary morning face wash with the icy cold water from the street tap. No house had its own water tap inside, or kitchen, bathroom, or toilet, for that matter; the toilet was in the woods, where we went with a bucket of water.

We lived five or six people together in the Indian house of which we rented the top floor. It was a huge room, absolutely bare save for a cylindrical stove at its center, hooked to the central pipe that rose up to the roof and stemmed from a similar stove on the ground floor. Attached to it was a beautiful wooden terrace and balcony that opened up on the Himalayan slopes.

From where most of our rented houses were—higher on the mountain than the village itself—it was a five-mile walk, half of it climbing hard, to get a hot bath. The best was to climb the mountain before the summer heat struck, and that meant early morning. But I was myself going there rather rarely. First, I didn't have the couple of rupees to pay for it, and second, I had found my own "Japanese bath pool" somewhere farther on the village mountain slope, past the forested area. In that patch of forest lots of ferns were growing; one day, looking at a young fern sprout, a thick stem at its center looking like a shepherd's or bishop's crook, I had the intuition it could be comestible. And indeed, when grilled in ghee (the local butter), it tasted like asparagus, something that enormously enriched our household's single daily meal of rice and onions.

Beyond the forest and before the rice fields a half mile further on was a creek flowing straight down from the mountain summit; the place was in wild nature and seemed totally deserted; the stream, unbelievably, was dotted with wild violet irises all the way down, growing in a low, grassy area. In one place, the brook that otherwise was no more than two or three feet of width, opened up in a large roundish basin. The violet irises in wild bunches against the flush green grass surrounding this pool of water shimmering in the sunrays—the scene could not be more entrancing!

And that was my immense pleasure, to take a bath in this surreal beauty under the hot sun. Then to linger at that spot to meditate, read, or write some poem or thoughts in my journal while my light cotton longyis would dry.

That morning, I had decided to go to the sulfur baths. I had already climbed up three-quarters of the snaking mountain road and I could see, between occasional bunches of trees bordering the road, the whole slope of the mountain I had climbed, all the way to the river at the bottom, and part of the laced road zigzagging down to it, with its hairpin turns.

I could see only one person on this road (some parts were invisible to me), and it was Karl, whom I had met earlier on climbing up. He must have taken his bath soon after dawn, because he was already way down the mountain on his way back to the village.

Karl was an Austrian hippie in his thirties who had been in India for five years already, learning with the sadhus, the itinerant Shiva yogis and ascetics. These were the wise men who held the highest knowledge about the mind and who inherited and transmitted India's millennia-old wisdom, a wealth of written and oral knowledge on human and cosmic consciousness unique on Earth and still amazingly alive and accessible to all.

On the road for more than a year, I had reached India hitchhiking in the early autumn about nine months earlier and had already made a round tour of India, clockwise, moving south to flee the cold in winter and going northward to escape the unbearable heat in summer. I was hitchhiking on the roads by day, barefoot and penniless, dressed in one white longyi and a top, another longyi around my shoulders and still another one wrapped as a turban around my head to ward off the deadly sun.

In whatever village or small town I was reaching in the evening, I would look around and walk to the first sadhus' temple whose red flag flying on the roof I could see from afar. Whoever was there, a solitary or a half dozen sadhus gathering for the night in the sacred temple, I would be greeted as one of them around the sacred fire, sharing their evening meal and hours-long meditation well into the night. Indeed there are *Mataji sadhus* (women sadhus) in India, even if they are rarer, and they are as welcome in the temples as men. The sadhus only care about individuals on their own quest for knowledge, the ones eager to attain the state of *moksha* or liberation. And these souls they will recognize and greet in their sacred circle.

Thus, just like Karl, I had been infused by the silent wisdom of these sadhus and had learned with them the secret science of kundalini energy—how to master one's consciousness and psychic energy, after it has been raised up the kundalini channel (the vertebral column) and gathered at the top of the head chakra (the crown chakra or thousand-petal lotus). I had awakened this crown chakra while learning with a Sufi master in Iran the previous summer, and since then my whole kundalini energy had been concentrated there. With the sadhus, and now with Karl, I was learning, in a strictly silent empathic state, how to operate it.

In between long months and stretches alone on the roads in India as a Mataji sadhu, I would reach some of the hot spots where the novel and first wave of hippies was gathering—Goa, Benares, Manali—and stay there for two or three months, before hitting the road alone again.

Back to my story. So, while climbing, I would occasionally perceive Karl in between rows of trees, down the slope and still descending. Karl being a yogic master whose silent teaching I was following, we were always in mental sync; thus I knew he was aware of where I was while climbing the road, as much as I was aware of him descending it, even with a distance of a half mile at bird's flight between us.

At one point, another bunch of trees hid Karl from my line of sight. I was still walking when, suddenly, I felt somebody's full weight pushing forcibly on my shoulders and grabbing me. An Indian man had jumped on me from behind to make me fall, obviously intending to abuse and rape me on this deserted patch of road.

My surprise was total, as I had not seen anybody else high up on the road nor sensed him following or approaching me. I let out a shriek, while he was violently clutching my shoulders and pushing me toward the ground. My reaction, as usual, was not anything physical or martial; I couldn't even see my attacker, although I knew he was a man willing to rape me (had he hoped to rob me, he'd have aimed at grabbing the bag loosely hanging by my shoulder, a real easy thing to do). I didn't try to clutch his hands on my shoulders, nor to aim at hitting him and disengage. Nothing of the sort; in fact, apart from one specific instance in Africa, I've never reacted physically to a physical aggression, even after mastering Aikido.

That time, I just put out a very strange shriek. It was not a very loud shout, not a cry for help either—just one of the strangest high-pitched shrieks I ever heard my throat utter.

It's at this very moment that the real anomaly happened. It was like a disruption of my consciousness stream, and a strange blank in my sense of self and perception of space and time altogether.

When I regained my awareness, I was standing strong on my legs (I hadn't fallen and was off-balance no more), and my face was already turned downward toward the side of the road and the very steep slope, where I could see, already about five or six yards down, my aggressor running straight down across the grass and rocks—something no man in his right mind would ever dare to attempt, even a mountain-wise highlander.

I had lost a few seconds and had not the slightest idea of what had given my attacker such a dreadful scare that, terror-struck and just willing to flee from me, he was now putting his life wildly at risk. The slope was so slippery and steep all the way down, maybe a 35-degree angle, that any stone rolling under his foot could have sent him to his death.

In the same glance, I could see further down that Karl had now appeared on the road past the trees that had blocked my view, and he was looking up at the guy zooming down like a madman—even if the distance between us was such that it's doubtful my shout had been heard.

At the time of this anomalous event, given that I was learning from Karl to develop my own mental abilities and that we were so often in telepathic contact, I spontaneously gave him the credit for this powerful psychic blow that had panicked my aggressor and had him take to flight. Karl, I had witnessed several times, was a well-honed telepath, a master yogi on whom I could see the double aura of the highest Samadhi (see plate 2), and he had an amazing range of other psi gifts, which is why I felt I had so much to learn from him. And when, after a year, I thought I had learnt whatever he could teach me, then I pursued my own path with the direct link to my Self.

So, the way I interpreted things at the time was that Karl had blocked the attack using one of his powerful mental tricks. Maybe he had been able to see the guy following me and decrypt his intention and then block him; or else he had grasped telepathically that I was attacked. And I didn't give further thought to this incident that was—given the density of my experience of the supersensible reality all along my Indian journey, and especially in Manali with Karl—just one more piece of learning. For one, I had already seen Karl being able to influence somebody's behavior (mine, as it happened) the hard way (against my will) from a hundred yards distance; and now I assumed he could do the same from much farther.

I now know all too well that distance is not a problem at all for syg-energy, that he could have sensed telepathically that I was attacked (even if I was hidden from view), and that he had the power to stop the aggression, because I've been able to do it too. So there was no inherent problem with my take on what a honed yogi's mind could achieve. However, this attribution of agency to Karl fell short when, while touring Thailand, I extricated myself from about the same situation of aggression with a similar mental feat, while no powerful yogi like Karl was anywhere around, as I will soon recount.

A Strange Blanking Out of Awareness When the Self Takes Over

I really had to assume, then, that it had been my own psi power all along that did it, a spontaneous surge from my superconscious Self. Unless Karl helped me perform the first time and I had learned then how to defend myself with syg-energy and became able to do it singly afterward. Yet, this attribution of agency to my own Self was reinforced by a mysterious detail of what had happened, namely the *loss of perception and awareness for a few seconds—those very seconds during which the syg-energy feat happened.* And this specific *blanking out of awareness* (without fainting) has been since then a repeated occurrence in several highly anomalous events that effected my avoiding danger, physical aggression, or even deadly harm in an accident. Here is a telling example.

As I recounted it in detail in *Living Souls*, as my car started skidding on an icy road in Provence, and I realized my wheel and tires weren't responding anymore, I entered a hyperawareness state while watching my car slide toward the side of the road bordering a precipitous hillside with a supernormal slowness (due to my decoupled mental speed). The last thought and perception I had (without any fear) was to be seemingly headed toward a bunch of trees planted lower than the road and seeing the approaching edge of the road and of the hill—the last yard or so before my car toppled over it. Then my next perception was to be (still in perfect mental calmness) sitting askew in my car, whose passenger door was impaled on these trees, with my driver door above my head and seeing only the snowy slope through a still intact windshield.

In that case, as in several other ones in which I had such blanking out of awareness, there is no loss of consciousness or fainting at all—just a few seconds missing in my conscious perception/sensation.

Based on these experiences, and being also proficient in astral journeys, my understanding is that on sensing the impending accident/danger, the astral body (with ego or I-consciousness) exits the body and merges with one's higher Self. And when our ego consciousness is merged with our superconscious Self, then it can deal with the crisis with a powerful syg-energy, so as to limit any possible harm or avoid it altogether; and, as a second benefit, it saves the ego from enduring a hard trauma. I also believe that, if unavoidable, the wounds endured by the body would be made less lethal and more prone to heal (if only because the psyche is not deeply traumatized).

Yet, this blanking out of awareness is not happening in all cases of reaction to a sudden aggression or danger. In the Aikido shop occurrence a decade later, in which I obviously was the one to give the blow, my awareness stream was not at all disrupted; I had no disruption of continuity, no break of perception, between the sight of the man's left hand reaching to my doorknob and clenching and raising his other fist, and his body being violently thrown backward with both his raised arms paddling the air—even if the psychic force, the blow itself, had not been perceptible to me either internally or as a beam of syg-energy. I have to say that I'm able to perceive these beams and fields, and their dynamic behavior as well, in many different settings and with great precision; I recount several instances of that in *The Sacred Network*, a 2011 book in which I analyze in depth these anomalous perceptions of syg-energy, in order to infer its dynamics and properties.

With decades of added experience, I can now reassess what must have happened on Manali's sulfur springs road.

Indeed, if it had been Karl orchestrating the psychic blow from afar, there is no way that could have caused a disruption of my awareness and perception for a few seconds.

In contrast, as I've noticed in several anomalous events, a blanking out of awareness sometimes occurs when I'm faced with an abrupt aggression or imminent accident, as a side effect of the instant merging of the ego consciousness with that of the Self; this ego-Self fusion allows the Self to deal with the problem using its superconscious and hyperdimensional psi capacities, and thus to figure and effect a (more) favorable outcome.

Furthermore, although I didn't have (or think I had) noticeable psychokinetic abilities (PK) back in my early twenties (apart from healing), I became able at a later age to consciously produce some of these PK phenomena on matter systems, and (as we have seen) to deliver such psychic blows myself—despite the fact that the process, definitely orchestrated by the Self, still remains partly mysterious and emerges only spontaneously, as if triggered and driven by the Self.

Thus, I am now more prone to give the credit of these psychic blows (even the ones at a younger age) to my own hyperdimensional Self—the supraconscious part of our consciousness, able to tinker with matter reality, as well as space and time.

FENDING OFF AGGRESSION ON A LONELY BOAT TRIP IN THAILAND

As I alluded to earlier, I have another instance in which a shriek conjoined with a mental blow had the powerful effect of putting two male sexual aggressors in a flight move. Let me note first that my life experience and community learning during my extensive travels have persuaded me that the worst a woman could do when sexually harassed was to be terrified, crying, and trying to flee. Any fearful reaction on the part of the targeted victim will only trigger a more violent behavior in sexually aroused males; it will also lessen enormously the victim's quick thinking and capacity to circumvent the trouble because a less strong victim's best strategy is to outsmart the aggressor; in that sense, the best reaction for a woman is to laugh the guy out, make fun of him, and put out ironic and demeaning remarks.

And by the way, do you know what the winning behavior is in front of an aggressive dog starting to chase you? Sit down fearlessly and stare him down. Well, actually there is another winning one: start to chase him—he will definitely take to his heels.

The event I'm going to recount now happened during six months of travel in Southeast Asia in my mid-twenties. I resided for a couple of weeks in Pattaya, Thailand, on the shore of the Gulf of Thailand, and had gone for the afternoon and sunset to the tiny island of Koh Lan facing this beautiful beach town (also called Koh Larn or Coral Island; see fig. 2.1a).

As was the custom there (since the trip to the island was a tourist attraction), I booked one of the fishermen's boats doing the back and forth on top of their own fishing activities. It took about forty-five minutes to cross the body of water, with a man at the front with a paddle and one at the back using one oar. (Of course, nowadays you'll find quicker options!)

When I started on my way back, night had descended on the body

a

b

Fig. 2.1 *a.* Koh Lan island, facing Pattaya bay, Thailand (detail)
Photo by Jtamad

b. Thai fishing boats at the beach
Photo by Sea Dave

of water and only the lights of Pattaya beach's buildings and shacks were visible at a distance; I found another boat boarded by two fishermen. I was sitting on one of the transverse benches, still drawn inward in a contemplative state and enjoying the scenery. We were now in the middle of the darkened bay, with no other boat near us, despite several visible quite far away. Suddenly, the man at my back jumped on me from behind and threw me in one swift move down on the wooden curved hull, immediately straddling me; he was lying on top of me, his weight on me, while starting to grab my clothing to tear it down; and on the side, I was seeing the dark silhouette of the other guy approaching menacingly with the same intent to get at me.

At that moment, I didn't struggle or push back on the man; I just uttered a powerful shriek. The man instantly jumped backward to his feet as if I was a fearful demonic entity and rushed to seize the oar to maneuver the boat again, and what's more, the other one followed suit at the helm. They just worked forcefully and hurriedly to cross the distance toward Pattaya's bay, without a word or a look at me anymore. When I uttered the shriek, there were no boats around us, as if they had intentionally taken the boat a long way off the usual route, without me being even aware of it. It was a guttural, deep throat shout that had nothing whatsoever that resembled my feminine, medium-pitched voice.

Despite the way I guarded myself, I felt utterly ashamed later that night at having been laid down on the wooden floor of the boat, with the man starting to grab my clothing. Yet they had both become fear-struck and the most aggressive one did heave on the oar like a madman to get me to the harbor, or should I say, to get rid of me as quickly as possible.

After having typed what happened that night in Pattaya—essentially describing my recollection of the events faithfully, exactly as I had committed them to memory—I went through a more precise reenactment of the whole scene a couple of days later. What prompted me to do so is the new global understanding I got about these anomalous events by reevoking them in one sweep, while they had been consigned to memory years apart. So I delved into comparing the way I fended off this Thailand aggression with how my Self acted in my previously written and analyzed ones, in Paris and Manali.

Reliving the Pattaya scene, how I was lying down on my back in the dark with the guy sprawled on me grabbing my clothes to tear them down, and the other one's shadowy silhouette lurking in threateningly on the side, I realized the next image I had was the guy back on his feet, standing in front of me, and then rushing to the back of the boat to the oar. It occurred to me that for him to be now standing straight near my feet, he must necessarily have made a few moves to disentangle himself, then get on one knee at least with a hand on the boat bottom or rim to propel himself up.

Yet none of those images had registered in my mind, and this despite the fact that any threatening situation propels my mind into hyperawareness mode. This is why I'm now convinced that, in this occurrence too, there had been a few seconds of a non sequitur, of an absence of perception, presumably at the moment my higher Self took control of my body to fend off the aggressor. And thus it was again a powerful psychic blow that propelled the guy from a lying position to standing backward on his feet then rushing to the back. The fact that it had a similar, utterly frightening, effect on the second aroused guy, an effect that didn't abate until they left me on the safe shore a good fifteen minutes later, is surprising too.

My inference that the Self's blow to the attacker was more efficient and crucial than the shriek is also supported by another element. As I realize it now, my recollection in Manali is one of a "high-pitched" shriek, whereas in Pattaya I described a "guttural, deep throat shout." What was more essential to their force must have been the psychic blow they accompanied.

After this careful analysis, it seems thus that in the Thailand instance, just as in the Manali case, we have both the power of the shriek and the Self delivering a masterful blow sufficient to frighten the aggressors out of their wits. And in both, a couple of seconds of a blanking out of awareness.

I must stress again that, apart from one exception, I have never in my life reacted to bodily aggression by using defensive or offensive muscular movements, even less so weapons, even after I trained in Aikido starting in my late twenties. This martial art was for me more about a mind-body harmonization. Besides, I never carried out the only instruction given, as an adolescent, by my mother, which was "hit the man in the balls." To the contrary, each of my reactions to aggression was different, spontaneous, nonphysical—and supremely effective. My baseline reaction, when I face danger or an unexpectedly risky situation, is to shift consciousness level and get instantly into a heightened state—in which, typically, my higher Self is the one dealing with the situation. As we have seen in these instances, whenever my Self takes over my mind and body, my I-consciousness (my consciousness flow) typically misses a few seconds of perception of the scene. Similarly, in my car accident in Provence, my Self was able to steer my ice-skidding car's course, while my mind was in hyperawareness and at hyperspeed for several seconds already (seemingly lasting minutes), all this before the actual blanking out of awareness during the accident itself, when my car flipped down the steep slope and crashed sideways on a lifesaving bunch of trees.

All things considered, above and beyond the crucial syg-energy blow delivered by my Self, the shriek must have had a powerful effect by itself. Indeed, we have two instances of a secret science of shrieks, in Celtic culture and in martial arts. In their book *The Celts and Extraterrestrials,* authors Edmond Coarer-Kalondan and Gwezenn Dana have explored the ancient writings of Irish Celts to find possible mentions of aliens. They notably sorted out several people (or ethnic groups) with traditions stating their ancestors "came down from the sky" and populated Ireland before the Celts' arrival around 1000 BCE. Such were the Fomore and the Tuatha Dé Danann. The Tuatha Dé Danann were a magical race of gods who lived in the other-world, and became *the Sidhe* faerie folk in Irish folklore (see plate 3). The ancient legends and texts (such as *The Battle of Mag Tuired* that recounts their overtaking of Ireland) describe many advanced technological tools and armament of these "gods" who regularly made war against peaceful human agricultural settlers, going as far as killing whole populations. In two instances, the Fomore (living in the island of Torini) used bacteriological weapons of mass destruction to wipe out in one blow the entire army of their enemies and decimate their people.

There are three more singular events in my life that could help shed some light on the way my Self takes over the reins of my body and mind to thwart a great danger. In the first, in Old Delhi, my Self shifted the sexual aggression mode of a group of men into one decent enough for their leader to take me to a rickshaw taxi stand. In the second, in New Delhi, my Self took control of my face to frighten a too-curious old ascetic in a dramatic way. And in the third case, my Self was strong enough to pull me out of an electrocuting circuit of four hundred volts, saving me from irreparable heart damage or possible death.

OVERTURNING GANG SEXUAL AGGRESSION BY UNTOUCHABLE MEN ON THE GANGES

It was morning in Old Delhi, where I lived for a couple of weeks in a shabby and low-rate hippie guesthouse, during my first journey to India. I was intensely meditating during this whole eighteen-month trip, and that morning, I decided I would walk and hitchhike, if possible, to the Ganges River to find a temple to meditate. Hindu temples are in great numbers along the rivers, especially on the Ganges, who is the most sacred river, and thought to be a goddess.

In fact, Goddess Ganga—referred to as *Maa Ganga* or *Ganga Mata*, Great Mother Ganges, in mantras and prayers—had been dwelling in the divine abode of the origin called Brahma's world. She was so powerful and free that, when she decided to come down to Earth, her

Fig. 2.2. Shiva androgyne, with Ganga flowing down from his ascetic bun (c. 1800 CE) British Museum

unbounded energy would have wreaked havoc there unless she touched down on a solid foundation. The god Shiva, the ascetic and yogi, had to receive her on his sacred sadhu's bun (see fig. 2.2). After canalizing her tumultuous descent, Shiva then let Ganga flow down from his bun unto the Earth. That maintained her sacred energy but with such a tamed strength as to be highly beneficial to Earth and humanity. Thus, from Brahma's paradise, through Shiva's bun, sprang down the Ganges, bringing water and life to Earth.

The yogis ascetics in India, called sadhus, vow to never cut their hair and it sometimes reaches to the ground. They form their large buns by twisting and rolling their thick dreadlocks (called *jata*) onto themselves. The sadhus' large bun and long hair are the symbol of their permanent state of ego-Self (Earth-Heaven) harmony, along the path opened by Shiva, the god of yoga, meditation, and spiritual knowledge (see fig. 2.3).

The bun expresses their activated kundalini energy (symbolized by Shiva's Naga or snake power, shown as wrapped around his neck) and their crown chakra operating as a sacred antenna to the divine hyperdimension's energy—while they strive to reach liberation (or moksha) (see plates 4a–b). Shiva's sadhus often wear a Tripundra, three ash lines across the forehead that symbolize the three sacred sounds of *AUM*, the mantra of harmony between the three dimensions of Being: cosmic consciousness (*brahman*, *purusha*), the Self (*atman*), and the ego (*jiva*).

Fig. 2.3. Statue of Shiva as a yogi, with bun and snake, at Murudeshwar, Karnataka, India
Photo by Thejas Panarkandy

I don't remember how I made it to within a mile or two from the river, in a deserted countryside. While following a dirt road, I must have missed the nearest ghats and temples of Old Delhi and gone astray toward a desolate shore of the Ganges.

That's when I asked my way from a nice Indian peasant with a white beard and a traditional turban on his head, riding a large wooden cart pulled by two immense cows. (Those huge Delhi cows, with a hump, have the most beautiful pairs of horns I ever saw, sometimes drawing a near circle; they are quite stunning.) When the driver showed me the path to the Ganges forward on the dirt road, I asked with a few Hindi words and lots of gestures if I could get on his cart, to which he agreed. I climbed in the long cart behind him, which was void of whatever vegetables or else he had brought to town. On we go, at the cows' slow pace, for quite a while indeed. Then finally we pass beyond an area of thornbushes and I discover a beautiful sandy shore along the magnificent river. The driver even pushes his cart on the sand punctuated by low greenery, then stops and, turning to me, gestures to the Ganges with a "Tikka, tikka!" (That's it, that's good). I thank him warmly and say good-bye with the usual sadhu mantra *Hare Om!* and a namaste gesture.

I watch him make a whole circle with his cart to depart by the same dirt road, before I even glance fully around me . . . and realize that I'm in the middle of nowhere, with no temple, house, or even anybody in view. All the while, I'm walking toward the river a good hundred yards away, on soft sand so hot for my bare feet that I shift to a way of burying each foot at each step to avoid being badly burnt; a larger landscape of open white sand bordering the river and low vegetation on the land side, opens in front of me. The sight is enchanting, but the large sandy area, and the absence of trees or anything that would offer some shade from the burning sun and scathing heat don't really make for a convenient place to meditate alone. Furthermore, there's a strange kind of oppressed nowhereness to this place, some sensation that I've never experienced in India where I deeply feel I'm belonging to any place in which I happen to be.

When, a bit disturbed, I turn back to the dirt road, the cart is already gone. What I see, however, is alarming.

A group of young and sturdy guys, four of them, seemingly emerging from the dirt road, are rapidly advancing toward me with dark looks and faces distorted by anger and affront. Within seconds they are surrounding me and shouting at me all at once in a tumultuous wave of aggression, in the broken English of the common people. I don't like the fact they are so muscular, in sleeveless tee shirts, like rickshaw drivers or coolies, arrogantly raising their balled fists and turning by the instant more sexually bellicose . . . as I sense any second they are going to throw me on the ground and gang-rape me.

"Here no Connaught Place"; "No hippie place here"; "You, no come here"; "Here, untouchables place, you no come here!"

Understanding dawns on me. So this is it: I just landed in a Dalit village—the oppressed lowest caste of people that nobody belonging to another caste would, traditionally, be allowed to even "touch."

They behave like the kings of the place, the strongmen, the gang of the young generation. I know for certain that not one person would ever get out of their houses or shacks and give me a helping hand.

All the while, I'm just standing my ground silently, weighing their anger, not reflecting any emotion—in fact, as I explained earlier, as soon as I sense some level of danger, I immediately shift to a heightened consciousness state and a fearless vigilance.

They are now a tight group closing in on me, their large shoulders cornering me, I smell their angry sweat. I watch, with total calmness, their sexually aroused eyes and gestures. I spot the leader—just in front of me, the closest and shouting straight at my face, the loudest, the most violent. The leader's head is inches from my face, his hands already getting on me.

That's when I, without any intention on my part nor any emotion, spontaneously do the most unconceivable gesture. Looking him straight in the eye, I slowly raise my right hand, showing my palm open in a peaceful (and sacred) gesture, and lay my fingers on his forehead a few seconds, then take my hand off and down my side, very calmly and neutrally, without uttering a word.

The leader is frozen, our eyes are still locked. I feel the whole group is frozen in shock. Nobody moves nor says anything for an immensely long couple of seconds.

Suddenly the leader straightens his head and posture; in the same movement, he takes my hand and says "Come, quick, you take rickshaw and go back."

And as unfathomable as it may sound, he actually pulls me *by the hand* back onto the dirt road, then a hundred yards farther into a spot where a bicycle rickshaw is parked, calling commandingly for somebody (the driver) to come, and then ordering him to drive me back to Old Delhi.

While doing this, he was telling me to hurry up, as if he had to save me from the other guys as quickly as possible, as if he had not been the most aggressive or hadn't been spearheading the behavior of the group all along, a group that altogether stopped harassing me as soon as he did himself.

Or maybe (as another way to look at it), he was just given a silent order from my own Self to take me immediately and hurriedly out of here and find the rickshaw. I add this possibility because, instead of being frightened by my Self (as we saw in other occurrences), the leader's aggressivity was overturned and inverted into an active will to help, to the point that he made a gesture done only for one's own family and friends: he actually took my hand to lead me to safety.

In this occurrence, we see the immense wisdom of the Self. First, because the Self always chooses the least dramatic path and the one costing the least, not only for me but for all the other actors. And second, because in that instance the Self broke a social interdiction, an enduring taboo—that of touching Dalit. And in doing so, it instantly rescinded the caste anger that had led to their aggressivity in the first place. It is worth noting here that, as a psychosocial compensation, the ones that everyone avoids and won't have any physical connection with—the outcasts in a literal sense—will forbid forcefully their own living spaces to anybody not belonging to their clan.

Let me take a moment here to say something about this caste system in India. Since the 1990s, the various Indian governments have launched positive actions to integrate the lower castes into the education system, job market, and government positions. It has been a laudable trend, as these social antics were devastating and impeding a healthy equality of people and voters in the most populous democracy in the world.

However ignominious we feel the antique caste system was—not only in India but in other historically strict hierarchical societies as well—this Indian society had, quite uniquely in fact, developed a way for any outcast person (man or woman) to be able to transcend it. Indeed, the wandering ascetics in India are considered outside and above the caste system, which doesn't apply to them. Sadhus are the ones who have totally cut all ties with society (and its norms) to pursue a spiritual quest. They are not supposed to work and earn money, as opposed, for example, to Tibetan monks, who generally work to sustain themselves. Sadhus must always wander from town to town, barefoot, and sleep in temples, but no more than a few nights in the same one; they must beg for food but no more than three times a day; they must cut all communication with their previous family and birth community and live up to the deep lonesomeness of their own Self in front of the cosmic consciousness and their god. Their only companions are fellow questers they meet in diverse temples along the road and with whom they share a few days and nights here and there.

My point is that anybody, at any age, can decide to be a sadhu, a saint, and devote one's life to the quest. Anybody can, in principle, suddenly leave their family—the more outcast the easier done—and become an extremely revered person on a spiritual quest (although in reality it's more difficult for girls and women). The Hindu system of old—despite the harrowing subjugation and suffering of the outcast—had left open an exit door while allowing for bypassing one's own birth caste, as a tribute to one's spiritual aspiration.

And similarly any married couple from any caste can, once their children have become independent, decide to dedicate the remainder of their lives to achieving the state of liberation (moksha); they will also cut all ties to their previous family and birthplace, settle in a sacred place, and live now mostly in meditation and from alms, being highly revered. They are called Sitaram, as they identify with the holy couple Sita and Rama, who achieved a shared liberated consciousness. Many such couples are seen in the sacred town of Shiva, Omkareshwar, on his sacred river, the Narmada.

MY SELF TAKES CONTROL OF MY FACE TO FRIGHTEN A TOO-CURIOUS ASCETIC

We'll now see yet another facet of the Self taking control over the body. It happened at the beginning of my first long journey to the East, at twenty-one years old. (Part of this story deals with the *superposed landscape phenomenon* that we'll explore in chapter 9.)

I was rescued by a young guru from being totally overshadowed by a malevolent immaterial entity with whom I had fought for several days and nights (mostly in a meditation posture, sometimes lying down)—after I had tried and failed to save another quester from its grip in the first place. We were both of us, as well as his friends, staying in a cheap hippie guesthouse in New Delhi.

The entity turned out to be too powerful for my three-year experience of meditation—and I finally ended up in the same place as the person, D, I had tried to help, having failed to overcome it. Apart from my clear awareness, steady soul, and unbending will to save myself from this terrible plight, my energy-body (my aura) had been wholly "taken," and this for a couple of days already, during which I had been desperately looking for some help in temples and with ascetics, to no avail.

That's when the friends who were traveling with D, and who had asked me to do something for him in the first place, told me a great young guru was going to give a speech that day at Connaught Place, the central plaza of New Delhi. I had never heard of him before, but they kept bothering me about it so much that I finally followed them. And now I found myself with them, in the fourth or fifth row among a dozen narrow rows of Westerners, set on the right side of the stage, perpendicular to the numerous and large rows of the main audience, a huge and overwhelming crowd of thousands of people.

When, on arrival with my friends, we sat on our chairs, the guru was already on the stage, talking with his group; then he came forward toward a set microphone, ready to start his address; his mother (the Mataji) was now standing sideways more than a yard behind him, and two rows of venerable ascetics were sitting at the back of the podium.

At that moment—I was in such a dire situation, my aura totally darkened by the entity—I thought to myself that if he was indeed such an enlightened being, then he should be able to hear me and help me. And with this thought, I sent a desperate telepathic call for help.

Immediately after my silent call, I saw him turn his head 90 degrees toward his right side and search through the rows of Westerners and spot me; for a fraction of a second, our eyes met. What's more stunning is that the Mataji, four feet behind him, did the same thing nearly simultaneously and spotted me too. Then he turned his gaze back toward the main crowd in front of him, still silent, while a powerful energy started to slowly rise up from my feet and, like a blanket, passed over my energy body and aura, slowly, all the way up to my head, purifying it and leaving my chakras alight with an intense white light. In a matter of a few seconds, not only was I back in my personal luminous aura, but I had received a gift of his own potent spiritual energy. (This surplus energy allowed me, on getting back later to the guesthouse, to free my friend from the grip of this entity, something that I had endeavored early on, about a week earlier.)

The guru never looked back at me (nor did the Mataji), and he started talking to his audience. That's when I had a vision of two superposed layers of reality—the higher one being the immaterial hyperdimension of Selfs (more in chapter 9).

Yet my consciousness remained centered in my body and I felt the best way to show my gratitude for the lifesaving help I had just received, was to remain in empathy with the guru and to support his inspired discourse to his audience. So I turned toward the crowd and remained with my eyes closed and in a meditative state for the whole hour of his speech, despite not catching anything of the Hindi words being said. The funny outcome was that, when I finally opened my eyes at the end, all the Westerners' seats were void, and I was sitting alone, in a vigilant and rigid posture, turned toward the audience instead of the guru, in what must have been a rather bewildering sight for the people gathered there.

When I did catch myself in this bizarre posture, and being so shy at that age, I just felt like disappearing as quickly as possible. All I wanted was to avoid interacting in real time with the guru and Mataji and anybody else. Being swept up in a group of followers was not my path at all, and all along I had avoided staying too near to gurus, allowing only a rare and evanescent crossing of paths.

Thus I swiftly walked toward the back of the stage, opposite to the main crowd movement leaving the plaza, to depart incognito. Yet, there were numerous people already pacing in all directions. That's when I caught sight of a venerable ascetic who was hurrying toward me with a look of astonishment, awe, and curiosity as to who I was—having probably understood some of the strange anomalous events that had just happened between the guru and me. And me, all I wanted was to avoid interacting in reality with anybody. As the old man was now hardly a yard from me, crossing my path diagonally, suddenly I felt as if my face was covered by a mask, a veil of sorts, an energy field . . . and I saw the ascetic stop short in his tracks with a look of terror, raising his arms in astonishment, and quickly turning around and walking away, as if he had seen a dangerous sight.

As to what I experienced myself: my only intention had been to escape incognito and avoid being scrutinized (or else), yet I was seeing the old man's curious intention filling his mind. My interpretation is that my Self, in that situation—which was not dangerous at all for me, but just bothering—created the specific mask and grimace that could frighten precisely this ascetic and make him go away.

Furthermore, my Self must have known that I needed to remain in this supraconscious state, with the hyperactivated and unperturbed energy flow given by the guru, in order to have enough strength to expel the entity from my friend's mind and body on my returning to the guesthouse. And any stupid or mundane interaction could have put this at risk.

MY SELF THRUSTS ME OFF A LETHAL FOUR-HUNDRED-VOLT ELECTRICAL SOURCE

The event I'm going to recount now happened in my late twenties, when I was living in Paris with Pat, the guitarist. My gynecologist was a young woman in her early thirties, a former medical university colleague of my sister. Psychologically speaking, this was important since my sister, at the time nearing the end of her dermatology specialty program, had had a substantial influence on me since my teens as regards to medical matters, and as she had been the one to suggest the gynecologist in the first place.

My sister was only two and a half years older than me, but a wide cultural gap was standing between us, a generational gap. My generation was spiritually inclined, consciously and intensely on a quest, while being anticlerical and anti-institutionalized religions. We were avid to travel to learn from the ancient cultures how to tap into our mind potentials. In contrast, her generation, nearly identical to that of my seven-years-older brother, was that of the sexually emancipated, loving exotic countries and travels, but hopelessly materialistic, down to earth, and with an endemic greed for riches and power. Of my two siblings,

I felt bullied and demeaned by my sister all along my childhood to the point that I went to live in our country family house in the south of Paris just to be by myself; the other one, my brother, was an alpha male who, fortunately, married early and didn't have much influence on me with his idiosyncratic pieces of wisdom such as "A woman can't realize herself completely unless she has a child!" This type of education didn't help two of his three daughters to maintain their professional activity. My brother was far from being up to my father, who would say (at a time when women were only starting to get to universities in large numbers): "As a woman, if you want to be independent, you need to have diplomas and a profession." My father, when adolescent, had been forced by his mother to get out of school and work at his parents' tea and pastry salon; his teacher came to their tea salon to plead with my grandmother, since he was an outstanding student, to let him pursue his studies up to a high school diploma. But she was the one to decide in my grandparents' couple, and she was adamant he should start learning the family profession. My adolescent father was devastated; all his life, he felt that this had been a missed opportunity and compensated for it by becoming an avid reader, a writer and painter as a hobby, self-taught in literature, art, and philosophy; then, once his catering house gave him the means, he became a modest art sponsor, loving to visit painters in their ateliers, and a collector of art and vintage literature books. Yet he who would have done anything to stay in high school (and who had asked his teacher to interfere), was able to empathize with my utter dislike for it, to the point of saying to me: "High school is really a bore, I get that; just find a way, get the notes to go through it as quickly as possible. Once you start university, it'll be exciting!"

My gynecologist was thus young, smart, competent, and perfectly self-confident. That appointment was a routine checkup that would be complemented with the mandatory cervical cancer test. We were only the two of us in the exam room and in fact in her whole medical suite, which was separated from the waiting room. And as usual, we, the women patients, would lie on the examination bed stark naked.

This bed was unusually high and featured a three-step metallic stepladder to climb and access the bed. She had already taken a uterine cervical tissue sample, had removed her apparatus to do so, and just told me I could get off the bed and dress up. Saying that, she had turned her back to me, now getting busy at a work table along the wall, to store the sample in a small, sanitized bottle with a tag to send to the laboratory. Her back was about a yard from the bed, and at the level of the steps opening on that side.

So, I'm a bit dizzy and out of it, because the procedure always hurts me (while I'm told authoritatively it shouldn't). As I put my feet on the top and then the second highest metallic steps, I see nothing to steady my shaky body on either side of the steps other than the extra-large metallic shade of the exam lamp that, bizarrely, has been lowered and is now just at the perfect level and position for me to put my left hand on it to stabilize myself. And gee! I get such an electric shock that I've never experienced anything that strong; I let out a low throaty shout and realize I'm glued to the shade—can't take my hand off, can't control my muscles. My vision is reduced to my hand on the shade (as it was while I came to touch the shade), in a hazy, nearly fluorescent light.

That's when I see a human silhouette, like a dark shadow, that crashes forcefully on me, with such force that it rips my body from the electrical bind, freeing me from it.

I gasp and let out a sigh, trying to catch my breath, and glance toward the gynecologist, who is turning her head around to look at me, and I say to her:

"I'm glad you pushed me away and out of this electrocution circuit! I just couldn't take my hand off the shade by myself!" And she answers, a bit too cool:

"Me? No, I didn't do anything of the sort."

That's when I realize she still had her back to me and is only turning now to face me.

I'm left wondering, gaping and still gasping for air, *If it was not her pushing me, then WHO did it?*

"Never had an electrocution with such a strong current! It was unbelievable!"

"Yes, I know, it's four hundred volts for our lab equipment; I know I've this current leak . . ."

She leaves her voice trailing, with a slight recognition that, indeed, she had the problem already—with another or other patients, plural—and that she should have taken care of it.

I'm befuddled. She knew and she didn't manage to call an electrician when such a voltage could be deadly, no less! She had some problem with other patients receiving a shock! She is not sorry or even pretending to be so! With all the money she makes!

I'm still gasping for air, shaken and feeling very feeble.

"It was really an incredibly strong current . . . normally, with the two hundred and twenty volts, it's just a jolt and that's all of it . . . I can't even stand up. I'll not be able to drive thirty minutes to go back home. I'll have to stay at my parents' house that's very near here, and lay down a while."

She finally, reluctantly, acknowledges my state and tells me (while I detect she's really annoyed at having to do that, and not at all sorry for me):

"Look, get dressed and go sit a while in the waiting room. I'll have a specialist come to your parents' house this evening to do an electrocardiogram check on you."

It took me about fifteen minutes to feel I could now walk more or less steadily, but I was still in no shape to drive. Pat, who had been waiting in our parked car all that time, took over the wheel despite having no valid driver's license, and we drove to my parents' flat, where I slept for a couple of hours.

Later that afternoon, the cardiologist, after completing his analysis of my cardiac rhythm, told me that there would be, from now on, a permanent signal on my electrocardiogram that would tell another specialist that I had suffered such an electrocution in the past.

On reflection, the carelessness of the gynecologist while dealing with such a high voltage system was really hard to believe, especially from a scientifically trained mind. Why did she wait to have the system repaired? And why would she, knowing there was a persistent electrical leak, need to lower the lamp and particularly near the bed and the steps—an invitation to touch it, even inadvertently? And why having everything metallic around the bed instead of insulated with plastic sheets or rubber, when her naked-feet patients wouldn't be protected by rubber shoes as she was? But more to the point, when she heard my guttural shout, why didn't she react immediately to check on me and push me away? (Of course, as we'll see, such a push would need to be done with great strategy to keep oneself safe.) And this negligence was on par with her total indifference to others, her lack of empathy to the point of being boorish and crude. Needless to say, I found another gynecologist for my future safety.

So, let's get back to this anomalous event and ponder the question that crossed my mind again:

If it was not her pushing me, then WHO did it?

Let's first assess what such a high voltage really entails in terms of current intensity and its effect on the heart, as it is the intensity in amperes that determines the gravity of the electrocution.

Medical examination lamps are usually 400 watts, divided by 400 volts, it gives us a current of 1 ampere.*

A Wikipedia article on electrical injury sets a current of 0.5 ampere for the duration of 1 second as enough of a shock to produce muscular contractions so severe that the person cannot let go of the

*According to Watt's Law, I = P/E, that is, Current (I, amperes) = Power (P, watts) / Voltage (V, volts). At 0.5 to 1 ampere, for a duration of 10 to 200 milliseconds (ms), there is already a possibility of muscle contraction (being glued to the source) with possible irreversible effects. From 1 to 2 amperes, the probability of fibrillation rises and reaches over 50 percent. Of course, the longer the time, the higher the risk of fibrillation (reversible or not), so that at 0.05 ampere, fibrillation may occur after 1 second.

wire or device that is shocking them; and at 1 amp, there's a good probability it will happen after 200 milliseconds. With a higher current (in amperes), breathing becomes labored, then ventricular fibrillation of the heart occurs—a twitching of the walls of the heart's ventricles that may be lethal if the person is not promptly treated with a defibrillator. But, at still a higher amperage, the shock clamps the heart to protect it from ventricular fibrillation, and the person's chances for survival are better.

It is well known that, if P witnesses somebody A being stuck and glued even to a low voltage circuit, if P touches A slowly, then P would get glued also and both could be electrocuted to death. (In case of high voltage, above 1000 watts, don't even think about it.) The sole possibility to save A from electrocution, if the current can't be turned off, is for P to have isolated shoes and to use a nonconductive wood or plastic stick to disconnect A from the source. Or else, to calculate a speed and a rush forward with such force and swiftness that he/she would be able to violently push A so as to break the touch to the electric charge, while both of them will be taken farther away by the impact force.

Let's consider what I saw was happening at the moment I was electrocuted: I realized I was being electrocuted by an abnormally high voltage when I perceived, in front of me, my hand glued to the lamp shade and couldn't, with a simple reflex, remove it; and simultaneously, coming from just behind my shoulder, I saw a body silhouette, rather indistinct, like a dark shadowy figure, that suddenly rushed in with great speed and collided with me (or just my arm) with a force and momentum so great as to interrupt the electrical circuit. Yet I didn't fall and my body wasn't thrown off-balance. As I had previously turned to my left side toward the lamp (to use it to steady myself), the shadow figure was coming from the side of the lab where stood the gynecologist—hence my first assumption it was her doing it—and anyway, there was nobody else in the room to push me that way.

My final assumption is of course that it was my own Self, with its immaterial *ki* force, who saved me from electrocution.

As a comparison to the other helpful and sudden interferences of the Self we have reviewed, here my Self doesn't fuse with my mind and take over the willful action; in contrast, in this case the Self uses the same type of ki force—syg-energy—that enables it to knock out an aggressor, but instead directs this force at my arm so that I may be yanked from the electrocution source.

But now, after reviewing the scientific data on the subject, I'm inclined to suppose that the "body shape" that collided with me in order to hurl me away from the electrical source may have done so in a small fraction of a second (and not a second), and that I didn't realize that my own frequency was decoupled. That would be consistent with the scientific fact that I didn't suffer major heart damage and didn't need to be treated with a defibrillator. With my mind in hyperspeed, what felt like a second was in real time only a fraction of a second. Indeed, mental hyperspeed is far from rare in peak states, where it is often associated with hyperawareness—for example, in Near-Death-Experiences; I have related such a hyper state during a car crash I experienced in Provence in my book *Living Souls* (chapter 2). Furthermore, there is no basis for assuming that the Self, who can control hyperdimensional, faster-than-light energy, would need as much time as a second to act. And if everything happened in a fraction of a second, then the doctor would have turned immediately on hearing my shout—only I was already disconnected from the source.

WHAT IS OUR SELF'S INNER POWER?

With the anomalous events we saw up to now, we reach an intimate understanding of our Self's inner strength and why this soft but immense power, while largely untapped, belongs to all of us. Why? Because it is the power of our supraconscious Self intruding in our conscious lives, and every one of us has such a hyperdimensional soul or Self. I want here to stress two crucial points.

The Power of the Self Defeats Physical Strength

The Self being immaterial, its power doesn't reside in physical fitness or strength, and to the contrary it is accessed and operated by all people connected and tuned in to their own inner soul. Yet the Self can defeat brute physical force and heal biosystems; it can also overwhelm complex matter systems and even technological systems.

In the decades following the collective awakening of the hippies embracing Eastern spiritual quest and yogic knowledge, to my watchful eyes it seemed that more women had collectively awakened to their Self than men. This is due in great part to the fact that we, the women, have been so systematically oppressed for so long, during several millennia of patriarchy and religious authoritarianism imposing their deeply seated biases against women. Just consider that even in the blueprint antique Greek Republic in Athens—a true leap in social organization and ethics at the turn of the sixth century BCE—women couldn't vote (apart from exceptions) and not all people were called citizens. (Athenian democracy was established under the leader Cleisthenes to eradicate tyranny and ran very stably for 180 years, from 508 until 322 BCE.)

Due to this terrible historical baggage, I felt it was important to stress that *the mind could override muscles*, and soul power could subdue and overpower material and physical might. It means a whole upturning of the patriarchy and macho paradigm based on *might equals right*. It means women, the disabled, and the kids, in order to defeat powerful opponents, don't need equal physical power but rather to explore their inner dimension and capacities.

Our HD Self Is Definitely Beyond Gender and Duality

Second, the Self is our hyperdimensional spirit, beyond duality and especially beyond gender. I am definite about this fact and all my experiences show that our Self reveals both masculine and feminine facets, as well as beyond-gender qualities, and this whatever gender (or no gender) we identify with in our social life.

Carl Jung came up with the concept of Self as a psychological conceptualization of the ancient spiritual and alchemical term of soul, or *anima* ("soul" in Latin, and feminine), and even *psyche* ("soul" in Greek). The Self, for Jung, was a clear-cut psychological fact, an assessment of the reality of a soul dimension that was based on principles of resonance and synchronicity, as opposed to the matter dimension bound to causal and physical laws. During his lifelong exploration, Jung attributed to the Self more and more autonomy and power, going as far as deeming it "trans-temporal" and "trans-spatial" (in brief, beyond spacetime) in his book *The Structure and Dynamics of the Psyche* (p. 413, p. 813).

In other words, he clearly understood, and especially during his collaborative work with quantum physicist and Nobel laureate Wolfgang Pauli, that the Self was, in each of us, a beyond-spacetime consciousness of the highest order.

Jung's monumental exploration of hundreds of alchemical treatises in several cultures allowed him to understand and translate in psychological terms the often symbolic language of the Self—our higher-dimensional being.

Jung attributed to men a feminine intermediary to their Self that he called the *anima*, and described it as a true angel, both a guide and a Hermetic opener of ways, messenger of the gods to our conscious. Now, being myself a Jungian theorist and a woman, I know that Jung attributed to women a masculine Self-intermediary, the *animus* (masculine form of *anima* in Latin); true to myself, I was a bit surprised that he gave it quite a poor power, and even negative qualities; one of his rare instances of shortsightedness, I must say. (And it could be why a woman, such as me, had to reply and reprove him by factual arguments!)

All my experiences in the domain of peak states and of my own Self's stunning interventions in my life, show that the Self is definitely beyond gender, just as it operates beyond bio-matter and spacetime. The Self displays qualities and strength both associated with predominantly feminine and masculine values. I want to emphasize that, as we now are aware of it (at last), there are natural variations among genders, as well as among psychological inclinations, and that if we call a certain quality, such as empathy, predominantly feminine, it does not mean that the other genders are devoid of it. My aim here is to stress the nature of the Self as being both masculine, feminine, *and* all shades in between; that is, a totality containing all possible variations. This is important because, again, I deem that Jung was quite biased on the question and got confused (by his own projections) when he confined the animus of women to mostly psychological traits and, moreover, negative ones (such as being obstinate, or in constant self-justification); in brief, he didn't attribute to the animus the same high spiritual level and guidance function as to the men's anima. As far as I'm concerned, I never related to any animus concept, and hardly to the anima one. From the start, my guiding entity was the Self—a She-He, de facto beyond gender. And regarding intermediaries, I prefer the concept of allies, women, men, and genderless, or asexual entities and spirits, including that of animals and plants.

Let's see some of the Self's characteristics (as demonstrated in real-life feats).

- It is a *soft power* as opposed to a warlike, competitive, and destructive one,
- It is a power that *works through harmony and synergy,* as opposed to manipulation and control.
- It always uses the *minimal and lightest intervention* needed to procure protection and avoid harm or danger, as opposed to abusive and overreactive force.
- It operates by considering the *global situation*, and by *caring* about not only the physical person it belongs to but all actual participants, and even a larger context; in other words, it uses a global defensive strategy as opposed to focusing on short-term interests.
- It *doesn't aggress or harm* the people posing a danger but instead finds ways to make them afraid or impotent, or else to circumvent their schemes, unless the situation is both extremely dangerous

and a potential threat to many people—in which case it will still choose the least action to stop the threat.

All in all, your Self and its soul power is your wise, soft, and strategic feminine ally, and at the same time, it is your strong, unbending, fearless, and imposing masculine ally.

3
ANIMAL ALLIES

Animal allies have been a constant help and source of guidance during my long trips alone, hitchhiking mostly barefoot and penniless. They appear of themselves to fend off danger, in situations of need, or else in moments of elation and harmonization, in so many ways that I wouldn't be able to remember them all. Sometimes they just convey in a quite forceful way that you are not taking the right road . . . as when an owl stood in the middle of a small road at night and wouldn't budge while staring fixedly at me (unafraid of my car lights), thus impeding me from following it until I backed away from it—only to realize this was not the road I was looking for. As we all know, owls are normally quite shy both of people and of cars, and it was a quite singular encounter.

Well, I'm not a Yaqui sorcerer and I don't cultivate animal allies. Yet they have abounded in my life, not only during my travels but also during some high-stakes spiritual and magical endeavors that sometimes kept me in heightened state for a period.

I'm going to recount here three significant encounters with them, which (at least in the first two cases) show how intelligent and inspired their behavior is, while it definitely departs from normal animal behavior.

A DOG ALLY LEADS ME TO A HIDDEN (PI GATE) TEMPLE IN SOUTHWEST INDIA

We were on our way, my companion Phil (not his real name) and me, to explore a large piece of land in Karnataka, along the southwest coast of India, where numerous ancient temples had been progressively overtaken by the sand. We had been told some temples were half buried in the sand, while others were still standing at ground level, this without any more information. On arriving at the small town bordering this terrain, we took a scooter rickshaw, explaining to the driver what we wanted to see, and asking him to take us to the beach nearest to the temples. He drove us through a large forest, on a dirt path.

We were a bit dazed when the driver left us on a pristine sand beach, quite extensive, pointing to the forest along it in a large sweeping gesture while repeating "tikka, tikka" (this is it, that's good) and pocketing his fee. Before we could realize we were in the middle of nowhere with no one in sight, he had already departed.

So here we are, both of us standing on this sizzling hot white sand beach, stretching for miles both ways and bordered by a large forest that's hiding any temple from our view. Everything seems immense—the perfectly flat and sparkling blue sea with the low whisper of subdued waves, the elongated beach, the thick greenery flanking it; the deserted landscape feels transcendent, undulating in heat vibrations. We're looking around us, mouths agape, and taking the measure of our problem. How in hell are we going to find these temples?

At which point I see, some 150 yards away, a slim dog, wild as most of them are in India, who has just emerged from the forest and, with a smart bearing, is crossing the sand beach diagonally on what looks like a straight line toward us. I zoom in on the dog coming, amazed, and somehow I know the dog is the answer—I recognize in him a shamanic ally. Phil's mouth is gaping, as if he were watching an apparition and wondering what's going to happen; none of us say a word.

The dog has a resolute and poised way of walking. I lock eyes with him as he is approaching, and he comes to about a yard and a half from me and sits on his hind legs right in front of me, his head turned up toward me, as if in expectation. His composed and self-assured way of waiting for me to ask him something further informs me he is such an animal ally.

An *ally* in the shamanic sense is ad hoc and impromptu help or guidance from the spirit world offered to the shaman, expressed through animals or plants, and sometimes even fellow humans. It is the deep connection of the shamans with nature, their seeing and engaging with the spirit of all living beings, including Earth as the conscious entity Gaia, that renders this type of communication possible. As soon as you are able to tune in to that soul dimension, not only is everything alive, but every being is communicating.

I know Phil is barely acquainted with this dimension of reality, his sole information derived from Castaneda's books on the Yaqui sorcerers' path in Mexico, not through personal experiences. And so I talk to the dog aloud, just for his sake, so that he may hear this shamanic communication. As for the animal allies, they pick up the thoughts and intent of course, and not the words per se, so that you might as well just send your thoughts to them or speak whatever language.

I still look straight at the dog's intelligent eyes and say aloud, with a friendly yet authoritative tone,

"Take us to the temple."

The dog instantly springs up on his legs (he had not moved at all till then), turns around, and starts walking slowly toward the forest. (Note that I said "the" temple, and this shows that my unconscious already knew that only one of them was the aim of this whole trip, as I will explain further on.)

So I immediately start to walk behind the dog, totally silent and immersed in my connection to the ally dog; and I just sense that Phil, now behind my back, locks step with me.

Now let me further explain that as soon as I recognized the approaching dog as an ally, my consciousness shifted to this shamanic dimension—the inner silence that allows direct communication with not only animals but also plants, and even with what our materialist science calls "inert matter" and which, in contrast, the shamans "see" as sacred rocks and high places endowed with a spirit or consciousness dimension. When I am in this higher frequency mode—in sync with the hyperdimension reality—I'm inclined to be entirely focused on it and to keep to myself silently.

The dog enters the forest in between bushes, and walks on virgin sand among the trees and thickets—and I follow him, and I feel Phil following me. What is truly amazing is that the dog will never look backward toward us, yet he walks at our own strolling speed, slowed by the fluffy sand, always remaining at a constant distance of about a yard and a half ahead of me. He does not follow any path but cuts through the vegetation. In the same fashion, I never look back at Phil, but sense him walking behind me.

About ten minutes later, I'm surprised to get to the edge of the forest and to discover a large field laid bare during this dry season, as crops will grow only with the rain of the monsoon. After walking along the edge of the forest for some distance, the dog cuts into the forest diagonally again (so that, for whatever reason, we followed some sort of triangular path).

After another ten or fifteen minutes, Phil suddenly lets out a big sigh behind me and declares that he is tired of walking and wants to smoke a spirited joint in this beautiful setting. And, as soon as it's said, he stops and sits under a magnificent old tree. Looking at him cozying up to the venerable tree, I think it's a great idea, and I go and sit next to him under the tree. I'm already in a natural high mode, and this will not break my state; I'll use it to enhance it, and both of us will attain a higher consciousness.

When I had stopped walking on hearing Phil, the dog had stopped as well in his tracks and turned around. Now he sits on his hind legs, facing us with alert and watchful eyes, immobile as a statue about three yards from us, right on the path toward the temple that only he knows.

I'm totally confident that he will stick to his shamanic course; I'm in an empathic connection with him, my ally, all the while keeping my intent as a buzzing antenna—and while I'm looking at Phil rolling the joint and then as we pass it between us, I don't let go of the ally connection nor the intent, and neither does the dog ally.

So here we go for about a half hour. At which point, we are both in a higher and more sensitive state and Phil is enjoying it tremendously. Me, I want to move on. But Phil declares that he wants to stay there longer and enjoy his expanded state. (It's possible that he didn't sense and trust that the dog was really taking us to the temple, and he preferred to be high rather than just walk around.)

I get up and try my best to make him stand up. The dog stays put.

"Come on, Phil, we've not discovered the temple yet! The dog is waiting for us, he'll take us there."

It's only at my second prodding that Phil finally agrees to get up. As soon as we take a step in the direction of the dog, the latter springs to his feet, turns around, and shows us the way (he had remained perfectly immobile and watching us during our whole break).

Here we go again, me following the dog, and Phil following me. And after a while, suddenly we distinguish a small, square temple, wholly clear of sand. The dog reaches the temple and sits about four yards to the side, and looks at us kind of happily.

When I get closer, I see the sure sign that this is indeed *the* temple, because it is flanked by the symbol that had been shown to me in a potent vision—the pi symbol—that appeared in the fire burning in the hearth of my writing house. The message had come to my mind then that this was the Pi gate, a powerful rite of passage that was going to happen in my life quite soon, and I had made a drawing of the logs that had taken this exact shape that I was seeing now standing in stone, in a sacred place, as the entrance to the Lingam-Yoni, the Shiva-Parvati, temple—the Pi gate to some higher connection and completeness.

About two yards in front of the small temple, and perfectly aligned with the two sculpted columns edging its front facade, was a large pi sign, π (or capital Π), with curved lines, made of finely sculpted stone. The width was the same as that of the temple—about five feet. And the pi (π) shape itself was made of thick curved tubular stones about eight inches in diameter. The height was a bit higher than its width. The legs of the pi were buried in the sandy ground, to keep it firmly standing.

As for the square temple itself, it was housing a Shiva lingam set at the center of a circular yoni—the perfect 3D symbol of the masculine-feminine complementarity and unity as fusion. The sacred lingam-yoni (phallus-vagina) symbolism is ever present in the oldest

Fig. 3.1. Shiva lingam and yoni temple at Lepakshi, Andhra Pradesh, India
Photo by Jeggi V.

temples in India and is the equivalent of the Taoist yin-yang symbol (see fig. 3.1).

With Phil, we were in awe while contemplating this magnificent jewel of a temple, approaching silently toward the Pi gate, and then the temple itself. Since the facade of the temple was adorned on each side with two columns of finely chiseled stone, we felt drawn to go and sit, each one of us silently and of a common accord, each with our back on one pillar, and got into a deep meditation while facing the Pi gate in stone.

I had found the Pi gate predicted to me, and during this meditation I indeed sensed that a new dimension, a new level of consciousness, was soon to be opened for me. I saw this immaterial gate as a sort of threshold, and I was approaching it in my spirit, standing on its edge, but still unable to pass through it. I got the deep certitude that soon another visionary state was going to unfold, that would signify my passing through the gate. (And indeed, it happened a few weeks later in Hampi.)

The Horned Gods Shiva-Pashupati, the Celtic Cernunnos, the Sumerian Enki, and Hermes

Strangely, despite four previous trips to India and two stays in Nepal (spanning nearly three years on-site altogether), I had never seen such a simple and man-high geometrical stone sculpture facing the entrance of a small Hindu temple. And it didn't cross my mind to compare it to huge elaborate torana gates. It was only years later that I discovered a dozen of them, of nearly identical shapes, at the Pashupatinath Temple complex in Kathmandu, some even with curved legs (see fig. 3.2).

Pashupatinath Temple is the oldest Hindu temple in the Kathmandu Valley, Nepal; it is an immense 246-hectare complex that has existed since 400 CE and that the Hindu religion deems "the Protector of the Universe." It is dedicated to Shiva, who took with Parvati a recreative and amorous incarnation as deer to enjoy dwelling in this beautiful Bagmati River Valley. When other gods finally located him

Fig. 3.2. A sort of Pi gate as a bell hanger. Shiva temple within the Pashupatinath Temple complex, Kathmandu, Nepal (detail)
Photo by Rajesh Dhungana

in the wilderness, Shiva declared he would henceforth be known as Pashupatinath, Lord (*Nath*) of all animals, to honor his incarnation as a deer (yet, he is often called Pashupati).

Interestingly, Shiva as a deer is the missing link to the European Celts—known to have emigrated to Gaul (France) and then western Europe from Scandinavia and northern Germany around 2000 BCE—and specifically to the god Cernunnos, the Horned God, who donned stag antlers (see fig. 3.3 and plate 5).

Fig. 3.3. *Top*: Shiva-Pashupati seal, Mohenjo Daro, Indus Valley, circa 2350–2000 BCE. Proto-Shiva, Lord of Animals, like the Celtic god Cernunnos
Photo by Aavindraa

Fig. 3.3. *Bottom*: Cernunnos with animals on the Gundestrup cauldron (detail). Denmark, circa 200–300 CE
Photo by Palnatoke

The Pashupati seal shows an early prototype of Shiva (or his Vedic predecessor Rudra, who also bore the title "Lord of all the animals"). The deity has a triple head and a horned headdress and is surrounded by animals. (The Elephanta caves also have a three-headed Shiva, the Trimurti.)

Pashupati bears several similarities with the Celtic Cernunnos:

- Both are a horned deity, Pashupati with the African buffalo's circular horns, and Cernunnos with rare straight and fanning deer antlers.
- Both are called Lord of Animals and shown surrounded by them.
- Both are sitting cross-legged in a yogic posture, with one or two feet precisely at the kundalini lower chakra.
- Cernunnos is holding a snake in his left hand, a symbol of Shiva, of the Sumerian Enki, and of the Greek Hermes, and in his right a torque (similar to the Sumerian ring of power).

This representation of Cernunnos is very mysterious. For one, no other Celtic god or goddess is shown cross-legged, or with horns. But the Anunnaki gods of Sumer, who came from a nomad planet attracted and captured by our sun, and lived for millennia, are all represented with horns that, for the greatest gods, make three or four rows surrounding the skull, as shown on Shamash, the Sumerian sun god and god of justice from whom the Babylonian king Hammurabi received his famous code of laws (see fig. 3.4).

Among the three children of King Anu, Enki/Ptah finally lived with his half sister Ninmah. Both were prominent scientists—in the hard sciences and life sciences respectively—and they founded the Egyptian civilization with their son Ningishzidda/Thoth/Hermes. It was at the time when the great gods and later demigods ruled over Egypt—before the human pharaohs—for a total of 17,520 years, according to the historian Manetho's King List (circa 270 BCE). The first of seven great gods was Ptah/Enki, who ruled for nine thousand years. Much later, Inanna,

Fig. 3.4. Sumerian sun god Shamash with Anunnaki horns, holding the rod and ring of power
Photo by Katolophyromai

great-granddaughter of Anu, inherited the Indus Valley and founded a realm there. She received the power of kingship from Enki and her link with him was strong. (Hardy, *DNA of the Gods*, 49–51).

Now, what is truly surprising is that only the Sambar deer, whose habitat starts at the Indus Valley and extends northward up to the Himalayas and eastward in Southeast Asia, exhibits such V-shaped antlers (see fig. 3.5). So the Indus Valley origin of Cernunnos is clearly revealed. And vice versa, Shiva-Pashupati's circular horns belong only to the African buffalo, thus revealing his origin in Egypt (the only stone-builders civilization in Africa at the time).

Let's also note that Enki's honorary titles were the Serpent, the Knower of Secrets, and his emblem was two entwined snakes, a blue-

Fig. 3.5. Sambar deer in Thailand, with V-shaped antlers
Photo by Lip Kee Yap

print of the caduceus that was later the attribute of Hermes ("Mercury" in Latin), as shown on fig. 3.6.

Both Enki and Hermes were of immense erudition and were polymath scientists, just like Shiva the ascetic and knower, and his son Ganesh, the god of wisdom and an erudite, sometimes represented as studying a book under the protection of the Naga King. Furthermore, didn't the tradition of the gods with animal heads start in Egypt?

Thus, just as we have recognized the Egyptian Ptah in Enki and the Greek Hermes in his son Ningishzidda, thus linking the original civilization of Sumer to Egypt and later to Greece, we now have to assume that Enki and his son Hermes could have been known in the Indus Valley, and later on in India, as Shiva and his son Ganesh.

Fig. 3.6. Mercury/Hermes with caduceus.
Metropolitan Museum of Art
Courtesy Rogers Fund, 1918

An interesting supporting tradition is revealed by Yogi Ramacharaka in his book *The Science of Psychic Healing* that expounds an ancient yogic healing based on breathing the *prana* (the cosmic syg-energy saturating air). This pranic healing was evolved into a science "over twenty-five centuries ago" by a mysterious "great Yogi teacher" who had taught the Egyptians, and later on "the Greeks obtained a similar knowledge from India and Egypt." Shiva was definitely the archetypal "Yogi teacher" while Hermes was also a god of medicine, a *therapeutes*, which is why his caduceus is the emblem of medical science.

In conclusion, Shiva the yogi and consort Parvati incarnated as deer are the missing link to Cernunnos with stag antlers and the European Celts, while Shiva-Pashupatinath's horns relate to the Sumerian-Egyptian gods Enki/Ptah (Shiva) and his son Ningishzidda/Thoth/Hermes (Ganesh), both outstanding erudite persons in all of these traditions. I dare propose that the primordial god Enki and his consort Ninmah the geneticist (whom he assisted in creating man) were also at one point living and venerated in Inanna's Indus Valley (as Pashupatinath and consort, or Shiva and Parvati); then, known as Cernunnos married to the Great Goddess Ceridwen, they were the ones starting the Celt civilization and Druidism, a civilization that would have its blueprint in the Indus Valley and from there migrated to northern Europe and later western Europe. A corroborating element is the Sacred Marriage rites instituted in her temples by Inanna (in Sumer and Akkad, and in the Indus Valley) and the same rites performed by Cernunnos-Ceridwen in Druidism (as I expounded in *DNA of the Gods*, 147).

An Eighteen-Hundred-Year-Old Unicornfish-Rider

As a cherry on the cake, there is another surprise for us on this eighteen-hundred-year-old Gundestrup cauldron; namely, the exquisite unicornfish-rider, top-right of Cernunnos (see detail on fig. 3.7).

Fig. 3.7 Unicornfish-rider on the eighteen-hundred-year-old Gundestrup cauldron
Photo by Malene Thyssen

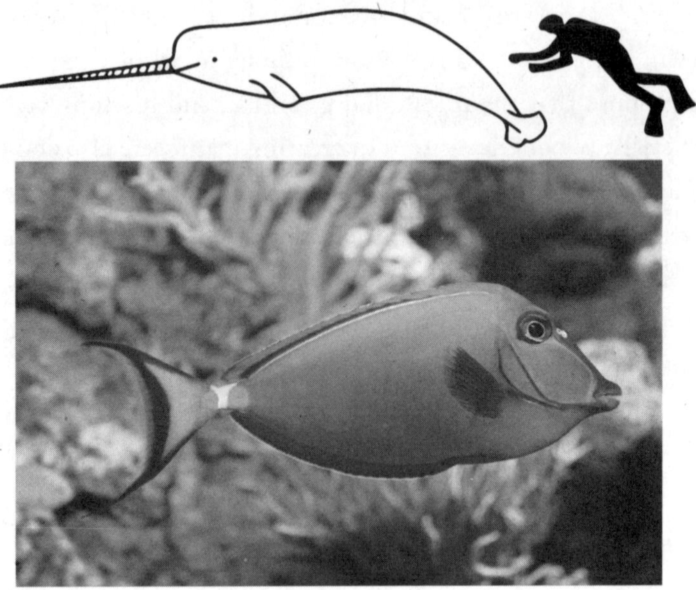

Fig. 3.8. *Top:* Narwhal shape and size
Photo by Chris Huh

Fig. 3.8. *Bottom:* The orangespine unicornfish (*Naso lituratus*)
Photo by Brian Gratwicke

Thus, the extremely sophisticated Indus Valley civilization, very urban—with large avenues, drainage and water supply systems, techniques of handicraft and metallurgy—had also the genius to domesticate a unicornfish.

From the size, it could fit the unicornfish of the dolphin family, the famous narwhal (whose spiraled unicorn is a tooth, a tusk), but it lacks the shape of the head and huge eyes and lives in the Arctic. The tusk is flexible and can bend, and narwhals use them to stun their prey. In contrast, the orangespine unicornfish (*Naso lituratus*) fits the head shape and huge eyes, lives in the Indo-Pacific ocean, and its spiraled yellow unicorn extends from the head backward, making a possible larger and longer relative a good candidate. In any case, a horn or tusk can be artificially bent and reshaped easily in order to be held by the rider.

A DOG OFFERING HIS PROTECTION IN HAMPI

At the end of that same journey in southwestern India, I had planned to stay in an inspiring spiritual retreat by myself for a full week and, after learning about Hampi, we opted to end our journey there. Since Phil had to fly back for a week-long professional assignment overseas, I had thought it would be a nice counterpoint for me to settle in a sacred place and indulge in a writing spree, instead of finding myself abruptly alone in Paris.

Hampi was the capital of the Vijayanagara Empire that flourished in the fourteenth century. After Phil left, I was spending several hours each day on a rented motorbike, exploring this magnificent land dotted with temples and ruins, in the midst of astounding rock formations. I was in a state of continual wonder—stopping here and there at stunning power spots to meditate, or to contemplate the sheer beauty of the place (see fig. 3.9 and plate 6).

Fig. 3.9. Rock formation near the Queen's Bath, Hampi
Photo by Surya Narayanan

And each evening, before sunset, I would leave my guesthouse at the center of town and walk all the way to the hill at the end of the large main street, where it stopped at a small temple accessed by stone steps leading to an inner columned hallway that in turn opened up, like a majestic entrance hall, on a wild high plateau abounding in outstanding rock formations. There was about twenty minutes of strolling along a maze of paths between the rocks, before getting to the edge of a long cliff that towered over a dry plain below, slanted toward the Tungabhadra River on my left. Giant rocks, a few temples, and some sacred ruins were sprinkled all around this vast desert and stony landscape, radiating a magical aura from its antique past.

I would sit at the edge of the cliff and dive into a deep contemplative state and meditation and, later on, walk back following clearly marked paths and using my torch light. In the first few days after the full moon, when the landscape was eerily lighted by the moon, I would stay there later into the night, entranced by the beauty and spiritual imprinting of this high place.

During the few days we were in Hampi together with Phil, we had come often to the plateau for sunset and had never been disturbed while haphazardly wandering around. Yet, as soon as he left, each and every evening I came there alone to take a stroll and meditate, I was met precisely at the entrance temple, under the columns, by a slim wild dog who would come toward me, and look at me with a friendly and jovial glance; then this very caring dog, with intelligent and soft eyes, would start happily walking next to me and enjoying it as it seemed. When I had finally found the spot at the edge of the cliff where I wanted to meditate that night, he would sit on his hind legs about two yards from me farther from the edge, facing inside the plateau, and just keep guard. He would stay there, as tranquil as me, and wait any length of time to accompany me all the way back to the entrance temple, now softly lighted by votive oil lamps, after which was the main street with its shops illuminated by petrol lamps and bulbs.

I have to state that I don't remember ever giving this dog food (and if it ever happened that was occasional), and to again stress the fact he used to sit away from me watching the opposite direction, toward the marked paths, unmoving for as long as I was myself seated on the ground. Quite a smart and intent behavior, you'll have to agree with me!

As it happened, the guardian dog was not without usefulness and merit. One evening, two smart, young, local guys found me as I was already sitting at the cliff edge—the dog had let me know of their approach by a low growling. When they became emboldened and started to bother me, by willing to engage in conversation and coming nearer, despite the fact I was not budging or answering them, the dog made its warning heard by barking loud and sharp, and dissuaded them from pushing their attempt further. They turned around and left, and I didn't have to abandon the terrain to them and head back, as would have surely happened if the dog had not been with me.

And as a last word, it wouldn't be fair on my part, just because I'm focused on animal allies, to leave this account at this sole watchdog level. I also have to say something about the rare level of empathy and friendly connivance that was shared between the dog and me—and the fact that this funny and happy dog was the one to offer it freely. How the dog knew about men possibly preying on women—especially those who love high states alone in the wild under the full moon—and that he could protect them, is a deep question. He was an inspired ally, that's for sure.

HOW I PROMPTED A DONKEY TO FIND A HIDDEN CHAMBER

The summer before I left for my first journey to the East, at twenty, I had a short but intensely harmonic love relationship with a soul-brother, Christian, that ended when we visited a Celtic Orthodox monastery in a tiny village in Brittany and he experienced there the spiritual call of his life. While we had been with the five monks forming this highly singular and far-reaching spiritual community only a few days—days filled with transcendent experiences for both of us—he abruptly felt compelled by his own Self to just join the monks, and realized that's how he wanted to live from now on. That implied terminating his medical university studies, despite having only his sixth and final year to complete to be an MD.

During our stay together at the monastery, I myself experienced for the first time the *telepathic field* the monks were sharing between them. It set a clear and constant telepathic connection while showing a definite field-like form; that is, it had structure and clear-cut boundaries in our 4D spacetime. This is a highly singular phenomenon that I have experienced again and again in my life of quester, yet it has presented somewhat different facets in variegated contexts and subcultures, as I recounted in *The Sacred Network*. The exceptional persistence and the stable reenactment of this field of shared consciousness (with consistent properties) led me to analyze it and model it (in an anthropological, then a hyperdimensional physics framework) as a telepathic-harmonic field of a hyperdimensional nature, or Telhar field (see Hardy 2020 (*PSTJ*)).

Fast-forward a few years later, and I'm visiting Christian, who is now living near Angers in France in another spiritual community that comprised another monk from the Celtic Orthodox order in Brittany, all spiritual questers. Three of them had opted to avoid their military draft (obligatory at the time, even if delayed for university students) and to switch it to a social service one. The clever pretext they had found was the restoration of valuable ruins, in this case an ancient network of caves that had been inhabited by ascetics maybe since early Christian times. The half dozen underground caves had been originally carved in the rock, and were disposed in a star shape around a central, round plaza. This plaza was now in the open, as well as the caves' doors forming a quasi circle around it, and its ground was just steeply slanted on one side to reach the level of the plain a few yards higher. What was stunning about these caves was that when crossing the large plain or when driving along the small country road, even from twenty yards away one was unable to see the caves or to imagine something strange was disrupting this monotonous and flat expanse of terrain with a few houses and trees dotting it. It had been quite a task to find them when I got there!

Christian and his friends were now happily living there, each with his own cave, having just upgraded them with wooden doors and furnished them with some basic practicalities of modern life, such as working tables, mattresses, bookshelves, and the like. These grottos were conveniently adjoining their teacher's property, where a communal kitchen was set.

While living in these grottos, they were indeed following the teaching of a very original woman guru, Lola, steeped in Celtic and Alice Bailey's theosophical initiatic knowledge, and highly psychic. Meditation, esoteric knowledge, the initiatic path itself, and more, were the stuff of dense exchanges each day, as they had been in the Brittany monastery, and of course, being myself a quester, I enjoyed them immensely. Our conversations, including with Lola, who was a personality full of enthusiasm in exploring the spiritual dimension, were extremely upbeat and congenial. Yet, all of them were like the core group around their teacher, whereas I was a visitor, and during these exchanges, I sometimes felt the air was dense around secrets they wouldn't share.

As it is, I was told they had a "secret chamber," a temple they had built or at least arranged to do their rituals, but they would not disclose its location to me, even less allow me to see it or participate in the rituals. In contrast, in the Celtic Orthodox monastery, whenever the head monk, Koulmer, was celebrating mass in the Christian Orthodox tradition, both I and Christian (before he became a monk) had always been welcomed to participate.

One afternoon when they had all departed by car for some undisclosed and mysterious endeavor of theirs, I was left alone in Christian's grotto and started pondering about the secret chamber. And suddenly I see the donkey standing at the edge of the plain overlooking the caves. An idea springs to my mind. I climb the slope to get near to the donkey, and start to pat him and stroke his neck and head while saying hello, and meanwhile letting him loose; then climbing on his back, I now whisper into his ears with a suggestive tone:

"Take me to the secret chamber."

And on he went, slowly but surely, across a large grassy field; he finally stopped in front of a white house set behind a wooden fence and that, sure enough, had an imprint of great spiritual energy. The gate in the fence was not even locked, and neither was the door to the chamber. And so I got in and could marvel at such a beautifully ornate spiritual lodge or church—remaining all the while very respectful of the sacredness of the place, neither touching nor disturbing anything, but just sensing and attuning to the semantic space. Then I returned to the donkey, now prodding him to take me back to the caves, which he did without any hesitation.

That night at dinner, after they all had returned, I suddenly blurted out mischievously:

"Your secret chamber is really great! Powerful energies there, for sure!"

A concert of surprised and skeptical voices erupted:

"What!? But how? You kidding!"

One of them, who knew better, simply asked:

"How did you find it?"

"Well—easy! I just climbed on the back of the donkey and ordered him to take me to the secret chamber!"

A few noses dipped toward their plates.

WHAT HAVE WE LEARNED SO FAR ABOUT ANIMAL ALLIES?

I'm sure that some of you, my readers, may find all kinds of rationalizations for the last two occurrences—that the dog in Hampi was looking for food (I never approached him by myself, never gave him food), or the donkey knew only one path (that's doubtful).

Yet remember the dog ally at the Pi gate. First, the injunction to the animal I used was nearly similar—half command, half friendly prodding; second, there were hundreds of temples half buried there in a vast swath of land; and third, the temple had a pi symbol carved in stone that had been predicted to me so precisely that I had done a drawing of it. And in chapter 5, we'll see in detail how this future journey marking the opening of a spiritual gate had been shown to me, not only one time with the pi sign, but in fact three times in the months beforehand.

So, what have we learnt so far?

First, animal allies appear all by themselves, at precise moments, and to fulfill a specific role or task, to help a shamanic or yogi soul who is involved at that moment in a spiritual endeavor.

They act intelligently and in a focused way, and they display an abnormal awareness of the whole situation and of the aim or purpose of the shaman. Once their task is fulfilled, they disappear (thus, when we came out of our eye-closed meditation, the dog-ally at the Pi temple had disappeared).

All in all, they are an expression of the collective consciousness (the whole hyperdimension of souls) that we share not only among us humans but with all of nature—plants, rocks, and animals—and crucially with the Earth as a living and conscious entity, Gaia.

4
ANOMALOUS BODY

The absence of pain during trance states is well documented in ethnological studies—specifically during possession trance, such as the Haitian Voodoo or Brazilian Macumba.

Sometimes, the head initiate (such as the *Madre de Dios* in Brazilian Macumba) tests the authenticity and depth of a novitiate's trance by quickly touching their arm's skin with a burning hot blade. If the novitiate reacts with pain, then she is not in a deep enough trance to allow her to be fully initiated.* Yet, within the cultural anthropology literature, I didn't see any specific mention of the absence of physical harm or bruises on the skin following hard blows, such as in the two instances I'll now recount. However, there were several reports of very aged shamans who, during their ritual trance, were able to dance for hours as if they were plagued no more with the arthrosis that was making even their walking a problem in their normal state of consciousness.

*Hardy, C. *La connaissance de l'invisible: le vécu de la transe*. Paris, France: Lebaud, 1991. (Le Dauphin, 1995–98). This book was the publication of the first part of my doctoral thesis in ethnology, on trance states and psi in ancient cultures. The second part, presenting parapsychological research on altered states and psi, was published as *La science et les états frontières*. Paris, France: Rocher, 1988. See also Bramly, *Macumba*.

Firewalking—walking barefoot over a bed of hot embers or stones during a trance state—has existed as a rite of passage or as a test of trance in many cultures. It is an example of an absence of pain and burns, thus an anomalous physiology, during trance states.

We have also lots of examples of trance states being used to cure a person in the ancient and First People cultures. See the stunning mural of Tlaloc paradise (Tlalocan) at the Palacia de Tepantitla, at Teotihuacan, Mexico (see fig. 4.1). Tlaloc is the god of rain, lightning, and earthquakes. In his pleasant paradise, water is in such abundance as to provide it plentifully to Earth, and it is where the people whose death was due to water and also leprosy dwell. We see shamans (with a headdress and mostly blue bodies) curing the sick with a powerful energy springing from their heads and mouths, represented by a blue ribbon with a bishop's crook shape that is directed to the sick person (see the pregnant woman) or organ (head, belly).

Fig. 4.1. Mural of Tlaloc paradise (Tlalocan), Palacia de Tepantitla, Teotihuacan, Mexico. National Museum of Anthropology, Mexico
Photo by Juan Carlos Fonseca Mata

The French psychiatrist Jacques Donnars devised a specific trance practice involving dancing to the music and rhythm of drums, and he was able to observe and verify over time not only the reduction of stress and anxiety (which had been his purpose) but also the spontaneous disappearance or lessening of a number of physical ailments (see Donnars 1981).

NO PAIN, NO BRUISES IN A HIGH STATE: HITCHHIKING ALONG THE NILE

In my late twenties, I embarked on a hitchhiking trip through East Africa with my boyfriend of the time, Pat the guitarist (whom we met already in chapter 2). The plan had been to take a flight to Cairo, Egypt, and then hitchhike southward along the Nile River all the way to Sudan's capital, Khartoum, from which we would head westward toward the Central African Republic (see fig. 4.2). Both of us knew Africa quite well already, and two years later we would engage in another long travel through West Africa, mostly by car, from Dakar in Senegal to Ivory Coast. Pat had spent his adolescence in Ivory Coast. As for me, it was going to be my second trip to Africa and my second crossing of the Sahara desert into the sub-Sahel. In the previous nine-month-long one, at twenty-three, I had hitchhiked alone across the whole continent from Morocco and Mauritania on the Atlantic coast to Kenya on the Indian Ocean, practically penniless and mostly barefoot. Then, after reaching Mombasa in Kenya, I crossed the Indian Ocean toward Bombay by boat and spent another nine months in India. We were in the late seventies—tyrants reigned unchallenged in some countries but the region was peaceful.

After landing in Cairo, we had eagerly explored the Giza pyramids and the Sphinx; then we had hitchhiked for a few days on the road that follows the Nile River.

That's how we had reached the exquisite and mysterious Luxor, some four hundred miles upstream, where we stayed for some time.

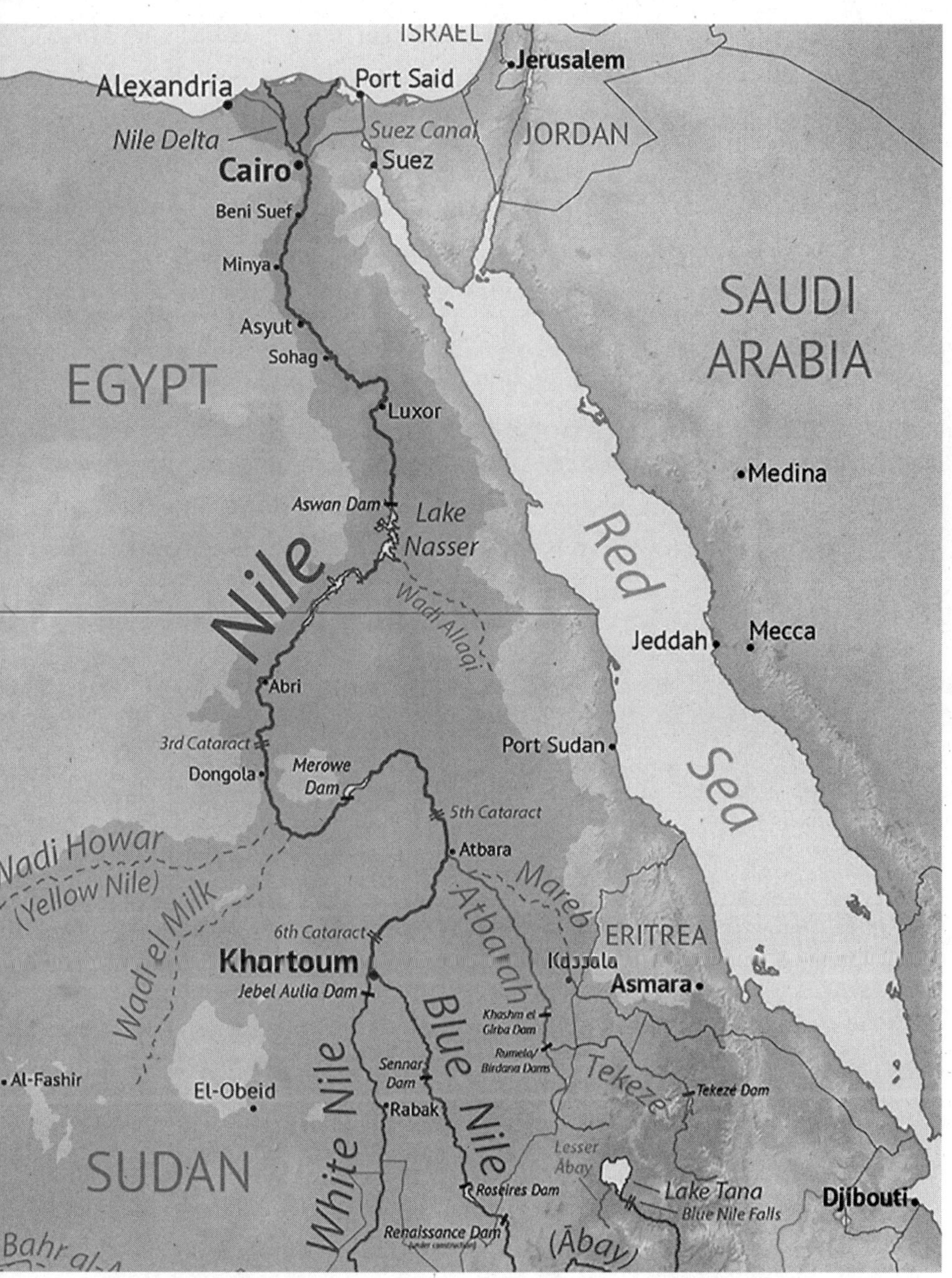

Fig. 4.2. Map of Ancient Egypt: the Nile up to the Fifth Cataract, and major cities and sites of the Dynastic period (circa 3150 BCE to 30 BCE), with Cairo and Jerusalem as references

Photo by Shannon1

In the city itself, we visited the Luxor temple, called the Amon Temple (see plate 7 top and bottom). Note on these two photos (from different authors) the very special energy generated between the central rows of columns (or in the central passageway), marked by a grayish upward and fanning outflow, contrasting neatly with the blue skies on the color photos; as well as (on *a*), strange oblique rays falling on the site and, if you stare at the two central columns, on their mid-height, and then look afar (defocus), you'll see the enveloping vibrant and bright blue aura all around them (lighter blue than the sky).

We explored also the magnificent Karnak temple complex of the antique Thebes, a few miles north, dedicated to the ancient Theban triad—the god Amun-Re, the goddess Mut, and their son Khonsu (see plates 8 and 9). The precinct of Mut is nested in the gracious curve of its sacred lake (see fig. 4.3).

Fig. 4.3. Precinct of Mut, nested in its sacred lake, at Karnak temple
Airbus, CNES/Airbus, Maxar Technologies map data

Fig. 4.4. Hypostyle Hall at Karnak Temple in Luxor
Photo by MusikAnimal

As we were both amateur musicians—Pat playing guitar and drums, and me mostly drums—we also connected with the local musicians for unforgettable jam sessions with their traditional instruments (and one extraordinary clairvoyant experience I'll relate in another book).

Then, one day, we felt it was time to get on the move again; the next leg of our journey was to follow the Nile southward for another thousand miles through the desert, down to Khartoum, the capital of Sudan.

Early the next day, we walked to the southern outskirts of the city to hit the road going farther south along the Nile. It was a stretch of desert all the way to Khartoum and there was only one road, the one following the river. We had the rare luck of being given a lift by a lonely man in a Land Rover who was heading to the capital. For him also, with a four- or five-day trip ahead, to have some people on board was a bonus, in case any problem happened.

The passenger seat in front being stacked high with his stuff, he told us to sit in the back, in the free space left in between his two large metal trunks. We thus had to sit cross-legged on the metallic floor, facing each other, and we managed to use our bags and some clothing to cushion our backs from the sharp edges of the trunks.

The driver was a bearded man in his mid-thirties, certainly very daring and well organized but not very talkative. He was by now driving along the Nile River on the dirt road (or piste) set beside the mostly deserted single railway track. The sight was of an unearthly beauty, the valley being like a continuous oasis with wild giraffes and camels, in the midst of palm trees and date trees, about one or two miles wide on each side of the river.

That first evening our driver stopped the car at sunset and we camped on the side of the piste that had thinned down progressively. In fact, we had not seen any vehicle for a few hours; as for the railway track, it had remained empty all along. We made a fire with dried twigs and date palm branches we collected around, and cooked some dinner out of dried soup packages he brought from the car with the water jug and pans. As hitchhikers quickly learn from traveling around the globe, never ask any question as to the private life of whoever gives you a lift—that alone ensures you to stay safely aboard. So we stuck to small talk as we ate dinner; then he retired to his minimal tent that he had set just next to his car, and Pat and I cleaned a spot of nice sand and arranged some cloths and longyis on the ground for our own comfortable sleep. The moon was nearly full, quite beautiful, but we were so worn out we didn't last long contemplating the scenery.

At sunrise, some noise woke us up as our driver produced a camping gas stove and a pan from his car. When we got up and saw the mostly blackened wood embers left from the night's fire, we discovered a very large silver and green snake coiled there, just the other side of the fire from where we had slept. On being disturbed, the snake moved away with a swishing sound in a silvery undulation, and we got busy making some instant coffee for breakfast. Still, we hadn't been asleep on our longyis and under our blanket that far from the snake! It felt like a wondrous sign that left us hanging in anticipation.

Around midday the next day, we had now entered Sudan and the Nubian desert. The piste running along the railway track became impassable, and our driver told us matter-of-factly we were now going to use the track itself as a road. By now we were persuaded he had done the trip up and down the Nile a number of times and knew what he was doing. The first difficulty was to find a point of access to climb the steep embankment, because the railway was built at a height varying from five to seven feet, to avoid it being covered by sand during sand storms. It took us about ten minutes to find a place where the ground was a bit higher and the slope less pronounced, so that the Land Rover, notwithstanding its four-wheel drive, could make it to the track by climbing in a diagonal fashion.

Here we were, but I couldn't help thinking that, even in this mostly flat terrain with only rare curves to the tracks that generally offered a long and straight line of sight of any arriving train (from the back or from the front), it would still require a lot of luck to find a workable passage in a few seconds in order to climb down from the earthwork. Of course, with only one track and railway stations in cities hundreds of miles apart, chances were that hardly one train in each direction was running each day.

Now, the perpendicular wooden planks supporting the metal rails were of course spaced apart from one another, and as we drove on them, it made the vehicle continuously bump up and down. Our bodies, as well as the two trunks, in the back were rising up and smashing down at the rhythm of the planks. We started in a hurry to better arrange our bags and clothing to protect our backs that were hurting the most, since we were leaning on the rough vertical sides of the trunks, but we had not enough spare clothing to also sit on them. As it was, we were, Pat and me, traveling with practically nothing, no food and not even a water gourd and very little money; each one of us carried a light shoulder bag, the way I had been used to travel myself for a few years. The driver finally found a speed minimizing the bumping, and we got used to it—both the constant banging and the hurting, and the deafening noise. We bet he had driven along this very piste before and knew all about using the track, or else he was just foolhardy but resourceful. Yet our mood, the three of us, was upbeat, taking it with humor. Was it not real fun? We couldn't exchange more than a few words above the noise, interspersed with roaring laughter and quick glances to the farthest ends of the track, checking for an eventual train.

The ever-changing landscape was a constant wonder of beauty and wild desert nature; for long hours I would just get immersed in the sight, as I had been while sitting atop the load in the back of the trucks while hitchhiking through the desert in Spanish Sahara and Mauritania, a place so much higher and farther back than the truck cabin where the truck driver and crew sat, that I felt like on a high throne contemplating and surveying the land. Protected from the deadly sunrays by a turban, with the hot wind, like an ally, constantly fanning my face and body, I had sat, eyes on the horizon, for hours, day after day.

On that second evening, one hour before sunset, we reached the third cataract, and he stopped the car for the night. The oasis was much larger, with a mud village inland, the river stunningly magnificent under the soon-setting sun. The landscape and river were strikingly similar to those of the fourth cataract, also in the Nubian desert, shown in fig. 4.5 and plate 10, here to let you dream. Again we lit a fire using dried branches and logs found along the river shore, and sat around it to share some light meal he provided.

Fig. 4.5. Sunset over the Nile from Sherari Island, Dar al-Manasir, Fourth Cataract
Photo by David Haberlah

Just like the previous night, as soon as we had finished eating, our friend went to sleep in his small tent, farther away and next to his car.

As for us, we had laid our longyis and blanket much nearer to the river bank, on slightly higher ground that offered us a magnificent view of the sunset on the river. It was breathtaking; I had rarely seen such an unearthly desert beauty, with the river's silvery shimmering ripples and eddies under a now reddish sun, slowly sinking behind the dunes and a peak.

And that night there was a full moon, which soon appeared rising to the east. We were so enraptured by the full moon now lighting the scenery with its magical touch that the only thing we wanted was to stay awake and revel in this paradisiacal harmony. We had brought with us some LSD trips in view of special peak moments and sacred places, and if there was one place naturally sacred and blessed by the full moon, this was it.

Let me dwell here on a facet of an LSD experience that is seldom described: the immersion in the stunning beauty of wild nature. Most people think that with a circular glance and a few snapshots of their camera, they have "seen" the beauty of a place—and it takes them no more than a few minutes after exclaiming "Oh, it's so beautiful!" before they move on, satisfied to have their memories-on-film.

As a poet in my teens, I knew that one has to "penetrate" into the beauty of a landscape, and get into a contemplative state to do so. And that demands time . . . to slowly tame and deepen our soul's connection and fusion state and take in the essence of nature.

First, you have to be totally still, sitting at ease, your mind void. Progressively you inch closer to harmonizing your inner being with the rocks, the trees and plants, the shapes and colors, until being fully immersed in them. Then you're really in tune and feeling the place from within, all in an infinitesimal constant transformation—like a minimalist, Steve Reich kind of music.

And at one point you merge and fuse with the landscape—every plant and tree and river is alive; the Earth's soul infuses you and the elements around you, and you breathe with them. You become part of a shared state of harmony and beauty.

That state of fusion, even for an experienced person, may demand half an hour just for tuning in, and it then evolves into an hour or more of sheer ecstasy. The difference with an acid trip, though, is that you'll remain in the contemplative fusion-state for six or seven hours. And each second will be like a timeless vision.

Dawn, with the instant-to-instant blossoming of colors, shade by shade, was a pure delight.

When one is in a contemplative state and, say, writing a poem or painting a landscape, it seems like time has stopped. It's the same with a contemplative trip, but with a stunning intensity.

Now—what is this dimension of time when we say "it's as if time had stopped"? It is not the clock time of Chronos, that's for sure. But it's not either "la durée"—Bergson's subjective, first-person dimension of duration. Nor is it the Kairos time of all opportunities—also called the "Indian time"—the precise timing that allows synchronicities, and serendipity, a flow of them, to happen. That Indian time would explain, for example, why we were in this magnificent oasis on the Nile precisely on a full-moon night, and also conveniently left to ourselves by our driver—perfect place, time, and situation.

Yet the depth of experience, when "time stops" is still another time dimension, that of *time as depth*; of time as a vibration of shared consciousness.

Beauty is not only in the eye; that is, the way we perceive. It is also in the sharing of consciousness. Being able to see beauty, as an inner depth, arises from one's empathy with the aliveness and the beingness of all that is, with the consciousness level—the semantic fields, the hyper-dimensional layer of all the natural systems bathing and mingling one into the other; it means participating in a shared field of consciousness and beingness.

When our companion got up, an hour after dawn, we were sitting on our longyis around the fire where we had retreated. Our consciousness was still spread over the entire landscape and even beyond, in the Earth-Soul dimension, in a deep feeling of oneness with all nature surrounding us. All through the night, each of us had taken a few short strolls around, both for discovering a new perspective on the river and to collect some dry branches to keep the fire burning, keeping us warm in the cold desert night; at sunrise, we still had incandescent red embers.

Just like the previous morning, we heated some water on his camping gas stove, and we shared an instant coffee with bread and nuts that tasted incredibly delicious in our heightened state.

After breakfast, with all the stuff secured back in the car, our friend got behind his wheel while we moved in a sort of fluid state to sit between the trunks, still facing each other but diagonally, our legs outstretched.

There we go, and the Land Rover is soon running on the lone rail track. We hadn't yet encountered any train, nor heard one during the nights. Neither would we, in fact, during the whole time we followed it or rolled on it. The car makes an impressively rumbling and bumpy start before taking up a cruising speed.

We now watch with bewilderment our bodies, in perfect synchrony with the trunks, being heaved up an inch and falling back harshly on the metallic floor, with only this sight and the staccato noise we hear to make us aware of it all. Unlike the previous day, it didn't even occur to us to arrange our bags and clothing to cushion us. We are now leaning with our nearly bare backs on the harsh edges of the trunks, rising up off the car floor and bouncing down on them with the weight of our bodies about forty times per minute.

"It's funny, I don't feel anything. Do you?" I ask Pat.

"Nothing at all—it's really weird!"

We laugh our heads off. Our bodies are limp, sprawled out and utterly relaxed, and we watch them being constantly raised above the floor together with the trunks. We feel as comfortable as if we were lounging on an armchair, and yet the awful noises of the shocks are like a steady drumming. And it went like that for hours in a row.

Not only couldn't we feel the impacts but, that same night, there were no marks on our vertebral columns and we didn't get painful backs. Around midday, we reached the then large village of Al Dabbah, and thereafter we drove on a clearly marked and wide piste going straight southward to Khartoum and avoiding a large curve of the river. Needless to say, no asphalt road crossed southern Egypt or northern Sudan in those years.

NO PAIN, NO BRUISES DURING A WHIRLING SUFI TRANCE

This instance by the Nile of a body-mind deep in trance being immune to (moderate) pain and, even more astonishing, not bearing any bruises afterward, is the most revealing one I've experienced so far, but it's not the only one.

Sometime in my twenties, I went on a summer trip to Côte d'Azur, the French Mediterranean Blue Coast. Côte d'Azur is renowned for its magnificent cliffs and Mediterranean flora. In Cassis, near Marseille, the coves or *calanques* are chiseling a marvelous deep blue sea into narrow indentations reaching deep inland, nested between high cliffs of white limestone that present an extremely beautiful stone relief (see fig. 4.6. and plate 11).

These rocks, mind you, were formed during the Jurassic Period and are dated between 201 and 145 *million* years ago. So, let me note in passing that I truly believe we don't appreciate enough the time Gaia took to carve these stunning landscapes, mountains, and canyons; especially when we consider the willingness of giant fossil fuel companies to frack them into dust in no time to add just a few more bucks in their own vast pockets! The land and rocks of Earth belong to humanity of all current and future times, not to a bunch of business people living in the early twenty-first century!

With my boyfriend, we had been invited by a couple of friends from Paris to meet them in the port of Antibes, where they would stay in a community for the summer months, and where we would also be welcome; we decided to go and stay there a good two weeks. They

Fig. 4.6. Calanque of Sormiou-Cassis, Côte d'Azur, France
Photo by Tobi 87

lived in this community each summer and knew the place and its surroundings very well. One day they proposed to us and another couple of friends to take an LSD trip in a very special garden situated high on a hill with one of the most striking views of the sea. They had done it already, because at that time, despite the very rich owner and the plush residence, the property had been unused for a long time and its garden abandoned and overtaken by weeds. It was no less than the property of the late Aga Khan and his beloved widow, La Begum, in Le Cannet, in the heights of Cannes. "Of course," they told us, "we will only sneak in the garden at dusk, remain there through the deep of the night, and then disappear at dawn without a trace." Let me confess here that, while the fascinating names of the Begum and the Aga Khan, and their exotic origin, were widely known and held in high esteem, I had no idea at the time of who they were exactly, and of the fact that the Aga Khan himself had died in 1957. I just figured they were so rich that somehow they were living in another one of their residences (which may have been the case for the Begum that summer).

We all found the idea very exciting, and a few days later off we went, of course on a full-moon night. The house was perched on the high hill of Le Cannet, overhanging Cannes, the seaside city where the famous film festival is held.

As expected, the place around the shuttered house seemed as if it had been neglected for months, its garden now running wild. We got in simply through an open passage. It was a jewel of Côte d'Azur's renowned "exotic gardens," featuring a beautiful arrangement of Mediterranean plants, with palm trees, scented flower trees, and bushes (such as hibiscus, jasmine, and laurels), among yuccas and cactuses (see plate 12).

We strolled around the garden and gathered on a flat stone terrace with a breathtaking view of the sea from high above, and sat there facing the sea. Our bird's-eye view was of Sainte-Marguerite Island and the Cannes seafront.

Soon, night fell and the full moon was now making the garden and the landscape stunningly beautiful, the immensity of the sea down there vibrant and enchanting, and we took it all in, for hours. At some point, I got up and moved to the back of the terrace to dance. This stone terrace was surrounded by an exotic patch of thornbushes and cactuses, nested gracefully between sparkling white natural rocks, despite being overwhelmed by wild herbs.

Soon, I got into a Whirling Sufi's dance with my arms extended like a dervish, one toward the stars and the other toward the ground—the Heaven-Earth transfusion of sacred soul-energy (see plate 13).

I swirled and swirled, taking up speed, while my face was turned up to the night sky, my eyes polarized on a very bright star; and now everything, it seemed, was turning around this star I took as a node.

I was in an entranced state, oblivious of anything else.

Suddenly, my spinning got out of control and my body was ejected furiously in one direction, and I fell against the harsh stones and thornbushes. Sprawling there in the rocks, I couldn't stop laughing (which reassured my friends). Still laughing and feeling just as great, I extricated myself from the stones and thornbushes in one fluid motion, only to spring back to the terrace floor. On I went to dance again, if in a more controlled fashion, feeling absolutely no pain from my fall.

At the very least, and given the velocity and momentum of my spinning motion and fall, and given the sharp edges of the stones, not even to talk about the thorns and cactuses, my body should have shown many bruises, scratches, and cuts, and the next day I should have been hurting badly, with blue and red bruises in places. Nope. Not a single cut or bruise, no harm, no pain at all.

My own experiences have thus persuaded me that during trance or a deeply altered state, the body exhibits a distinct physiology in high states and that it behaves according to a different set of laws.

However, heed my warning about it. There's a red line as to, firstly, the depth of the trance and secondly, the severity of the wounding. In another instance of such a Whirling Dervish dance (while in a milder, nonpsychedelic trance), I was hurled against the metallic frame of the DJ's platform, hitting it with full force just below the arc of my

Fig. 4.7. Whirling Dervishes: Statue of Mevlana (Rumi) in Buca, İzmir, Turkey
Faik Sarıkaya

eyebrows. I immediately got back to my feet and resumed dancing, now avoiding swirling, and at first felt no pain; however, I quickly developed a searing pain on my eyebrow bone and, as it turned out when I looked at myself in a mirror later, I had badly gashed my arc and had to get stitches at the hospital the next day.

The Whirling Dervishes (Mevlevi Order) are a mystic Sufi order whose tradition goes back to Mevlana Rumi (Molana), a thirteenth-century Persian poet, mystic, and theologian, born in present-day Tajikistan (see fig. 4.7). He was fond of poetry, music, and dance as a way to reach the state of oneness and divine harmony. The Mevlevi Order, a reference to his name as *Molana* ("my master" in Persian/Farsi, *Mevlevi* in Turkish) was founded after his death by his son in Konya, Turkey, where he lived and taught after a period of travels. Molana emphasized the deep unity of all humans; he writes, in a quatrain of the *53 Secrets from the Tavern of Love*,

> *On the seeker's path, the wise and crazed are one.*
> *In the way of love, kin and strangers are one.*
> *The one who they gave the wine of the beloved's union,*
> *in his path, the Kaaba and house of idols are one.*

In Sufism, the law (*sharia*) is the first and exoteric-only stage of the spiritual way, the second being *tariqa* (esoteric path); the third, *haqiqa*, refers to the mystical truth; as for the fourth, *marifa*, it is the attainment of the state of fusion with the One, of mystical union and knowledge.

5
FIELDS OF SYNCHRONICITIES

In my life as a potent sensitive (by now you know I'm a psychic weed!), I came across a phenomenon that is an amplification of the synchronicity that Carl Jung analyzed at length in his famous book *Synchronicity*. Already, Jung was amazed by the fact that, in our human personalities, the unconscious reaches far beyond what Sigmund Freud had assumed in his psychoanalytical theory. Freud thought the unconscious was a tumultuous cache of libidinous drives that the ego and superego (the repressive father figure) had repressed. Yet already, at the start of the twentieth century, psychologists William James and Frederic Myers had fathomed that we were all connected through an underlying level of reality. "Like islands in the sea hang together through the ocean's bottom, (. . .) there is a continuum of cosmic consciousness (. . .) into which our several minds plunge as into a mother-sea or reservoir," James had written in a 1909 article.

Jung went further, bringing proofs that the unconscious extended—beyond the personal and emotional unconscious—into the collective unconscious, a deep layer of reality through which all our psyches are interconnected with all living things on Earth. It is from this fabric of interconnection that archetypal dreams emerge whose symbolism belongs to faraway cultures unknown to the dreamer. It also allows synchronicities—the meaningful coincidences we experience—to happen. When quantum physicist Wolfgang Pauli worked with Jung on synchronicities, he had a dream showing a split blackboard with one side titled "Quantum mechanics" (with nothing else), while the other side was titled "Deeper reality" and showed the design of a grid—hence the term *deep reality*. (More in chapter 10.)

It is this underlying deep reality, the dimension of our personal Selfs or souls, that I've modeled as a hyperdimension of consciousness (called Syg-HD) organized by a hyperdimensional energy, the syg-energy. Syg-energy is a high-frequency sub-quantum energy (sub-Planck scale, thus beyond spacetime) that pervades all biological and matter systems, down to all molecules, atoms, and particles. Syg-energy is thus faster-than-light, and this is why, beyond seeding synchronicities, it is also the source and means of psi experiences that defy matter and causality laws.

In chapter 1, we saw the suites of synchronicities that I experienced during my nine-month-long crossing of Africa, but here I want to recount another phenomenon also related to the layer of interconnection of all the souls (including those of animals, plants, and natural systems), that of a *field of synchronicities*.

To give you a psychological definition of the term: A field of synchronicities is a complex network of unconscious information about a distant or future event that somehow keeps emerging into the conscious stream (through dreams or signs), thus alerting the person to the probability of such an event and preparing them for it. All in all, the questers will (retroactively) decrypt the prodding and guiding influence of their own Self, and will eventually realize that they had an unconscious knowledge of the future or distant event, whose source was their own Self.

A THRICE-PREDICTED JOURNEY TO SOUTHWEST INDIA

The *southwest India* field of synchronicities I'm about to relate here involves three separate precognitions (the ability to see or sense a future event) that happened to me in the six months preceding Phil and I deciding (apparently) out of the blue to take a three-week trip to India's Kerala coast. These precognitions were indicating important events (with a date and a consciousness portal) and a rare landscape, yet they provided no specific clues as to what they were really referring to and in which country they would occur. As I was able to assess it later, they all pointed to the same future journey, yet I didn't sense they were related, nor interpreted them that way, at the time of these precognitions.

This field of synchronicities is complex in the way the three precognitions implied were so precise as to be unmistakable, but where it becomes truly surprising is when the information about the future journey emerges in two different ways; namely, two precognitive dreams and one vision in the fire. Moreover, this latter vision itself entailed PK (psychokinesis)—the ability to modify the organization of matter, or mind-over-matter.

So let's see these three occurrences.

The "Hugest Trees in the Southwest" Dream

My first precog of the Indian journey was a dream that predates this trip by several months. Let me emphasize that with Phil, we had, at the time of the dream, absolutely no plan to go on a special journey or even to take a holiday in the months or even year ahead. In fact, we were generally so deluged with work, each of us, that we couldn't afford holidays each year, and when it did happen, it would invariably be in the summer. Or else if we attended a conference together in a foreign country (because each one of us was a speaker), we would use this opportunity to add a few days afterward to visit the country. Our great travels to exotic places occurred only every four or five years in the winter, in order to enjoy the cool season in the tropics; and these were never decided more than two or three weeks in advance, when we saw a rare time lapse in our activities, as in this typical case.

It was a long dream showing three distinct parts, all of them concerning the future.

The first part puts into play an immediate problem in the family (that was indeed happening at the time) and predicts its quick and easy solution in the near future, which also became true. The family trouble was represented in the dream by a huge traffic jam of all cars (about a dozen) belonging to parents and relatives at what seemed to be a grand family gathering. The funniest part of this comic-like description of a real family hurdle is that the congestion happens in the middle of a huge expanse of flat land, with absolutely no obstacle whatsoever, apart from the stubbornness of the drivers. While the cars that converged there from all directions block each other, making any further move impossible for each one of the vehicles, my (deceased) father suddenly arrives on foot, with a resolute expression on his face, and comes to stand at the worst point of congestion, which is right in front of my blocked car. I'm at the driving wheel and my aunt Denise (also deceased) is in the passenger seat. (My aunt, during a decade or so after her death, was appearing often in my most essential and symbolic dreams, as a good genius and ally.) My father, with a dose of exasperation at this stupid situation and an utter confidence that he can and he will straighten it out right away (in character with his past personality), stands at the center and plays the traffic policeman. With large gestures, he orders each car, one after the other, to move this or that way, and in hardly three or four movements, the family knot is dissolved.

This first part of the dream thus predicts a quick fix to the problem plaguing my family and affecting me firsthand at the time, and indeed, some psychological knot was soon resolved. While the dream mostly shows that what's needed is quick and decisive action to redress the situation, it is still interesting that two deceased parents decide to interfere to help. (As I recount it in *Living Souls in the Spirit Dimension*, my numerous interactions and dialogues with the deceased leave me no doubt about their survival as intelligent and self-driven persons, and I therefore consider most of their cogent appearances in dreams as intentional.) This first part, and this is the reason I'm recounting it, shows that the dream involves the very near future (the imminent time of the solution) and thus is precognitive in nature. This allows me to treat the next two parts as also showing the future, something that was invaluable in my interpretation.

In the second part, the one that interests us here, I'm still accompanied by Denise; we are strolling together in Paris and entering a small park situated in my ancient Censier university quarter. (Censier was an annex to Sorbonne, where I did my first bachelor of arts year in French literature; then I changed course and pursued a BA degree in sociology in another university.) While we walked through the large entrance of the park, following an alley bordered by beautiful oaks and laurel trees (typical trees in Paris and at this latitude), a voice-over, that doesn't belong to Denise, says: *"The hugest trees are in the southwest!"*

In the third part, after a hiatus, I am again strolling with Denise along streets in the Left Bank (south of the Seine River). This fragment, unrelated to the subject, similarly involves the future.

While writing down the dream the next day and then analyzing its second part, I know it clearly refers to the future (due, as I said, to the first part). Yet neither "the hugest trees" nor the "southwest" could fit the small Paris park with its all-too-common trees, and given that Censier quarter is center-east in the south within Paris proper. I'm thus drawn to interpret the voice-over as a prediction about a future travel in an unspecified country, where I (or together with Phil) will discover gigantic trees in the southwest of this country. However, I've no way to know, from the dream elements, how far in the future this journey will happen, or what country it refers to.

The Pi Gate Vision Appearing in the Fire

I was in my writing house on the Cher River, and as usual in the winter months, after an evening siesta, I had lit a fire in the large, traditional fireplace. My writing house was a two-century-old stone house and the antique stone chimney was about forty inches wide, as we see in ancient castles, so that I was able to burn several quite long and thick logs at a time. I used to write each and every night until dawn or later, and when in this house in the summer, I was writing in a tower overlooking the river, but during the winter, I had my table set in the living room downstairs and facing the fire. I had devised a way to arrange big logs interspersed with small ones, in a triangular shape, so that I would need to tend the fire only one or two times during the night. Needless to say, angled or curved logs were extremely rare (since they were oak wood), and I don't remember seeing any such strange, evenly curved, logs ever before, or noticing them to prepare the fire that night. I was in the habit, around dawn, to stop writing and come to sit on a cushion on the thick carpets just in front of the fire, to contemplate it and meditate for a while; but that night, it attracted me much earlier.

I was still writing when, my eyes resting on the fire, as often while pondering an idea, I was awed by its beauty and the astounding, regular figure drawn by the burning logs. Leaving my writing table, I went to sit there to contemplate and decipher the pregnant message. It was a magnificent pi symbol, of a flamboyant red against the darker shades of burnt wood. The shape was drawn by three now incandescent logs; not only was the pi perfectly geometrical and balanced, but all three logs were slightly curved—drawing an upward curved pi, π, as the Greek letter used in geometry goes, yet with the vertical lines also curved (and missing the bottom line).

Indeed, this very particular shape, with the lintel curved upward, was reminding me of a huge sacred gate called torii that stands in the sea in Japan—a shape so striking and spiritually evocative that, in my adolescence, I had spent many a time looking in awe at photos, notably of the torii at Itsukushima Shrine, which is a Shinto shrine; this torii, in wood and painted red, is of Ryobu style, meaning that its two pillars are buttressed by square posts (see plate 14).

Interestingly, one among several speculations about the origins of the Japanese torii, as explained by the Wikipedia article on torii, proposes that they "originated in India from the torana gates in the monastery of Sanchi in central India" and that their design was brought to Japan by the Japanese monk Kukai (774–835 CE), who founded

Shingon—the Japanese branch of Vajrayana Buddhism that originated in the university of Nalanda, India, in the fifth century BCE. And indeed, huge elaborate torana gates are found flanking many temples in India, of very elaborate design (see plate 15).

The torana nearest to a (straight) pi sign in India is the Hindu torana at the Fort of Warangal—the capital of the twelfth-century Kakatiya dynasty, in Telangana state (fig 5.1).

But the Pi gates fronting the façade of Angkor Wat in Cambodia, as shown at the center, and especially the one on the right on the drawing by Henri Mouhot, are even more impressive (see fig. 5.2).

In my chimney, the vertical logs, showing an opposite curve, were slightly slanted backward toward the engraved metal fire plate isolating the stone wall at the back; these logs were about sixteen inches high, while the bigger horizontal and curved log at the top, on which the other two rested, was about twenty-two inches long.

It was so astonishing, such a beautiful, curved pi, and so gracefully symmetric, that I couldn't not take it as a sign of something of great import. But I was wondering what exactly it was a sign of.

I started to draw the perfect design, using a black pencil for the dark and brown logs and red markers for the pi logs that were glowing red. Below and behind the three flaming curves was a core of flaming embers, and the whole picture evoked a secret entrance toward a flaming core, right through "the Pi gate." And so I called my drawing such, noting the date. My interpretation, written on the bottom of the drawing, was that I was at a moment in my life where I was soon to encounter this "Pi gate"—that I took wholly symbolically, as prefiguring a spiritual change or a passage in terms of consciousness—and that I was meant to pass through this gate. To be more precise, the pi symbolized the gate and the flaming core at the center farther back (the "inner sanctum") denoted its high spirituality.

The sign in the fire was thus showing me that a threshold lay before me in the near future, and that I should anticipate to undergo a consciousness leap.

Fig. 5.1. A Pi gate: the Hindu torana at the Fort of Warangal, India. Called Warangal Gate, circa 1200 CE
Photo by Santosh Korthiwada

Fig. 5.2. Pi gates on the façade of Angkor Wat, Cambodia. Drawing by Henri Mouhot, c. 1860
Photo by Henri Mouhot

At no point did I expect to meet the pi sign in real life, and especially not as a large stone structure, as I recounted earlier when Phil and I, guided by a dog ally, found in the southwest of India a temple among several dozen half-buried ones, that had this very Pi gate as a man-height stone sculpture set facing its porch.

The Japanese torii nearest to my Pi gate in the fire that I found is on the coast at Oarai, Japan—the spectacular Kamiiso-no-Torii, meaning "gate at the beach of the gods" that is facing the shrine called Oarai Isosaki Jinja (see fig 5.3).

Now, the most fascinating part about the torii in Japan is that, as I just discovered roaming the Web, they were *meant to mark the entrance to a sacred site, and to trigger a shift in consciousness toward a heightened state*—from the mundane mindset to a receptive spiritual one. So we have here, beyond the precog, one among many proofs of Jung's collective unconscious: my interpretation of the vision in the fire was congruent with the Japanese torii symbolism, of which I knew nothing.

Fig. 5.3. The Gate of the Gods: Kamiiso-no-Torii at Oarai Isosaki Jinja shrine, Japan
Photo by Saigen Jiro

Precognition, Divination, and Psychokinesis

Let me note here that I'm accustomed to having significant and ominous designs appearing not only in the fire but also in the shapes taken by the melted wax falling out of the candle in front of my writing table, and even (although more rarely) in its wick. To give you an example, I was astonished one night to see clearly in the wick the silhouette of a slim woman skier in the posture of sliding down a slope, with astounding precision; the skis, the feminine body with delineated breasts, the torso bent forward over her thighs, the position of the legs with folded knees, and the angle of the sticks for speeding down, all were there, as if it had been a sketch showing the speeding skier from the side.

What was utterly perplexing to me was that I didn't follow sport news, nor was interested in sport at that time, apart from ice dance, and I never watched or even followed real-time competitions, even for the Olympics or involving my Aikido practice. So I was really bewildered by the theme of the sign, a first of its kind for me, and asking myself why I would get a skier appearing. Yet the next day the news was all over the

French media, impossible to miss. Our great world champion alpine ski racer Régine Cavagnoud had just sustained a high-speed collision during training in Tyrol; she died two days later, on October 31, 2001.

The precognitive visions involving precise shapes and figures in the fire, or in the candle wax and wick, imply an added psi element to the simple precognition—even one using a divination system, like Tarot cards. Let's take for granted (or let you accept for a moment) that a divination system is able to offer the "reader" information relevant to the question asked. In other words, let's assume that our unconscious knows something about the future and that a divination system provides a means to put it out in symbols, in brief, to express this information in a way we can interpret it. (I've used the Tarot often and have even invented a few divination systems, enough to know by experience that the predicate is right.)

With the Tarot system, a researcher may argue that a mind uses only precognition (either fuzzy intuition or precise knowledge of the future) plus some clairvoyance to pick up the precise cards bearing and pinpointing the relevant information. Yet, if one uses a technique in which the order of the cards being drawn follows a prior reshuffling of the deck, then we have to add also some type of reorganizing force, belonging to mind-over-matter or PK.

Now, as far as spontaneous shapes in the fire are concerned, many a time I've watched *designs so neat and precise* that, when possible, I take photos or draw them in my journal, and sometimes I may realize they offer a prediction (as with the Pi gate). Then we can't explain them away as mere interpretations or projections made by the mind on otherwise totally fuzzy and ill-defined shapes. As for the candle-wax sculptures, they are sometimes so well-drawn and recognizable that I detach them from the support and keep them; see, for example, the Chinese light-bearer sage holding a lantern and a Madonna accompanied by her naga ally in fig. 5.4.

The question arising is: how are the burning logs, the wax falling

Fig. 5.4. Spontaneous candle-wax sculptures during writing: Chinese light-bearer sage holding a lantern (*left*) and a Madonna accompanied by her naga ally (*right*). In the background, a statue of the Naga Queen on my altar table
Photo by Chris H. Hardy

off the lighted candle, its wick, or the card order (re)arranged? This feat, in my view, does imply the ability of the psyche to (re)organize matter; in brief, PK. This ability is clearly evident in psychic healing, or bio-PK—a feat amply proven by more than a hundred double-blind experiments (as we saw earlier).

This is why, in the Pi gate fire vision, we have a complex interweaving of different facets of psi: a synchronicity, a precognitive vision, plus a PK influence driven by the unconscious (the Self), as well as a correct, ulterior left-brain interpretation.

Now, the deep question is why would the psyche have such mind-over-matter capacity, both as PK and bio-PK? In my systems theorist's view, we need to invoke a layer of deep reality as predicated by Jung and Pauli; precisely, a *hyperdimension of consciousness* in the universe existing beyond space and time (as in my cosmology theory), in which the psyche and Self are a negentropic force; that is, a force creating order based on intent and meaning (more in chapter 10).

A Stunning Date Prediction: The Two Towers Dream

The third prediction of our journey to southwest India involved a precognitive dream stating the precise date of a turning-point event in my life. This dream happened about two months before we suddenly decided to go on this trip.

The dream, save for the precise date, is highly symbolic.

It also shows a unique trait in terms of dreams, in the sense that I'm not an acting and speaking character within the dream. Usually, we are an "I" in our dreams, interacting with other dream-people and situations, feeling our movements from the inside, while we don't see our own face, just as in real life. But in this Two Towers dream, my "I-consciousness" is watching the dream characters interacting with their environment. I have thus an observer's perspective and during the dream, my point of view as an observer will shift, and I chose to call "north" the perspective facing me in the first dream image (that is, the narrow wall with the two towers). I'll thus see the scene from above, first from the south, then from the north, then from the south again, and finally I'll be at the level of the ground.

> *In a wild property, a large rectangle of mostly raw earth enclosed by high stone walls, two tall and beautiful young men are, each one, building his own (square) tower with cut stones, at the two corners of the small northern side. They work in parallel, while keeping a*

Fig. 5.5. Sun god Helios, stone relief
Altes Museum, Berlin, Germany. Detail on face
Photo by Yair Haklai

friendly interaction, like talking to each other once in a while; and their building of the towers is about at the same low height. I come to interpret them as two facets of my psyche, "the Vigilant" (the scientific and theoretical research facet) and "the Voyant" (or seer, the psychic-meditative-artistic facet). Through this interpretation, I now understand that what I feel in real life as a conundrum of widely different vocations and frameworks, that I sometimes pursue in parallel, are indeed meant to be that way, and that, moreover, my work is advancing in an orderly, constructive fashion, in each domain.

In the second part of the dream, the two builders have moved and are now taking a break and relaxing at the back side of the terrain (the south), where there is a tall stack of hay, seemingly left over from the harvesting of wheat. From above, I contemplate (from the north), on the stone wall delimiting this small south side, a bas-relief in bronze set high up and featuring the head of a sun deity who serves as a sundial (see fig. 5.5). The place is now bathed in sunlight.

My interpretation of these two dream scenes, later on, is that the work on both facets/domains in my life is advancing in a sacred (solar) time frame and now comes the period of rest.

> *Changing my observer's perspective, I'm now seeing the scene with my back to the south wall, maybe at the level of the sundial, high up. In a strange inversion of their functions, the Vigilant is lying down in a slack position, his back resting on the pointed stack of hay; in contrast, the Voyant is sitting on the ground in a controlled, cross-legged posture.*
>
> *Suddenly, in a parallel dimension superposed to that of the dream, a short, slim, and young man, "the eternal youth," crosses the dream scene (the terrain between the long walls), as if sliding or flying low, from left to right (or west to east) along an oblique path, passing in front of each of the two young men in turn, who don't see or sense him. (Note that the eternal youth's appearance is not happening in the same dimension as the one of the dream the builders belong to.)*

This eternal youth is the symbolic Chidder-the-Green, the mysterious Al-Khidr ("the Green One") of the Sufis—the guide and initiator in secret knowledge and wisdom. Represented as an immortal old sage or an eternal youth, he's a beyond-time figure and also an expression of Hermes/Thoth/Mercury, as messenger or gate opener of the divine dimension (see fig. 5.6). Indeed, Hermes Trismegistus describes in his books the attainment of the sphere of The Ninth, the fusion with cosmic consciousness. (See *The Discourse . . .*)

When appearing in my dreams (rarely but very significantly), he forecasts a world-shaking change in my life. Strangely, Hermes/Chidder always cuts across the dreamscape, generally flying. Even within my dreams, his appearance always denotes a higher dimension than the dimension of the dream per se. In two dreams (this one and the "New Temple" one I analyzed in *Living Souls*), he was flying across the dream-

Fig. 5.6. Archetype of the eternal youth Hermes/Mercury: *The Genius of Liberty* by Augustin Dumont (French, 1801–1884), topping the July Column at the Place de la Bastille in Paris. Gilt bronze, 1833
Photo by Marie-Lan Nguyen

scape without belonging to it or interacting with the persons or scenes in the dream; in a third, 1998 dream, "The Opening of Neptune," which marked (in a first part) the ending of my relationship with M, he appears out of nowhere and soars here and there above me and a group of sensitives; we are lying down on our backs and meditating in an open-columned yet roofless temple and, while flying, he sprays us with ashes as we get into a higher "Neptunian" musical tone and trance. The thought traverses our now telepathic group-mind "This is the opening of Neptune." This dream thus forecasts a collective leap in consciousness.

I understand this Hermes/Chidder dream entity as the higher-dimensional figure of my own Self, who is able to make direct intrusions into the spacetime dimension (where the building of the towers, representing my conscious life work, is elaborated).

> *(Back to my dream.) My observer's perspective shifts anew; I'm now at the level of the ground, still watching from the south and listening to the dialogue between the two builders.*
>
> *The Vigilant speaks first. "In exactly two months (day to day), on the fourteenth of March, a very important event will take place."*
>
> *To this the Voyant replies: "This was correct, but due to some new factors, this event will be pushed back exactly one month to the fourteenth of April."*

Thus, at the beginning of the dream, two distinct facets of my personality and mind—the Vigilant, left-brain, and the Voyant, right-brain—are working independently on a parallel task (building or creating something), and yet relying on friendly interactions. But in the later part of the dream, the logical and scientific facet of my mind (the Vigilant, left-brain) is developing its intuitive and psi abilities (right-brain). As for the Voyant (right-brain), he is even more precise and sharp (left-brain precision and factors analysis) in his psi and notably his predictive abilities. The dream thus tells that the Voyant is also undergoing a leap in his intuitive and psi abilities. Altogether, some kind of exchange or swapping is taking place in their respective role, which forecasts a consciousness leap consisting of a blending of logic with intuition.

Third part. The scene changes totally, and I now see myself on a country road, alone in an old gypsy's cart drawn by a horse. I'm driving the cart downhill while a large storm drawing dark heavy clouds is looming, approaching from behind, from beyond the hill I just passed. (I'm observing from the valley the horse cart rolling down the hill, conducted by myself, and the dark sky beyond it. In other words, I have both an observer and an actor perspective.)

In my interpretation of the dream later on, the third part meant that my life was going to be drastically changed, and I would be "on the road again"—as Bob Dylan's song hailed it; that is, as a state of utter freedom, something I had experienced for many years. I'd be alone with myself again, as I had loved to be in an earlier cycle in my twenties. Yet this time, somber events would be lurking on the horizon.

At the time, I had concluded that my scientific theoretical work was going to become more intuitive and visionary, a blending of right- and left-brain capacities (and, seeing it now from a distance, it certainly moved more and more that way, especially with my hyperdimensional cosmology theory).

As for the precise date that was predicted, I could infer that a dramatic event was going to happen that day, that much was clear. However, would it be a positive or a negative one in my life? That, based on the dream alone, I wasn't able to clarify. The storm approaching in the third part was casting an uncertain and ominous shadow lurking above this new life cycle. Yet, the conversation by the stack of hay had been bathed in sunlight and carried on under an auspicious sun god bas-relief. I remained altogether wary about what this momentous day would bring me.

Of note also is the fact that in this whole dream, I'm in an observer position, yet I perceive a higher-dimensional entity, divine and highly propitious, crisscrossing the dimension of the dream. The passage of Hermes, who links and connects the material dimension with the spiritual hyperdimension, reveals that this life-turning event was clearly concocted by, and under the auspices of, my higher-dimensional Self; that is, guided by Hermes (as a living archetype).

The Journey Itself, as It Turned Out

So, what happened after these three occurrences, which I didn't know were precognitive and interconnected? After another couple of months of a heavy work schedule, with Phil, we abruptly saw the possibility to take a three-week travel break, decided to go for it, and started mulling over diverse destinations. And we chose, seemingly out of the blue, to travel to the coast of Kerala, meaning the southwest of India. The final plan, as it turned out, was to fly to Mumbai, take a direct train to Trivandrum (at the southern tip of India), and then climb up the western coast slowly, to finally find a great place near Mumbai where I would stay alone a bit longer. But Phil had to fly back to France on the fourteenth or fifteenth of April. As I remembered the ominous date predicted in my dream—for which I didn't know if it was going to be an ordeal or an elating event—I asked him to stay with me on that date and depart for Mumbai only on the morning of the fifteenth. And we booked plane tickets according to this.

What we both experienced during this quite astounding journey was a steep heightening of our consciousness state while we were progressing north along the southwestern coast of India.

After a few days relaxing on the exotic beaches above Trivandrum, we moved to explore the Cardamom Hills. The next morning after our arrival there, as we were having breakfast on the terrace of the guesthouse we had found, a man came to propose to us a day of trekking in the tropical forest toward a secret temple deep in the forest, about three hours of walking one way. He would take us with his jeep to the edge of the forest and already had a couple of tourists booked for today, but could accommodate another two people—were we interested? The prospect of the secret temple in the jungle couldn't be more exciting to both of us; the departure time was in a half hour and we got ready.

The way in, along a large dirt path going steadily down that obviously was trodden by religious pilgrims at specific dates, was sheer bliss. I had never seen such gigantic trees, tall and straight, whose consciousness I could sense and hear, and I did some shamanic sharing with some of them. I recognized immediately that these trees were "the tallest trees" mentioned in my dream, and it just occurred to me that, indeed, were we not in the southwest? In contrast to the trees, the temple was rather gloomy and nothing exceptional compared to the dozens of magnificent temples I had visited in India. As for the way back, I must confess that it was an excruciating four hours of climbing that reignited such a harsh pain in my previously damaged knee that I was able to endure it only by putting myself in self-hypnosis. So, in contrast to what their name suggests, there are gigantic trees in the Cardamom Hills; of course, there are also gorgeous fields of cardamom bushes on numerous hills around, extending to the horizon.

Then, a week or so later and farther up the coast, we were told of a large forested terrain, several miles wide, of half-buried temples, and couldn't resist the call to discover some of them. That's when we fell upon the "Pi gate temple"—a small but exquisite one in the forest that featured, in front of the temple and aligned with it, a magnificent pi made of stone, and where we experienced a high meditative state. As I recounted earlier, we were guided to it by an animal ally.

Finally, we learned about Hampi and planned to spend our last few days together there, where I would stay one more week alone. Hampi is an extended field of temple ruins on bare and scorched earth, with some magnificent ones still whole—such as the Vittala temple, with its musical pillars, also called "singing pillars," near the Tungabhadra River, where I was to enjoy a fantastic music jam on the full-moon day after Phil had left (see plate 16).

I must say that, given the daily wonders we experienced on that trip, by the time we reached Hampi, I had forgotten all about the fateful date. (It's hard to fathom how this could happen, but I guess our trip was so rich and blessed with extraordinary encounters and heightened states that indeed we were just moving with the here and now.) We realized that Phil's needed departure for Mumbai was the day of the full moon and we wanted to have a great eve together somewhere special. Meanwhile, just two days earlier, we were told about an exceptional place farther west along the river, with magnificent natural pools created by an underground river emerging within a field of boulders of extreme beauty. We decided to spend the full-moon eve and night meditating in that place. For both of us, it was a breakthrough meditation, each one perched on top of a boulder, in that surreal field of stones and boulders on the river's shore.

That night, I saw a line of sadhus (yogi and ascetics), issued from Shiva himself, who were keeping alive and alight the connection between the higher spiritual realm and Earth—and I was integrated in it as the last one in the line. I had indeed lived with sadhus and as a sadhu myself, a wandering ascetic, for more than two years in my early twenties, even remembering a past life in Goa as a sadhu; and all along I had felt I belonged to their community of timeless questers, and was always greeted by them as such (see fig. 5.8 and Plate 4).

Finally, at dawn I reunited with Phil on the river shore and we experienced a state of oneness and fusion with the magnificent wild nature, as the colors in the landscape were slowly appearing one by one and deepening in minute shades.

And this is how the three predictions came to be realized in this single trip to Kerala and Karnataka. *The tallest trees in the southwest* in the Cardamom Hills, then the *Pi gate* in the terrain of buried temples, and finally, on the momentous *day predicted by the dream*, we achieved the highest state of consciousness in our whole journey.

To put things in perspective, I've been a globe-trotter and have ventured, mostly alone, to a lot of high places on a number of different trips. Yet, this is the only one of all my journeys that has been clearly predicted. Moreover, it was forecast three times, by different means, including (1) the mind-over-matter feat of the perfect sculpture of the pi

Fig. 5.7. Vaishnava sadhu in Kathmandu with locks falling to the ground and an Urdhva Pundra mark on his forehead
Photo by Wen-Yan King

in the fire, and its interpretation as a "Pi gate," a threshold that I would, at some future point, pass through; (2) the message in a dream about the precise future date that, in a mysterious way, had been pushed back one month; and (3) another message in a dream about the existence of a magnificent forest of immense trees.

Lastly, we didn't know anything before we arrived in India about the terrain of sand-covered temples, nor about the secret temple in the huge forest, or even about the extraordinary site in Hampi; we learned about them while in India, either through the people we met on the road or via the globe-trotter guide we bought on our arrival in Mumbai.

So the question we can ask ourselves is: How can we be so finely and precisely guided? And yet, these predicted events were not thoroughly predetermined, given that some factors in real life had led to the ominous date (and therefore the whole journey) being pushed back one month.

My way to figure this out is to attribute to our Self—insofar as we have harmonized ourselves with it—a permanent and real-time guidance of our ego within its physical and social environment. Our Self would thus be able to concoct some events—such as crucial encounters or visiting a sacred place on a specific day. Our Self would also be able to tweak some lines of probability in our future, to help us and coach us into achieving our spiritual goals. As we saw, I do believe such a subtle tweaking of events happened to force me to pass my bachelor exam (chapter 1). The tweaking involved not only two accidents that stalled me from hitting the road, but the place where they both happened, next to my parents' house, reveals clearly the signature of my Self.

THE BON-PO SHAMAN'S RING AND THE DHOLAK DRUM

After a three-month stay in India for the turn of the millennium, and now separated from M, I took to spending one or two months each winter in the state of Goa, depending on how much time I could snatch out of my usually heavy work schedule in Paris. It was always a crucial breathing and rejuvenating time in terms of getting disentangled from the exclusively Western zeitgeist pervading my scientific and literary milieu and my own penchant for recoiling in solitary writing and theory-building. Goa was like turning the glove inside out, a Klein-bottle trip during which I reveled in the transnational crowd of free-wheeling sensitives, globe-trotters, multicultural artists, nature- and planet-lovers, and in expressing myself freely in trance dancing and drumming—that boosted a heightened creative space feeding some exceptional writing sprees.

That year, I landed first in Bombay and had decided to get myself a new dholak—the double-headed, barrel-shaped drum of Indian classical music—and to offer myself a classical music one (see fig. 5.8). Its body, the shell, is carved in mango wood; as for its two membranes, the smaller one is made of goatskin for treble, while the bigger one is a thick buffalo skin for bass. Sure enough, I wasn't playing the dholak the Indian classical way; from my immersion in so many cultures, I had developed a free style that ventured far beyond any typically allowed gestures. Thus, instead of tapping the beat on the two skins simultaneously

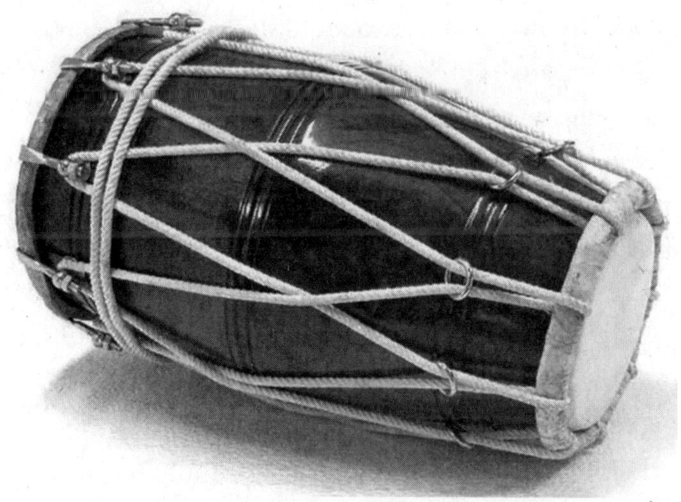

Fig. 5.8. The Hindu dholak drum
Photo by adil113

(which I loved too), I adored sending the sound from one head to the other while getting in a rhythmic dance of my body, sitting cross-legged. Yet quite often I played on the bass head only (definitely a weird style), as it afforded a rare melodic array of sounds when tapped at various spots with different fingers. I used predominantly my right thumb near the rim, while I modulated the sound by pressing more or less hard on the edge of the leather skin with my left hand. This is why I wanted the dholak to be of the highest quality and went to one of the best classical instrument shops in town. Having found there a dholak with a really great sound, I headed straight to Goa.

But when I started to play the drum in Goa, I realized the rim of the shell, where the leather skin is rolled on itself and tightened with ropes, was abnormally high and hard, seemingly made of metal under the skin. And it was hurting me badly, especially on my right thumb.

When tapping the skin the hardest with my right thumb, the metallic rim kept banging on the left side of my second phalanx and joint; nevertheless, I got into a high state and forgot all about the pain. But then, after playing, my thumb was so sore as to be nearly numb and it would keep hurting for hours. I was really frustrated and upset, especially since I had never had such problems with dholaks before. So how was I to play drum in an entranced state for hours if it hurt me so much, and the next time the pain would be even worse? Would I have to relinquish this marvelous sounding and expensive dholak and find another drum of lesser quality? The mere thought distressed me.

A couple of days later, as I went to swim, the sea was tranquil and flat that afternoon, the waves very low. I usually swam quite far into the high sea, slowly, getting in the feeling I was one with the ocean; I kept my body very flat, like sliding above the water while minimizing gestures and creating the least friction possible. I called it the *yoga of swimming*, the art of fusioning with the sea. Then, when I was far enough to feel I was alone with the elements, I would turn on my back, extend and spread out my limbs, and let myself float still, in a meditative and immersive state, feeling one with the immensity of the sea around me, one with the sky extending to infinity. Beyond enjoying this heightened state, it helped also to gather strength before swimming back to the shore.

That day, while floating perfectly still on my back in the high sea, I suddenly had the utterly strange sensation of a soft squeezing all around my right thumb, in the depression in the second (proximal) phalanx, seemingly by a torus-shaped sea creature. The feeling was like silk stroking my finger, wrapping itself around my thumb, and then a warm, very delicate squeezing around the depression of my phalanx; the image popped up in my mind of an annular kind of jellyfish that had gotten around my thumb. Despite the incredible softness, I was suddenly filled with a terrible memory of a very serious burn by a jellyfish, and instantly shook my hand and got it free even before I could get a glance at it; and meanwhile I assessed that this creature, jellyfish or not, had not been poisonous.

But the mysterious sensation remained, that of the very soft, silky, caressing squeezing all around the soft depression space of my thumb. It had been so gentle and delicate, so sensual in fact, that I regretted my abrupt reflex. I wished I had felt it longer and had a look at it to understand what it was.

Another two or three days later was the weekly flea market on Anjuna Beach. I wanted to get myself an antique Tibetan ring and specifically looked for some Tibetan stands. One Tibetan woman had a full case of silver rings—and one attracted my attention by its beautiful aura and shape. It was the only one of its kind, with an oldish patina despite not being a traditional Tibetan form I could recognize, amidst an array of modern and more flashy silver rings. It was an annular round ring engraved with perpendicular coils. It was curiously large, seemingly fit for a thumb. As the idea flashed in my mind, I passed it over my right thumb. Not only did it fit absolutely perfectly in the depression of my phalanx, but the sensation I got reevoked that of the annular jellyfish. I was spellbound and started to realize that this could be the solution for my drumming plight.

The Tibetan woman, in her thirties and with her toddler on the mat next to her, had a very friendly and openhearted personality. We bonded spontaneously and I knew she was not going to lie to me. (This is also one thing about Tibetans, they are generally utterly authentic; they are not playing salesman's tricks with you.) I could see the ring was pure silver, the whole of it, and I asked genuinely:

"Is it an antique ring?"

"Yes," she answered. "It's a Tibetan shaman ring, the Bon-Pos use these rings for drumming."

My mouth dropped in bewilderment.

I looked at the ring on my thumb, turned it on itself—it was amazing; the coils rounding it were so smooth as to feel like a caress, just as the jellyfish had stroked me. As if the ring had been made just for my thumb. I checked for it not to slide off my finger inadvertently; I had had to squeeze it past the joint to put it on, and sure enough, it wouldn't get loose when swimming.

I explained to the Tibetan woman that it was exactly what I needed, and we chatted a little more while I paid, just keeping the ring on me. (To this day, I still wear it.)

The ring did marvels. It gave my thumb the extra protection against the hard ridge of the drum, and moreover, I could use it to produce an extra sound, sharper—no doubt the way the Bon-Pos used it. I left the flea market chuckling, while thinking to myself: "The jellyfish was used to precisely measure my right thumb width! What an extraordinary feat!"

I don't know who the good genie was who came to my rescue and allowed me to keep playing my dholak. But the magical interference of the sea creature has been one of the most enigmatic experiences in my life.

A MAGICAL TRIP TO MEXICO

A couple of years before publishing my cognitive theory book (*Networks of Meaning*) on my Semantic Fields Theory in the late nineties, I felt confident enough to belong to some international scientific societies on whose frameworks this theory was based—chaos theory and systems theory—and to present my work at their annual conferences. I was thus reaching out to new communities of scientists, beyond my previous inclusion in the parapsychology and the transpersonal psychology fields.

Joining the chaos theory researchers and, soon after, the systems theory ones felt like a gust of fresh air. As I was all by myself in these new fields, I enjoyed being recognized on my own ground, as I was now able to take my full dimension as an independent researcher, and I made great friends. It gave me a lot of incentive to develop my Semantic Fields Theory in greater depth, on specific topics, for each new conference. These scientific societies were publishing, ahead of the conference, the program with the presenters and the title of their papers and sometimes put all the abstracts on their website. It was the very beginning of these scientific societies creating and using websites—and these were all open access for anyone interested (just for lack of any alternative)—and providing, with each researcher's abstract, their research lab and email.

And so it happened that one day I received in my mailbox an email from a Mexican university student who was enthusiastic about an abstract posted on the website of the Society for Chaos Theory in Psychology and Life Sciences (SCTPLS).

As I'm writing this story, I pause to fumble through my old files of presentations and articles, to find the precise title; and now I'm laughing my head off: believe it or not, the email addresses were, at that early time, still made out of numbers, and not using real names!

It was the Boston 1998 conference and the title ran "Synchronicity: A Transpersonal Dynamical Process," and it showed the research association we had launched in Paris a decade earlier with my ex-husband (by then we had been separated a year).

As Juan, the student, explained, he had launched a search on the Internet with the keyword "synchronicity" that returned a link to my abstract on SCTPLS's website. He had been so enthusiastic about it that he contacted me right away. He was a philosophy student who loved Heidegger (just like me) and Carl Jung (my paper referred to him, of course), and, what topped it for me, he was a Yaqui Indian on a shaman path. And, with a background and PhD in ethnopsychology, plus a personal quest, I was deeply connected with the Yaqui Indians' sorcerer path that Carlos Castaneda had expounded in his books. We were definitely on the same wavelength and we started a back-and-forth communication via email.

That was the first synchronicity I had with Mexico and, funnily, it had been triggered by this very same term! But it was far from the last, as Mexico suddenly became a sort of attractor for a string of synchronicities. The word *Mexico* or things related to Mexico kept popping up around me. For example, a new car on a display in a commercial center was linked to Mexico by its name. When I paid a rare visit to a friend of mine, Matt, in France, he spontaneously showed me his photos of the Maya pyramids in Yucatan from a previous trip. He was fascinated by Mexico and couldn't stop talking about it.

Meanwhile, integrating these new fields and meeting so many researchers had given me a powerful momentum for my own research and I was planning to attend several international conferences to present papers there the next summer. After a European Parapsychological Association (PA) meeting in France, it so happened that year that three of the annual conferences I loved to attend were happening in California that summer, which made it easy and affordable for me to show up there. There was a chaos theory one in June in Berkeley, then a systems theory one early July in Asilomar, and finally the annual PA meeting was scheduled in August at Stanford University. Fortunately (because I wouldn't have been able to afford a hotel stay for that long), my great friend Linda Dennard, a researcher in chaos theory who was at the time a professor of public administration at California State University at Hayward (now CSU, East bay) and living near Berkeley, welcomed me to stay at her place. (See Morcol and Dennard 2000.)

While I was scheduling these three conferences and writing papers for them, I kept having this ongoing synchronicity connection to

Mexico that brought my mind back on this track regularly. So it was only a matter of time for me to realize that, being in California, it was just the perfect opportunity to take a trip to Mexico—especially when I learned that Juan was living in Tijuana, right on the border. I asked him if, as a Yaqui shaman, he would "open the gate to Mexico" for me; he replied he would be thrilled to do that.

I decided to fly from France to California with a one-way ticket and, after the last conference in Stanford, to take a cheap flight to Tijuana and meet with Juan. Then my plan was to roam around the country freely and intuitively, and when ready to go back to France, I would book a flight from Mexico. When I told Matt about my plans, he was so excited that he decided to head to Mexico that coming summer also, and we would meet in Mexico City where he had made great friends.

I stayed a couple of weeks in Tijuana, in a hotel nearby Juan's home, and we had a lot of exciting exchanges in English on the many topics we both loved, while I tackled Spanish at top speed. It turned out that Juan was part of an extended network of philosopher-shamans, and he gave me several contacts all over the country. Then I started a slow tour around northern Mexico, visiting many interesting places and people—including the famed Tarahumara—hopping from bus to bus, staying for the night at cheap hotels wherever I happened to be. By the time I reached Mexico City, I was already deeply acquainted with the country and the people, and was able to have basic interactions in Spanish.

This long tour of northern Mexico alone before I reached Mexico City prepared me for the essential incursion into Maya territory and the exploration of the Yucatan pyramids, which I pursued alone, after a rich fortnight in the capital with Matt, his friends, and Juan's shamanic contacts. With my new Mexican friend and Matt, we visited the magnificent Teotihuacan city complex (see plates 17 and 18). Built between 100 BCE and 250 CE, Teotihuacan was multiethnic and the most influential civilization in the Americas, and the sixth-largest city in the world until its destruction started around 550 CE. Its unknown builders are the subject of debate, but this culture predates the Toltec one in Tula by about eight centuries, and their descendants, the Aztecs, by about a thousand years.

All in all, with this field of synchronicities, not only did Juan introduce me to Mexican ways in Tijuana, but his network of philosophers, who were also shamans and poets, had been a fantastic way to penetrate deep into this culture. Thus, funnily, the concept "synchronicity" opened for me in Paris a field of synchronicities around "Mexico," which in turn led me to a network of shaman-philosophers and to exploring high sites in Mexico.

6
THE POWER OF INTENT

We are now going to explore a theme well-trodden by practitioners of positive thinking and positive psychology, namely the hard-to-believe effectiveness of a focused mind with a plan. As one of these practitioners, I've already published two books about it and meditation practices, with loads of real-life examples. Yet I'll recount here only my strongest experiences to date, which happened in such outstanding and fringe situations (not to speak about questionable practices) that these had no place whatsoever in books of practical exercises. While recollecting and comparing them, I came to finally attribute the best part of the agency, I mean what or who steers their effectiveness, not solely to my previously stated powerful intent but largely to the Self, or more precisely to the ego-Self fusion-cum-intent. So let's see the cases.

MAKING ONESELF INVISIBLE TO GET FREE ENTRY

I had just gotten the news that there was going to be an extraordinary concert by David Bowie at Porte de la Villette's huge tent-framed concert hall, north of Paris, in a couple of days. For a music lover like me, this was a unique occasion, something I couldn't miss. The problem was: I didn't have any money and the ticket price was not cheap.

For whatever reason, none of my usual concert-going friends were in Paris; I was alone and I had to find a solution. There would be several thousand crazed fans crowding the place, reinforced security lines, and several checks on tickets, and even the tickets sold at the entrance by people trying to make a bit of money would be above my means.

After a furious review of any possible way I could borrow this sum or find it somehow, I concluded it was a nonstarter. Yet, one thing was sure: I was going to attend this concert! I was going to go there, to La Villette, and try to get in. But how? There was not the remotest chance one could climb a wall or get over a metal fence—all were tightly guarded. After a decade or so of such pop and rock concerts, the security was hermetic, seamless.

Then suddenly a bright idea dawned on me: "I get it! I'll make myself invisible! If I don't let out any psychic energy, not a fleck of it—don't look at anybody and anything, don't perceive anything, nor feel, nor think—then I should be invisible."

As soon as the idea crossed my mind, I felt confident that this should work, and I became totally invested in it. Again and again I weighed and pondered the many instances in which I had remarked that looking at someone makes the person aware of you—they will turn their head even unconsciously until they spot you. People feel unconsciously the perceptions, emotions, and thoughts focused on them; because these are psychic energies (and I mean real energies), they do have an impact on others' psyche. And in the same manner, these energies leave a print on objects that are cherished or held sacred—one I'm able to perceive sometimes as an aura or glow.

This sensitivity to other people's good or bad "vibes" had suddenly sprung up in the first hippie generation of the late sixties and early seventies; similar linguistic expressions emerged in many different cultures and languages simultaneously. As for myself, (but you already know that) I had had the strange gift since eighteen to see this energy of consciousness as rays and auras around people and objects, including monuments. I could also sense energy fields in places of power, with a definite feel about their uplifting or else negative psychic influence.

And in meditation, since that age also, I had learned how to get into a state of perfect silence, being withdrawn and inward, and thus reaching a state of heightened consciousness in which one doesn't feel one's body anymore—perfect transparency. However, this inner-silence state was also accompanied by an extended consciousness (beyond language and words), hypervigilant and hyperconscious. And that went with an extended aura that I was able to perceive on others who were meditating, as a field of intense immaterial light.

I knew from experience that such an extended field was attracting undue attention from people, unconsciously. I remembered all too well the problems I met as I had just come back to Paris from my first eighteenth-month trip to India: each time I would enter one of the large and packed cafés in Montparnasse, even one with a glass-enclosed entrance like Le Select, everybody would just look up to stare at me, even turning around, from their seats way inside the place. The first time, I thought I must have been making too much noise or being too flashy in my behavior. Next time, I reduced my field intensity before reaching the door, lowered my head, and slipped through the door noiselessly. But the effect was just the same.

So, an extended mental field such as in meditation was precisely what had to be avoided.

In contrast, I reflected, to be truly invisible, one has to quiet any type of bodily, psychic, and mental process. No perception at all—not seeing or sensing anything; no thoughts, not any awareness or brightness of any sort. Let's be totally transparent, and void, and surely I will become totally invisible.

The more I was thinking about it, the more I became convinced this was indeed the reality of mind and perception. . . . We were emitting psychic energy, sparks and puffs of it, while sensing, perceiving, thinking . . . and others were unconsciously sensing our output, becoming aware of our presence. And while I became more confident this was it, therefore my plan was going to work, I strengthened my intent about watching the concert and getting in the hall by my being invisible.

The evening of the concert, when I took the highway northward toward Paris, then the circular Périphérique to get to Porte de la Villette, I was already getting myself into the right mood—the subdued countenance of a nonshining body and mind. I parked my car and slowly walked toward the large crowd holding prepaid tickets and queuing toward the entrance.

Void mind, unfocused eyes, just barely breathing and moving with the bodies around me—as part of a common collective body—as if I was just an extension of the arms of my neighbors left and right in the four-person-wide file, just remaining at the center of it. On and on.

There were not one but three checks on the tickets, with screening going on left and right of the file. And yet, I passed them all, totally, absolutely unnoticed. As if there was nothing there to be seen.

I let out a sigh of victory once I was inside the huge hall, mingling with the excited and impatient fans: I had done it! I was right: a perfectly void mind is indeed invisible!

READING THE EXAMINER'S MIND AT AN ORAL EXAM

I would never have gotten where I am now—devoting most of my time to research and the scientific modeling of consciousness and psi capacities—if I hadn't succeeded at my end-of-high-school diploma, the *bac* (le baccalauréat), in the first place. It's not that, had I failed to pass it the first time, I wouldn't have replicated my last high school year. As I was a brilliant student and intent on going to university, I surely would have. But as it happened, just after I graduated (in June) and was in my first year in the literature department at Sorbonne University in Paris, major, earthshaking events in France and in my life started unfolding at blinding speed. And if I hadn't been already at the university, I would have missed out on them all.

Among these events: I dove into the oneness philosophy (with the Upanishads) that very summer and started exploring meditative states; after I started university in October, I had a kundalini awakening at Easter in Tunisia (a trip to her home country imputable to my new university friend); and finally, I was active in the student revolution in May—all this taking me through repeated leaps in understanding and awakening. And looking back, I definitely had to be a university student and participate in these momentous events that were going to shape a whole generation.

And yet, without a stunning anomalous event happening to me at the oral session of the bac, I would have missed at least two of them—I would never have met my university friend Danièle, who invited me into her family in Tunisia, and I wouldn't have been a revolutionary participant and a nonviolence voice in the student movement. Moreover, if I had had to spend my whole summer still studying to pass the second-chance exam in September, I wouldn't have started meditation, nor explored my emerging psi talents, and therefore I wouldn't have been ready for a kundalini rise.

Allow me to give you a bit of context and explain in what frame of mind I was that last year of high school and regarding this diploma, because it surely made my feat at the exam possible.

At fifteen years old, I was writing poetry, had decided I was "a writer," and was living nearly exclusively among my preferred poets and writers, feeling myself as a bohemian soul—à la Rimbaud—daydreaming about my future travels during classes. (As a result, I was ahead of my age intellectually but a bit backward in social skills.) That's when I got obsessed with traveling to India; I couldn't wait for when I would live my own life and go there. For now, and since I was fifteen, I was going on hitchhiking sprees, mostly at full moons, alone or with friends. But this was far from enough for me. What I impatiently wanted was my full freedom; and that meant being at last out of high school and at the university. As my father had suggested to me, "Try to make it through high school as quickly as possible; try not to have to repeat a class year." I thought it was sound and decided to follow through—studying minimally what didn't interest me and only for exams (I would study a couple of days ahead of them, and get an impressive grade; otherwise, I wouldn't even open my books and sometimes get some resounding zeros). I thus managed to steadily be the second, sometimes the first, of my class, the best in literature and later philosophy and quite good at math.

Then came at last the final and crucial year of my end-of-high-school degree, the bac, which, as a one-day national exam, each student has to take in a remote and unknown college and surroundings. I turned eighteen that year. I devoted a couple of months to studying intensely for it. My fellow students were constantly voicing their fears. When asked about mine, I would answer, "I don't have time to spend one more year in high school; I'm going to get this bac diploma." And I really felt that way: something in me knew that I had to move on with my life at high speed. Therefore, failing the exam was not even a possibility in my mind. I was looking ahead to the university.

The first part of the bac, the written session, went very well, and so I was called for the second part, the oral exam (another one-day national exam, in still another unknown college). And I knew I was so shy that I could lose countenance totally, to the point of even shaking all over and being rendered incapable of talking or delivering a presentation (despite knowing my stuff thoroughly)—even among my own classmates. But as I had noticed, when discussing with someone one on one, all shyness disappeared because my attention was on the ideas, and not on myself.

I devised a strategy. I was going to look straight into the eyes of each teacher (there were going to be about six or seven of them, one for each subject matter). That way, I was going to open a communication channel and forget all about myself.

It worked marvelously for the first few subjects. But then I got to the math test. While the student ahead of me was passing the test, the teacher, a small and thin woman, handed me the test question on a piece of paper, telling me I had about ten minutes to study it before being called.

As I'm reading the three lines of the problem, I realize I don't have the slightest idea of what it means. The terms are wholly unknown; we haven't even broached the subject during the whole year. Having attended a school of good standing, where teachers were extremely thorough in preparing us for the bac (and betting the school's reputation on it), this was in itself highly unusual; but this wasn't something I had time to think about at the moment. I was good enough at math to know I couldn't even try to improvise an answer. And, as math, together with the main subject matter such as philosophy and literature, was given three or four hundred percentage points, even in my literary section, a low math grade, let alone a zero, meant failing my high school diploma.

And while I'm thinking full speed, suddenly I have a bright idea. "Okay, the teacher knows the solution. Then I'll pick up the solution in her mind."

Now, it's already my turn. (I'm still able to see the scene.) The student preceding me is walking away. The teacher turns to me—I make eye contact, but this time I've the intent to reach out to her mind, to the solution; she tells me to go to the blackboard and complete the math problem-solving. I'm very calm as I walk toward this giant, double-size green board while sustaining a line of contact with the teacher's mind; I get hold of a piece of white chalk and move to the left of it. At that point, there's a very calm and supporting voice in my head: "Go on, start writing; don't look at what you write, don't think at all about it." I'm starting to write, or rather, I see through a haze that my hand is writing, extremely slowly; I'm just sticking to a horizontal line. Following the inner voice's advice, I avoid thoroughly looking at or trying to make sense of what my hand is writing. I just listen to the continuously talking voice (repeating the suggestions), but I'm also branched on the teacher (now behind me, invisible), connected with her mind. It's like there is an energy beam, whitish, that runs from the back of my skull to her head, and I'm maintaining my intent and focus on it, even while hearing the voice. The voice keeps talking, repeating the message "Keep going; don't look, don't try to understand, just keep writing." My hand moves incredibly slowly but continuously, white signs appear, blurred; I have no idea what they are; I reach the right end of the board and walk back to the left for a second line. I remember I had just started on the third line when the teacher's voice, seemingly exasperated by my slowness, interrupts me.

"Okay, I see that you know your subject well; no need to go farther. I give you fourteen," (out of twenty).

That was an excellent grade in math, where the highest would be seventeen. After this test, I still had several more hours of testing to go through.

But then, that day, another anomaly happened: no sooner had I left the math-test room than I totally erased the whole telepathic episode from my mind. To my parents and to everybody, I would later recount my great grades in math and other matters (I got an award for this exam), and never mention that anything unusual had happened. Not that I tried to hide this fact; the memory was just not there. In fact, it was only in India three years later that, one day, I relived the whole interaction again.

Let's ponder this episode a bit.

First, let me explain that the whole time I was involved in academic psi research (that's since starting a PhD on the subject), and despite being convinced of the reality of telepathy and other forms of psi I had already partially mastered, I didn't think it possible that a telepathic thought, and especially one involving numbers or math, could be received with 100 percent accuracy. As if, in my rational and conscious mind, my bac feat had never occurred. That is, until I had an hour-long discussion with the soul of physicist Wolfgang Pauli that included a precise date I could check on later.

Let's now dive in the phenomenon proper. There seems to be a discrepancy between the "bright" idea that occurred to me—"I'm going to get the solution in the teacher's mind"—and what actually occurred after that; namely, the voice telling me "don't look, don't think"—which is the opposite of an intentional retrieving, or picking up, of information in someone's mind.

What I did that day is nearer to automatic writing. This is a feat some channels or mediums perform, and they generally attribute the writing itself to discarnate spirits or immaterial guides and ascended masters. During these sessions, the medium is generally not aware of whatever they are writing. I have tried it occasionally to get an answer to questions I badly and urgently needed, all the while addressing my own Self. And I can tell you that, as hard as I tried to let my mind blank and not interfere, I couldn't not "hear" the words passing through my mind while I was writing them and interpret the answer all along, while the words kept pouring in. (Incidentally, the answer to such a question in India gave me a 95 percent correct prediction running along four or five short pages about which town to go to next—an unknown name, two times out of three written correctly; where exactly I was going to find a house to rent for a couple of months—a description of the house on the seashore, roadmap, directions, distance, time to get there and find it, and all; and the fact it was going to be a fantastic place to write, which it turned out to be.)

So my feat at the bac was akin to the ideal automatic writing (some entity driving the medium's hand, medium without awareness of what's written and not hearing words before writing them), yet it differed from it in the way a voice was giving directions to me, to my active mind, that is, instead of superseding itself to my mind.

Of course, as I know for certain, whatever psi feat the Selfs of the discarnate can do, can also be done by my own Self (given that all Selfs or souls pertain to the Syg-HD), and thus by a living and embodied mind at least theoretically. In brief, our own Self has supraconscious powers and knowledge—the very capacities of the hyperdimensional consciousness.

Yet, simultaneously, there definitely was also an energy-link to the teacher's mind, with my intent and focus to keep it steady. So how to interpret what seems, again, a quite paradoxical psi event that evades a strict definition of telepathy?

How could I, simultaneously willfully pick up and "read" information in somebody's mind (by an energy link) and have my hand write it faithfully enough to earn praise, while both the "reading" of the information and the writing were done unconsciously? As a first assessment, the answer escapes me. I've just learned, through this anomalous event, that such a strange feat is possible.

An added question is: Where do all these apparently "bright ideas" come from—ideas that I immediately put to the test with confidence, despite never having had any such notion beforehand?

The more I think about this bac feat, the more bizarre it appears, even with so much more real-life experience. Here is my informed guess:

My Self, being supraconscious, (1) knows I need to get my bac for future events to unfold; (2) and seeds the idea of reading the teacher's mind (just as it had seeded the idea of making eye contact to overcome my shyness); (3) my Self knows the math solution of course, can also see it in the teacher's mind (the way she expects the solution to be given), and is perfectly able to drive my hand, but nevertheless my Self requires me to be confident enough to go to the board and start writing blindly yet boldly. The telepathic intent will allow both. Being multidimensional, the Self can both guide my hand while giving me constant suggestions to buttress my focus and state of consciousness.

Yet, this interpretation of what happened leaves out the fact that I created an energy link with the teacher's mind.

I'm starting to fathom that my recent cosmology theory (the *Infinite Spiral Staircase Theory*, ISST) may allow us to understand such psi feats. ISST states that our mind, for most of its higher operations, is hyperdimensional and using the hyperdimension's (HD) syg-energy: great ideas, creativity, innovation, spiritual and artistic inspiration, all this is driven by syg-energy. Thus syg-energy is interwoven at a sub-quantum scale with our brain's neural networks and the habitual paths of our conscious thoughts. This framework is much more complex than the old dualism or interactionism paradigms that posited the mind as a separate entity on its own plane, and driving our brain/body. With ISST, the problem shifts to one of ego-Self coordination, and what the ego is conscious of. So, let's see where that leads us.

(1) My Self needs to solve the unknown math problem, in order for me to have the bac; (2) my Self takes hold of my mind and body, seeds the intent and confidence; (3) that part of my HD mind that is my Self launches the eye contact and creates simultaneously the energy-link to the teacher's mind—because the best-rated answer will be the one as phrased by the teacher, and also because this will teach me how to create such a link (since it has my unwavering attention), and this skill will be needed later on in my life; (4) then my Self's crucial task is to keep me (the ego) in the right frame of mind (confidence and "let it happen") so that it may keep driving my hand; finally, (5), my Self judges that for my adolescent ego to remain fully conscious of what had happened would be disturbing, and manages for the memory, once I'm out of this ego-Self-fusion altered state, to be relegated to unconsciousness.

This definitely seems more coherent and self-consistent as an explanation, as it takes care of all the facts. Now, there is still one more possibility, namely that instead of (1), we may have (1a): My Self wants to use the enhanced and heightened state of consciousness of the intense two-month bac preparation, to teach me something about mind contact, telepathy, and energy-links. And it arranges the perfect unanswerable question to fall on me, in the first place; after the feat, it erases my conscious memory of it, knowing that the crucial knowledge was imprinted deep in me. This latter scenario seems the most plausible, given what I now know about our own Self.

As we saw, my Self's interference to secure the completion of my studies in due form and time didn't stop at the bac; another strange event followed, that forced me to get my BA diploma (see chapter 1).

SKYROCKETING OF AN IT BUSINESS, THEN CRASHING IT, WITH PERFECT INTENT

It had been years already of constant struggles to make ends meet, with my companion, M. Despite the fact my books were selling well—and I'd had two years of magnificent royalties, but that was long ago—the intense social life needed to keep the buzz going and new opportunities arising was generally beyond our means. At the very beginning of the Internet, France's still state-owned phone company was pricing our access to the web at obscene rates, and this bill, conflated with the phone bill, was crushing us every month, reaching half of our suburban house rent.

Our financial, accounting, and administrative burden was mostly on me for a number of years, as M dedicated himself solely to research in our research association. Daytimes, I was running around giving courses and conferences, as well as weekend workshops; as for my nights, I spent them writing whatever book or research article was on my desk until dawn, with a narrow five-hour sleep as had become my habit.

One night, as I was mulling over this constant financial stress, year after year, I just couldn't take it anymore. That night, I started reflecting differently. Instead of bearing this constant weight on my shoulders while pursuing one book project after the other, would it not be more productive to stop all creative work and aim exclusively at solving the financial problem once and for all? I knew what would make it happen: it was to focus on it—with visualizations, meditation, and intent—day and night until the solution offered itself.

As soon as the idea took hold of my mind that night, I had to admit that it was flawless . . . and the path crystal clear. At that moment, I took the decision to get on with it and I set to work immediately.

I had no doubt about the power of visualization techniques I had devised myself and used regularly for pinpointing objectives. I knew they operated amazingly. Therefore, if we were still trapped in the same dreadful situation, it was only because I hadn't focused on solving the core problem itself.

In fact, just a few days earlier, as I was discussing with a friend of mine, a video artist himself also constantly struggling with money problems, I had told him, from the top of my head: "Maybe it would be better to spend three months of our lives to solve our financial problem decisively, instead of spending countless hours worrying about money week after week!" So it seems I had planted the idea in my mind myself genuinely, and it just struck me some days later as *the* solution indeed.

I devised and launched a work session on the spot. I first got into meditation to strengthen the link with my higher Self and enter a heightened state, until I reached a peak of concentration. Then I improvised a lengthy visualization technique on the global problem and its ideal solution—with lists and a drawing specifying what type of financial situation I was aiming for. Namely, a constant influx of money (of the royalties type), which doesn't need any added work and constant attention so that I/we could remain in a creative flow. Finally, I meditated on this visualization and its drawing, thus projecting my intent outward.

The next morning, I explained to M what I had decided to do (and already started), and I told him that from now on—and until we got some results—I wouldn't engage in any new project and would just fulfill whatever commitments I was already bound to.

And night after night, day after day, I sat on my meditation futon and figured and performed new techniques of visualization.

In the years previously, whenever I had done a visualization for a specific purpose, the effect or answer had generally taken just a few days to present itself. Based on this experience, yet bearing in mind the task at hand was clearly more considerable, I was not expecting to spend three months to get a result (as I had thrown out to my friend), yet I would do it if need be. My mind was set and my will unbending, hard as steel: I would perform visualizations for whatever time it took for me to reach a solution, and I would do only that from now on.

One of these past commitments was a one-hour live talk show for a small suburban radio show, and it fell about a week into my ongoing visualization work. My already published books had covered the domains of scientific psi research and trance in ethnology, which I had explored for my doctoral thesis and as a research assistant in the Psychophysical Research Laboratories (PRL) in Princeton (before we moved to set up our own lab in France as a newlywed couple). My ethnopsychological thesis for Jussieu University (Paris VI) had been on psi (paranormal phenomena) during trance and altered states. Thus, a first part covered experimental psi research using altered states (as at PRL, investigating telepathy through the hypnagogic ganzfeld state). And the second part was ethnological; namely, on trance states in ancient cultures evidencing psi capacities, including yogic meditation, shamans' out-of-body journeys, and ancient divination techniques—all domains in which I was a proficient adept myself, even if the doctoral context barred me from talking about my own experiences. Of these two parts of my thesis, I had derived and published two books, and then I included the small section on ancestral divination techniques into a third book on divination practice (and principles) that was just published a few months earlier. This radio show was the latest in a string of such media shows in the follow-up to the book's release.*

My radio host was specifically interested in widely used divination techniques such as the Marseilles Tarot deck and the ancient Chinese I-Ching, and this is how I came spontaneously to describe, in the last few minutes of the show, how I had devised a Tarot divination program running on computers (in Basic and running on the Apple-IIe I had bought for myself in the United States before moving to France), and how I had created a totally original divination program. This novel divination system, which I named Ellora, was based on several hundred sentences (which I had composed), one of which was chosen randomly by a pseudo-RNG (random number generator). I had conceived it so that the user could discuss whatever topic they wanted with the

*Hardy, C. *Le livre de la divination.* Ed. Lebaud, 1990. Partly reedited as *Votre futur avec les Tarots.* Ed. du Dauphin, 2001.

program—since what was really happening was that the user was, in fact, drawing answers from their own unconscious. (To make this fact crystal clear, I had subtitled Ellora "Dialogue with Your Unconscious.") On the show, I gave a couple of examples about how incredibly well the system was working, indeed really on par with the Tarot cards, provided that the random selection algorithm be of the highest quality, which it was in my case, since I had brought it back from the lab in Princeton.

After the show, my young host was eager to prolong our discussion and soon asked me if I thought such divination programs could work as well on an Internet-like platform. To which I replied that, surely, it would, as long as the ultimate Princeton algorithm was inserted in the program adapted to the Internet provider's machines.

In France, at that time, the government had decided to launch nationwide an Internet-like system called the Minitel, and the national phone company, France Telecom, was providing a free terminal to whoever was interested (while the users would pay for the communication time). In parallel, they were encouraging all kinds of service companies to set up their own websites and post their information online; and soon the Minitel offered tickets reservation for trains, metros, travel tours, flights, and more. And this encouragement came in the form of a hefty percentage of the phone bill users were paying per minute of Minitel use being given back to the services providers.

My host then told me that he knew the heads of a start-up who were launching divination services with real one-on-one readings by psychics, and that they would probably be interested in divination programs as well. As I left the radio's recording studio with the phone number of the couple heading the start-up in my bag, I had a strong hunch that this was it. And indeed, from that moment onward, everything unfolded at blinding speed.

When I called them the next day, the host had already contacted them, and they gave me an appointment right away. I went there and showed them the printouts of conversations using Ellora. For this divination system, I had devised three options (business, love life, and social relationships), each with about two hundred answers evenly distributed with 40 percent positive, 40 percent negative, and the rest neutral. During the past year, I had refined the grammar so that it could readily reply to any type of question; it could even refuse to answer, stating that the user lacked sincerity or clarity in their questions (their thoughts did not have the power to elicit a pertinent answer). As a result, the game was stunningly on target, giving prescient perspectives and tips. Thanks to M, who was much more competent in programming, my initial rough but perfectly working program had been upgraded to a more user-friendly and sophisticated version, still in Basic.

I had also a Tarot-reading program ready, one for which I had devised an interpretation for all possible sets of two conjunct cards, which gave a pool of several hundred possible answers in clearly defined domains (such as the seven-card standard Tarot reading and the twelve astrological houses). As a result, the readings became quite sophisticated, and their predictions were specific enough to be tested in real life.

As I had discovered myself with extreme delight, provided the random algorithm was state-of-the-art and initialized anew for each card-answer, then the accuracy of the reading relied on the great number of possible answers. To give you a comparison, other Tarot games on the Internet or Minitel were giving the user's question only one answer—in the form of one of the major arcana. Since there are only twenty-two of them, a recurrent user would see a lot of repetition, on top of receiving only simplistic and vague answers. Furthermore, these other programs utilized the built-in random function of computers that the user's unconscious psi couldn't influence because it was too fixated and biased, not allowing a re-initialization at each probe.

At this first appointment, they were enthralled by the idea and my programs. They could see, just reading through the printed exchanges I had myself with Ellora, that it was working very well; the questions and answers were enough to realize this was really a coherent and meaning-laden conversation.

Plate 1. *Princess Bari Holding the Flower of Resurrection.* Eighteenth-century painting used in Korean shamanism.

Plate 2. Double aura of Padmasambhava, seated in his pure paradise. Tibetan thangka, Kathmandu Valley, Nepal, c. 1931.
Auckland War Memorial Museum from the collection of Mrs. F. E. Foster

Plate 3. The Tuatha Dé Danann, as depicted in John Duncan's *The Riders of the Sidhe* (1911).
The McManus Galleries, Dundee

Plate 4. Sadhus of India.
Top: Vaishnava sadhu in Kathmandu with locks falling to the ground and an Urdhva Pundra mark on his forehead.
Photo by Wen-Yan King

Bottom: Shaiva Sadhu in Varanasi (Benares) with bun and Tripundra on his forehead.
Photo by Pierre-Emmanuel Boiton

Plate 5. Celtic god Cernunnos with stag horns and unicornfish-rider (Gundestrup cauldron).
Center: Cernunnos, with stag horns, holding a snake and a torque (ring of power).
Top right: unicornfish-rider. Denmark, c. 200–300 CE.
Photo by Malene Thyssen

Plate 6. Granite boulders of Matanga Hill, Hampi.
Photo by Vyacheslav Argenberg

Plate 7. Temple of Amon in Luxor city, Egypt, and extraordinary auras and rays.
Top: photo by Fran Ferrer (looking north)
Bottom: photo by Elias Hallak (looking south)

Plate 8. Thoth-Hermes, god of knowledge and science, with an ibis head. Frieze in the precinct of Amun-Re, Karnak Temple.
Photo by Djehouty

Plate 9. Hypostyle Hall at Karnak Temple in Luxor.
Photo by MusikAnimal

Plate 10. The Nile River near the Fourth Cataract:
Dar al-Manasir as seen from the top of Gebel Musa, Northern Sudan.
Photo by David Haberlah

Plate 11. Calanques of Sugiton, Morgiou, and Riou Island, from the Candelle mountain pass.
Photo by Pablo Sievert

Plate 12. The Exotic Garden in Eze (near Nice, Côte d'Azur).
Photo by Berthold Werner

Plate 13.
Whirling Dervishes by Jean-Léon Gérôme. Oil on canvas, c. 1895. Private collection, Houston

Plate 14. Japanese torii (Ryobu style) at Itsukushima Shrine.
Photo by redlegsfan21

Plate 15. Torana from the Satavahana period (first century CE) fronting the Sanchi stupa dating to the Mauryan Empire (third century BCE). A UNESCO World Heritage Site.
Photo by Swapnil Karambelkar

Plate 16. Singing pillars of Vittala Temple, Hampi.
Photo by Vyacheslav Argenberg

Plate 17. Teotihuacan, Pyramid of the Sun, completed by 100 CE. Mexico.
Photo by Francisco Anzola

Plate 18. The Great Goddess of Teotihuacan, from the Tepantitla apartment complex at Teotihuacan.
Reproduction, National Museum of Anthropology, Mexico City
Photo by Thomas Aleto

Plate 19. Kukai, "Child Grand Master," flying to heaven on a lotus. Japanese Vajrayana Buddhism. Muromachi Period, fifteenth century CE.

Plate 20. Meteora, Greece. Striking monasteries atop stone pillars: Rousanou Monastery (*foreground*) and Agios Nikolaos (*behind it*), with part of Grand Meteora (*top right*). Note the road at the bottom of the valley.

Photo by Stathis Floros

They were in their mid-thirties, just like us, and truly passionate about divination and precognition; we bonded right away. It was going to be a pleasure to be working with sympathetic and authentic persons.

We made a deal. They offered to give back to me seven francs (about 70 percent of what the phone company was giving them as a percentage per minute. The only thing needed was to transcribe our programs in Basic into the computer language used by the Minitel systems, something that their own system engineer was going to do with M. They took less than ten days to have the two programs ready, while I worked with M to create the website environment, the section housing our programs, with visuals and all. Meanwhile, I devised at great speed an I-Ching program—the antique Chinese divination system that gave sixty-four hexagrams multiplied by six lines; that's 384 differentiated answers.

The start-up (which I will call "the company") took off like a bushfire, immediately grabbing the emergent market for Tarot readings, and it remained the giant first of its kind, well ahead of all other competitors for a long time.

As for us, there was no limit (other than the server's capacity) to the number of people who could simultaneously interact with our divination programs, and by the end of the first month we had already gathered a hefty benefit. Thus, the programs began generating money barely five weeks after the initial talk show. In the computer world, everybody and everything was already very fast-moving, but the Internet sphere was a gear higher, rushing at breakneck speed, things being set up at the snap of a finger, people (us included) working day in and night out until completing whatever task was at hand. Moreover, the Internet computer nerds were constantly adapting their systems to the growing demand and traffic.

We had entered a new social dimension, a very speedy and demanding one, which was going to stay with us for many years.

❋

Meanwhile, as we hadn't given our programs' exclusive rights to the company, we were soon solicited by other websites and providers, notably a major TV channel, and I signed with two of them. Yet, the other two companies—despite giving us about the same rate of reimbursement were not anywhere near our previous hours per month; they were gigantic websites, our programs lost in them, unlike our company, which was uniquely dedicated to divination and readings.

The inflow of money was now steady. We were working like crazy in the daytime, yet, after the initial months, I persisted in dedicating my nights to meditating and writing. Apart from regularly spaced wide-audience books, I had two long-term projects going on for nearly a decade each; one was a literary biography of a specific period in my life and travels and the other the elaboration of my theory of consciousness—Semantic Fields Theory, in a cognitive and systems theory framework.

M was always involved with parapsychology research and we ended up being members of a different set of scientific societies, participating in ongoing research and annual conferences.

The Minitel robust income had been rolling for about two years when, one night around 3:00 a.m., I decided to pause my writing and get into a meditative state; I moved to sit cross-legged on my meditation futon at the side of my desk and put on some Zen music in the background.

As I was raising my state of consciousness to get into fuller contact with my Self, and started harmonizing with her-him, I entered, as usual, into a heightened state.

But that night must have been very special because I suddenly remembered vividly how, years earlier, I was able to get into a state of fusion with my Self. I reevoked how I would feel, my mind receiving a dense influx of high energy from the cosmos on my crown chakra; how my spirit was totally open and free, breathing in these high frequencies and sensing the vast expanses of a collective consciousness.

And I realized that, at the moment, this highest state was not accessible to me anymore. And at that point (eyes still closed), I perceived, all around my head, filaments of light that were issued from my head chakras and were cascading all around my body toward the floor, where they plunged underground.

Despite seeing these luminous filaments for the first time ever, as soon as I saw them I knew what they were. It was the way my mind, through visualization and intent, was steering specific forces—born out of my consciousness—in order to manage the many facets of my professional and social work, and particularly our Internet financial endeavor.

I then knew for certain that these syg-energy filaments connecting me to the social networks existed for real. Before that, I had only guessed and sensed that energy-links existed, visualizing them as loose waves and ethereal, but I would never have imagined that they presented this sort of filament reality, especially linked to the head chakra. And it was now crystal clear that I had created them in the first place through my visualizations and that they also impeded me from attaining the highest states of consciousness—the fusion with my Self.

And at that moment, I felt thirsty and longed for experiencing again that blissful liberated state.

I pondered the problem briefly and concluded that, by now, things with the Minitel were running by themselves. The seeds had been planted long ago and there was no need for me to keep steering and watching things so closely.

And with this decision, I visualized that I got hold of virtual scissors and, with a large sweeping and circular gesture, I just cut them all at once.

Instantly, I could now feel the dense flow of energy from the cosmos—like a cascading river falling on my crown chakra, rejuvenating me. And I entered a fusion-state with my Self, exhilarated at sensing it expand and experiencing it again.

A long time passed in this blissful state, and finally, I just reclined my body on the futon, covered myself, and slid into sleep, still in this heightened state right there.

❋

Next, my work (landline) phone erupts and rings raucously, hardly three feet from my head, waking me up the hard way; and as I raise myself on an elbow, I register it's just a few minutes past 8:00 a.m.—a time at which, in our media and research sphere, nobody is ever calling anybody. It's so ominous that I answer it.

The caller is the cohead of the company, by now a friend, and yet I hardly recognize her voice, so stressed and sharp is it. She delivers a message in quick and chained sentences. They had problems some time back with her husband; they finally split and decided to sell the company. Now the company has just been bought but they are not allowed to say by who. The change of CEO is immediate and the buyer is keeping the company's team but will decide which divination programs they want to carry on and which ones they will drop; thus, she has no idea if my divination programs will be retained, and she warns me that our payments may be stopped anytime and soon.

And this is it. Her quick delivery hasn't allowed me to step in. I dispute the fact she won't tell me who is now in charge and give me at least a contact or phone number to discuss with them. She replies it's not an option and ends the call rather abruptly. The line goes dead. This call was hardly three minutes long.

As I realize fully what's happening, I let out a groan.

"Whoa! Such a mistake I made! The effect's really drastic!

Company sold; no interlocutor; no way to discuss things with the new CEO; funds slashed anytime . . . and the guy may choose to just not tell us of his decision! Really wild!!

Is such secrecy and such cavalier behavior vis-à-vis subcontractors even legal? . . . Never heard of anything like that.

So, this was really a mistake of mine of grand proportion! Grabbing imaginary scissors and cutting all the filaments, the links, took me hardly two seconds. And now I have to immediately get visualizing, to try to rebuild or create new links. Can I repair the situation? How long could it take? No idea!"

With that thought I went to the kitchen to make myself some coffee, eat a quick bite, and prepare for hours or rather days of visualization. M was still sleeping; I would inform him later.

And I set off right away a new round of nonstop visualization and meditation. *The problem, I was saying to myself, is that in the first round to solve our financial problems, I had some notion, even if gross, of the time it would take to obtain results—like two to three hours of daily visualization, and expecting something to happen within two to three weeks; in contrast, I've no idea if and when I'll be able to reconstruct the broken links. I'm cornered and have to be uniquely concentrated on it, day and night.*

I was of course furious about the secrecy clause and swore to myself that—given our large social network—it wouldn't take me long to find out who the buyer was. And indeed, it was a matter of a couple of phone calls and hardly two days to discover the well-known business and luxury mogul, the company's name and plush address in Paris. As it happened, the grassroots business of our friends had been overtaken by Paris's cream of the cream.

The Hyperdimension Steering Spacetime Events

Allow me a digression here to explain how things work with the hyperdimension. Many of you may think that the crashing of my business, as it was announced a few hours later, was only seemingly related to my visualization; because it doesn't make sense at all, since selling a company does take weeks and months of preparation.

I agree. Yet, I've observed time and again—I'm talking about real-life experiences—that mental and psi states enable us to change things and overturn tables in our 4D and social dimension in a way that fully contradicts the laws of matter and spacetime physics and the normally causal and sequential course of social affairs.

So much so that I'm now convinced that meditation, visualizing, and psi at large operate via the faster-than-light syg-energy of our hyperdimensional mind and Self. In other words, part of our consciousness belongs to the Syg-HD and doesn't abide by the past → future arrow, nor by the cause → effect linear process.

As I have argued in several systems science papers and my book *Cosmic DNA*, our hyperdimensional mind, by operating beyond the 4D spacetime, can plant seeds in the future but it can also work in a present → past, or retrocausal, manner (see Hardy 2021). Thus, a meditation on Sunday may plant seeds days and weeks earlier. The cause will generate a retroactive effect in our 3D+1D spacetime, because the source—the HD thought-impulse—exists within the timeless hyperdimension.

The best way to picture it is to imagine an HD pebble falling from the HD into the spacetime lake on a specific day in June. It will send concentric ripples across the whole spacetime fabric, many of which are moving backward in (1D) time, thus seeding events all the way back to February. This happens because the hyperdimension is pervading all 4D matter and all of the lake's waterdrops.

You have thus to picture the consciousness hyperdimension—which is cosmic consciousness (Syg-HD), interlaced with hypertime and hyperspace—as pervading and extended in our 3D-space and 1D-time; thus, the syg-energy's influence impacts all instants of our time, in the past and the future. And since our own Self is the part of our consciousness that belongs to the HD, it operates in the same fashion.

Indeed, my cutting the filaments had been a HD pebble in spacetime, creating a new course of events for my business, as many other situations could have happened. For example: Even with our friends facing problems at home, things could have turned another way for M and me. Also, even their couple breakup wouldn't necessarily lead the CEOs to sell their thriving business. Or else, the new buyer didn't need to be such a stingy businessman.

How I Remedied My Catastrophic Visualization

So, was I able to redress this terrible mistake of mine? To some extent, yes. But we definitely lost some feathers in the process.

Figure that I was meditating day and night, trying to weave new filaments (now that I had been able to clearly see what they looked like). I was also testing strategies, and since I had found the address of the buyer's company—in an upscale quarter—I was building my own strength and intent to go there and confront this powerful man of the Parisian elite one-on-one, running full frontal against his secrecy clause.

In the course of two or three days, I had worked out, using the Tarot cards, the day, hour, and details of my visit, in order to find out the time at which this many-faceted man was going to be there—at one seat of his many business operations. I had also patiently sorted out my best arguments; they had to be appealing to his business mind, yet without diminishing my own work, research, and confidence in my programs. Fortunately, the magnate—let's call him X—also had an artistic bent. And as such, even if he didn't believe in precognition and using divination systems to make the psi information emerge to the conscious, at least he would give some credit to authentic research and an original creative product. In terms of arguments, I also had the backing of experimental psi research in the United States, and M's and my doctoral theses on the subject.

Finally, I make my move. So here I was, entering the upscale building and facing a front desk hostess, to whom I gave the name of the top Minitel operator of the company—let's call her Nathalie—as the ex-CEO had told me X was keeping the team running the website. I explained she was a friend and I wanted to see her. I was directed to pass through a smoky glass partition and discovered a vast hall with a half dozen desks, widely spaced. At the first and largest one was sitting Nathalie. I also perceived a large square room embedded into the hall, all in smoky glass where, no doubt, the boss had his private office.

I maintained the large toothy smile I had presented at the front desk and walked toward Nathalie, who looked both surprised and rather uncomfortable at seeing me. I had to remain standing (there was no chair) and opened the conversation by genuinely discussing the buying of the company, trying to convey my sympathy to her. After a few minutes, I showed my cards. I told her that I firmly intended to see and talk to X. She countered immediately that it was not going to be possible, that he was not available, not even there . . . (she was a bit confused in the way she tried to shield him); that, anyway, he wasn't accepting any appointments at the time. And now, of course, she was quite upset at my strategy.

So I answered, looking her in the eye, as cool as I could muster:

"Well, I see a chair there, next to the hall door. I'm going to sit and I will not budge from there until I am received in his office by X."

And I went to sit on the said chair, which was conveniently overlooking the exit: nobody could get out of this hall without passing in front of me. I had no idea what the man looked like (photo unobtainable in these early Internet times), but I had a view of his office door and the whole team.

I took out a book from my shoulder bag and went on reading while clearly standing watch. I figured a one-way mirror partition afforded X a roving view over his team working, while he remained invisible (which was proven right). And I was sure my stance had not escaped him.

(Note that I was so confident in my Tarot readings that I knew he was there, despite Nathalie trying at first to suggest he was not.)

About ten minutes later, I saw Nathalie engage in a phone conversation. She now trod the dozen steps toward me and restated that X had said he had no time at all and wouldn't receive me, no matter what.

To which I answered courteously but firmly that I wouldn't budge from this chair until I talked to X, no matter what. And I dove back into my book. She apparently relayed my answer.

It took another forty or fifty minutes. The atmosphere was quite dense in the workroom as all had watched with eagerness the ongoing standoff. Nathalie walked again toward my chair and this time told me that X was now able to receive me; she led the way toward his office door, knocked politely, and let me in.

Just like the hall, X's office was a vast and imposing space. I was composed and focused, surfing on high gear on the crest of four days of intense meditation. I sat on a chair in front of his desk.

He played the big boss apparently amused by my stand. I presented myself as the creator of the divination games and programs, a dedicated researcher with a PhD thesis on the subject who had worked in a psi research lab in the United States. He cut me short and blurted out, with a gaslighting smirk:

"The point is, I have bought several divination companies, and thus I have a half dozen *identical* Tarot programs. I'm going to keep only one, and that's going to be the cheapest one."

He was thus confirming my hunch that, for him, divination was just crap, especially on the Internet, and this whole business affair was just that, business as usual. The company's ex-CEO had warned me about an array of divination programs.

I was unfazed and went on explaining why my programs were different and why they were working, and how I had spent about a year refining the linguistics of Ellora so that it could answer most questions coherently, whatever the grammar and phrasing being used. I spelled out how enormous my pool of Tarot answers was and how such programs needed a perfect pseudo-random algorithm, one that I brought back from the lab in Princeton.

He was a bit taken aback; he had not expected to have a real interlocutor making her case. And, being smart, he started listening . . .

I then pointed out that it was because my programs were delivering on-target answers that people got hooked and would come back to use them. And because there were several hundred detailed answers, they were spending more time on them than on any twenty-two-answer digital Tarot filling the Internet. And even more time on the open-answer discussion program, Ellora.

I detected a shift in his mindset. And now he proposed this to me:

"Okay, I could choose your programs, but there's no way I would give back seven plus francs per minute per customer. I can and will offer you only one franc. Take it or leave it."

That's when I was so shocked I overreacted and told him, squarely looking him in the eye:

"There's no way whatsoever that I will bring the price lower than six francs per minute." (That was about one dollar.)

"Then, this is it. We have no deal," said he with a final tone.

There was nothing for me to add. I was outraged. I swallowed hard and took my leave, thanking him for having received me. He wasn't budging; I was not. It was a dead end.

On the way back, I was not really sure of what I had accomplished. In the readings I did as a preparation, the Tarot cards had shown me that I shouldn't give in to his pressure and that I should instead stand my high ground. As went my mulling on them, it was psychologically sound that such a powerful and superrich social figure—yet smart and refined—would immediately crush and checkmate anybody displaying meekness and servility. You had to stand your ground and even rebuke them just to be considered a worthy interlocutor.

I had stood my ground. Would that work later on? I was curious to check it with my Tarot deck.

That night, after a short rest and now in a deeply concentrated state, I asked the Tarot where I stood at that point, and what to expect next.

The answer was stark and rather brusque.

All over the twenty or so cards I pulled was shown my utter defeat: I had burnt all bridges; it was an absolute catastrophe; there would be no deal and he was going to choose a cheap program. We were ruined and back to the poverty line.

My mind went into overdrive.

So, I've to backtrack at top speed. Will try to save whatever can be saved from the deal. A lower price is better than nothing . . .

How am I to explain to the boss my about-face?

Well, he had enjoined me to understand his pragmatic and financial reasoning. I'll call him next morning first thing, explain I had mulled over what he told me and wanted to propose a new deal.

After that, I spent the next hours working on this new strategy and saw in the cards that it was doable. I checked with the Tarot each and every potential move and what price could entice him . . . a midway offer.

Next morning, I apprised M about what I had worked on and told him I was readying myself for the call. Generally, when he sensed that I was fully in charge of something and taking it all on myself, he didn't try to interfere in any way. When, on my return from Paris the previous day, I had recounted to him my meeting with X and the final deadlock situation, he had just empathized, expecting, like me, that things would finally turn to our advantage in a second round of talks.

I made the call to X. Siding at first with his business perspective, I then proposed to consider three and a half francs per minute. He counter proposed three, and we agreed on that.

It was going to be a drastic reduction in our living standards, but I had avoided a free fall and ruin.

Now, something very bizarre happened: we both totally forgot to set an appointment to sign the new deal, and the problem didn't even cross my mind afterward. And very quickly it was the start of the winter holidays and the superrich were not in town anymore.

In the aftermath of this deal, I reviewed anxiously one evening the accounting of both our research association and our personal one, trying to figure how to manage our now high-expenditure life with much less money, given the new deal basis. And that's when I made a fantastic discovery. I checked the two columns of benefits and expenses again; there it was! Unbelievable!

I jumped up from my cushion, burst out of my workroom, and joined M in his own workroom in the basement—the Lab—where I found him glued to his desk computer as usual.

Excitedly, I cajoled him into going upstairs to our music and meditation room, explaining I had such great news to discuss with him that we had to pour one out for it!

And once seated in our late-night cozy music room, with a vodka served, I went on a stand-up comedy stunt, claiming theatrically that I had just "invented right-brain accounting" and that it produced a fantastic outcome. "Cheers!" I said, clinking my glass with his.

"Come on, spell it out!"

"OK, I was checking how to deal with our lower income. Figure that our working expenses for the phone, Internet, and car gas every month are so high—and given that we don't need to be in town for the money to fall into our account—I calculated that if we spend our time in a cheap-living country like India or Indonesia, after only two months and a half we would actually start saving money! Can you believe it!? Just two and a half months to pay for two pricey flights and hotels, and we start saving money! And then, the longer we stay, the more we save."

He was flabbergasted.

"Look," I pursued, "we have nothing retaining you or me at the moment in Paris. We can't let that opportunity pass! Any moment, we can be chained again to some longwinded work . . ."

We agreed and drank another toast at the thrilling idea; and then, opening the atlas on Asia, we went on deciding where we were going to spend the next three months. We opted for a grand tour, arriving first in Thailand, then traveling through Malaysia, Indonesia, and finally Bali for the remainder of the trip. His next commitment, in the United States, was more than three months ahead; it was just a perfect interlude.

It took us hardly a week to get on the move and we had a marvelous trip, especially in Bali.

But here is the cherry on the cake that awaited us on our return: I found out that X's company had been obligated by law to keep paying us for three more months at the old price because we were not there to sign the new deal. X, despite his initial (and failing) avoidance strategy, had kept his gentleman's agreement.

7
ENERGY AND FREQUENCY ANOMALIES

We are now going to explore fascinating anomalies that expose the reality of extremely high frequencies belonging to the hyperdimension. These HD frequencies, being sub-quantum, are revealed only through their interaction with our material world in which the electromagnetic (EM) energy spectrum reigns. Two other forces above Planck scale (the first quantum) operate within the nucleus of atoms: the weak and strong forces. As for the fourth fundamental force, gravity, it is sub-quantum and still mysterious. The EM spectrum runs from the lowest frequency range (radio waves), up to the highest one of the cosmic rays reaching above 10^{24} hertz (Hz) (see fig. 7.1).

Just so that you understand what is at stake here (and for me to make no false claims), the hyperdimension—aka hyperspace and/or hypertime—(1) has been proposed in several physics theories but hasn't been proven yet; (2) is de facto integrated in all superstring theories (i.e., as soon as you go over 4D, you include some sort of HD). Moreover, since its integration by Theodor Kaluza in 1919, and especially in the superstring theories, adding extra dimensions to the 4D of spacetime is an indispensable acrobatics (in terms of math and physics) in order to build a unified theory of physics—that is, an integration of Einsteinian spacetime physics with quantum physics or, put differently,

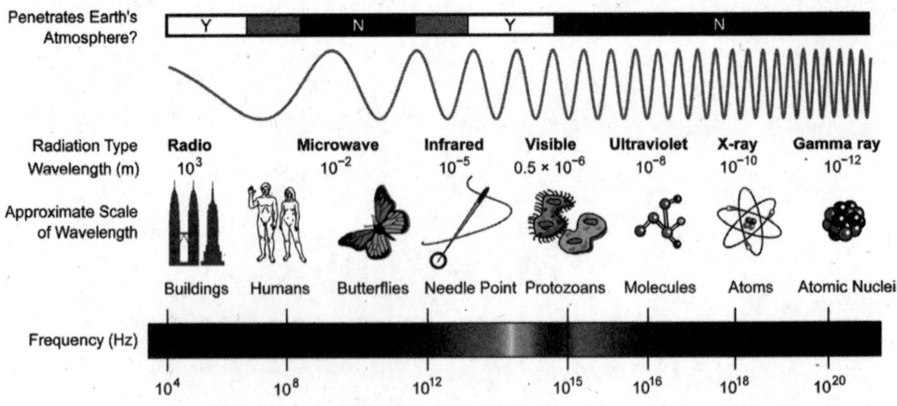

Fig. 7.1. The electromagnetic spectrum. Milton diagram. The wavelengths are expressed in meters; the spectrum goes from the low frequency and longer radio waves, at 10^3 meters to the shorter gamma rays, at 10^{-12} meters. Next, the various wavelengths are compared to sizes found in everyday life.
Photo by Inductiveload

a unification of all four fundamental forces (hence the eleven dimensions of Witten's leading M-theory). But, as it took me some time to understand, math is so central to the reality of the universe that a math necessity reveals nothing less than a necessity of nature and a physics reality. Thus, in my (nonhumble) view, expect nothing but the vindication of these hyperphysics theories in the future; not of the whole of each one, but substantially as regarding their "hyper" part (this doesn't include Leonard Susskind's multiverse hypothesis based on randomness alone; see Carr 2009).

As noted by several psi researchers (me included), the experimental research on psi capacities has also given us solid proofs that psi (thus, the mind) operates beyond spacetime, because psi often contradicts the spacetime and matter laws. In short, psi works in a beyond-space way (as in clairvoyance at a distance) or in a beyond-time way (as in precognition)—that is, it is nonlocal (Hardy, 2017). Moreover, psi also contradicts causality, meaning that it is *acausal,* as Jung has defined synchronicity.

What we'll now ponder is another set of evidence, not based on laboratory experiments but on real-life experiences in high states of consciousness. The anomalies in terms of frequencies and EM fields do reveal the existence of a non-EM type of energy, obviously a hyperdimensional energy such as the HD syg-energy I modeled. But they reach way beyond that and also reveal the workings of this syg-energy, and especially within our chakras and acupuncture meridians; thus, in our energy-body as well. Let's remember that in Eastern religions and shamanism, this energy-body (or astral body) is able to become independent and exit the body, with our full I-consciousness; it can thus be the vehicle of part of our own Self, itself nothing less than supraconscious.

As a reminder: With ISST, I have proposed a hyperdimensional cosmology positing a universe endowed with cosmic consciousness, in which our Selfs are the hyperdimensional and eternal entities. The energy filling this consciousness-hyperdimension is syg-energy, which belongs to another energy spectrum than the EM one—the syg spectrum. Syg-energy has frequencies vastly higher than the highest gamma rays, and a speed much greater than light (and all EM energies that are moving at light speed). The syg spectrum starts below and before Planck scale, at which scale space, time, and, later, particles (e.g., electrons) and atoms came to exist; and this is why it is unbound by spacetime and EM laws (which mostly rely on electrons). Syg-energy is also the energy of our HD Self, and what constitutes our energy-body and the best part of our mind.

The accounts below are highly anomalous experiences for which I don't have all the answers. This is why I have to be as honest and precise as possible when recounting them, because some of their facets may reveal some workings of the HD and of our Self-consciousness that may become decipherable by future science; in which case, they may offer precious highlights. Yet I'll propose some ways of understanding some of their facets. Let me first start by reviewing the ancient knowledge on the cosmic immaterial energy (prana) and energy-body.

ENERGY-BODY AND CHAKRAS IN ANCIENT ORIENTAL TREATISES AND IN CURRENT RESEARCH

The Eastern traditional medicines—such as acupuncture in China and ayurveda in India—are derived from the accumulation of knowledge on the energy-body through millennia of practice. They are a corpus of knowledge expounded in ancient oriental treatises and based on the practice of meditation leading to the awakening of the energy-centers or *chakras* (Sanskrit for "wheel"). Medical and philosophical treatises have gone to great lengths to map the energy-body, its chakras and acupuncture points, as well as its energy flow through *nadis* and meridians, and their relationship to organs and somatic systems. While there are notable differences between various oriental traditions, they all state the existence of five to eight chakras on the central channel along the vertebral column, as shown on fig. 7.2. (See the translation of an ancient

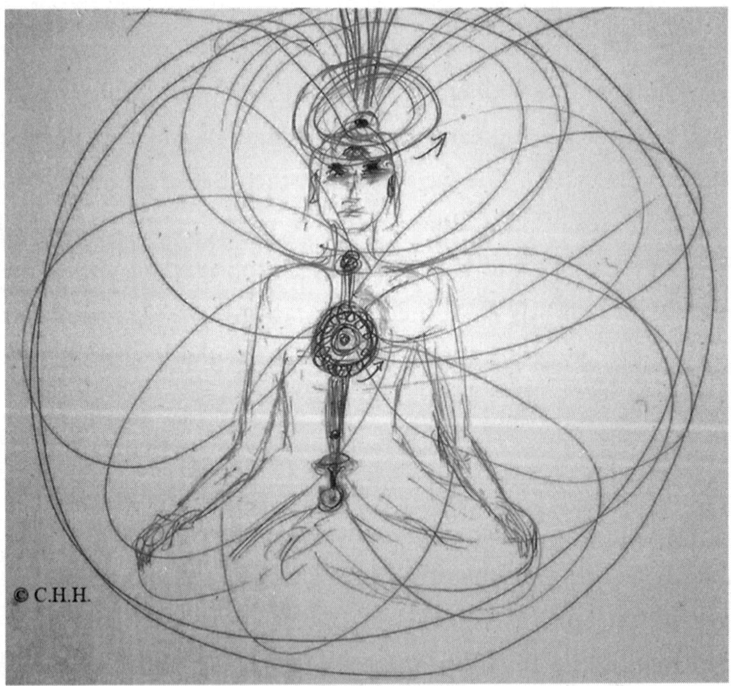

Fig. 7.2. The higher chakras and their energy field
Concept and artwork by Chris H. Hardy

treatise on chakras in Arthur Avalon's *The Serpent Power*.) In Hindu Tantra and the Upanishads (the philosophy of nonduality; i.e., of oneness), there are two lesser channels or flows (*nadis* in Sanskrit, plural of *nad*) running left and right of a central kundalini channel called Sushumna, which connects the base chakra (Muladhara) to the crown chakra at the top of the head (Sahasrara).

Now, what interests us most here is the "subtle energy" of this energy-body—called chi or qi in China, ki in Japan, and prana in India. Prana (or kundalini energy) belongs to another dimension altogether than matter and the body. It is described as existing before our matter universe and in fact birthing it and surviving it (this being the closest lay description of a hyperdimension). Prana is said to be immaterial, ethereal, and steered by our higher Self or atman, itself belonging to the divine realm (aka the HD), where dwell both the goddess Shakti (who guides the kundalini awakening) and Shiva (her consort).

Thus *Varaha Upanishad* (circa thirteenth to sixteenth centuries CE) states:

> *The nadis penetrate the body from the soles of the feet to the crown of the head. In them is prana, the breath of life, and in that life abides Atman, which is the abode of Shakti, creatrix of the animate and inanimate worlds. (Varahopanisad V, 54/5*)*

In the terms of ISST, this would translate as "the energy-body is formed by, and filled with, cosmic syg-energy (prana as consciousness-energy), in which abide all the individual syg-fields (the atmans), in which dwell all the Selfs (the Shakti, as one and multiple), whose ensemble, as the One-plural cosmic hyperdimension, created the matter universe." Indeed, given that a person's syg-field contains their Self, their energy-body, and all their bio-matter (body and brain

**Varaha Upanishad.* Visit the "Hindu Online" British website (.co) and see the original text of the Hindu scriptures under the Upanishads tab.

system) information, it is thus a larger system than their HD-Self per se, even if "I" usually equates the individual atman with the person's Self (like Jung does).

Each culture and country has its own knowledge, science, and creative genius, as well as specific cultural influences. For example, Tibet has been mostly influenced by India (and the birth of Buddhism in Nalanda University), and later by China; moreover, as we saw, it also had its own ancient shamanic religion—the pre-Buddhist Bon that reached predominance in the tenth and eleventh centuries, with some scholars dating it to 100 BCE. Yet all Eastern cultures and religions, as well as all ancient shamanic traditions worldwide, have observed that, in heightened consciousness states or trance states, the energy-body was able to exit the body, passing through any matter barriers (such as walls, ceiling) and travel at the speed of thought. The scientific research uses the neutral term *out-of-body experiences* (OBEs) and has included experimental and clairvoyance testing.*

The flying energy-body is called the astral or etheric body in Western esoterica, the "intermediary body/vehicle" by the Tibetans, and the dreamtime body by the Australian Aborigines. Let's note that in Hinduism and Tibetan Buddhism, there are several such immaterial intermediary bodies—with frequencies corresponding to different levels of divine consciousness. In the triadic Christian concept of a body-soul-spirit, the energy-body corresponds to the soul and the spirit to the immortal Self.

The Indian yogis, just like the shamans, are prone to travel in their astral body for the sake of knowledge, while meditating or in trance states. The shamans use it also for healing and clairvoyance sessions. In contrast, the martial arts masters of Vietnam, Japan, and Asia at large, will strive to be able to exit with such force as to give their opponent a powerful blow at a distance of one or two yards—as we have seen in the self-defense chapter.

*On OBE research, see Tart 1969, Monroe 1992.

Here is the point: prana, being immaterial, has a higher dimensionality (and frequencies) than the matter (and EM) dimensions; the prana, which Indians saw as the vital and conscious energy of the cosmos (beyond matter), fits perfectly the HD level filled with the syg-energy spectrum (in ISST).

The experience I will now recount gives us an inkling of how distinct the two domains of frequencies are—the electrical grid at 50/60 hertz, compared to the hyperdimensional and astral body domain. It shows also a strange interaction between these two frequency domains.

A FIGHT AGAINST THE ELECTRICAL GRID DURING AYAHUASCA

In 2004, I attended a conference on psi research organized by the spiritist university of Curitiba (FIE) in Brazil a high-quality scientific research university.* I was there to present a paper on synchronicity, explained through my Semantic Fields Theory (SFT). Actually, by positing a dimension of consciousness beyond the matter and spacetime manifold, SFT could bring a new perspective on synchronicities by invoking instant (faster-than-light) meaningful connections happening through this *syg dimension* (Hardy 2004). (As a parenthesis, all terms, dynamics, and properties of this syg-energy and semantic (syg) dimension were put forward in SFT before I developed their hyperdimensional facet in ISST.)

Spiritism—a doctrine positing the existence of a realm of spirits, which allows for mediums' contacts with the deceased—was spearheaded by Allan Kardec and has the status of one of the predominant religions of Brazil. That made the audience an attractive one for me, since the scientists teaching there, as well as the students, were likely to have explored self-development techniques.

*The University of Curitiba, FIE (Faculdades Integradas Espirita) held its second psi meeting in Curitiba, Brazil, in 2004. Besides its classical scientific (and large-spectrum) census, FIE is notable for its specific research focus on psi and parapsychology, states of consciousness, and spiritism.

The FIE had organized a second conference on states of consciousness, interlaced with the first one, which was to take place in the evenings. And we, the staunch and serious scientists presenting their research in the daytime, were taken each night to discover a different, homegrown creed and its rituals composing the rich and variegated spiritual landscape of Brazil. What an experience and what a genius idea! I truly loved it!

That night, a dozen of us who had been both volunteers and cleared for this specific exploration (via a scientific and medical evaluation) were to participate in an ayahuasca ritual of the Santo Daime Church (the "Holy Give-Me" church). It was such a significant experience in perspective that I decided to retire to my hotel room earlier in the afternoon to spend a couple of hours meditating. At lunch, some young students whom I had befriended and who had already participated in several such rituals at this church offered to take me with them to the mountain site of the church, as they planned to drive there in their own car, instead of waiting for the bus dedicated to the scientists' evening trip. We had been instructed not to eat that evening and very lightly at lunch, and to be dressed in white as much as possible and warmly. Indeed, the large church was set at the very top of a mountain, and it was freezing cold there, in perfect contrast with the stifling hot weather in town. I was happy I had, as a last-ditch idea while leaving the room, grabbed the cotton bedspread that happened to be white!

The church was a very large octagonal hall (about sixteen yards wide) in which the rows of wooden chairs were disposed in concentric circles around the "altar"—a tall pillar set at its very center (at least twenty-five feet high) and supporting a geometrical roof whose beams, fanning slightly downward from this center, created an inspiring octagonal mandala. I grooved on this sacred architecture reminiscent of Native Americans tepees and of shamans' huts featuring a central pillar and a hole in the roof at the very center of a round tent.

These circles of chairs were crossed and spaced by alleys forming another geometrical design. As I was told, the women were to be seated on one aisle of the church, and the men on another one; they turned out to be quite far away, since the hall was so large.

As it happened, I was sitting a bit diagonally two rows behind the head of the church, an astonishingly young woman in her late teens, quite reserved, who probably had attained the highest state of consciousness in their whole community. I mention this because, during the whole three hours of this intense altered state, we experienced a close telepathic contact between us, with her sometimes turning her head backward to look at me at key moments when I was connected to her state (despite the chairs all around me now being filled up). She was obviously the high node of the large telepathic-harmonic field that included all participants in the ritual. And that Telhar field included also the dozen or so "helpers" who, on our side, were a handful of young women; they stood guard in the largest circle near our door, at the ready to escort outside anybody who would, as is customary for newcomers, feel an urgent need to throw up.

I had never experienced ayahuasca beforehand, but I had read accounts and knew it was an entheogen rich in the psychoactive compound dimethyltryptamine (DMT). In the Santo Daime creed, it is a mix of two plants, the ayahuasca vine (jagube, *Banisteriopsis caapi*), and the *Psychotria viridis* leaf, the Queen of the Forest (also rich in DMT).

After the bulk of the scientists arrived and sat down, we had a moment of meditation in silence; then we were led to get in a file and walk toward a table behind which stood a man dressed in white and green, who was handing, to each person in turn, a certain amount of the sacred beverage in a small glass. First, the initiated women belonging to the creed were served, a full vodka glass. Then we, the neophyte women, approached. I could see that the man in charge was not giving the same amount to the first-timers ahead of me, hardly a half glass. Yet, after he sized me up, he did fill my glass with the initiates' dose.

I swallowed slowly while welcoming the spirit of the plant in me, making an ad hoc harmonization with it, and walked back to my seat. (I believe that was the reason why I didn't have any retching reaction to it.)

Then I got absorbed in the heightened state quickly setting in my mind, with such an extremely rapid and high mental frequency, the like of which I had never experienced before. After a while, my spirit lifted up and exited from my body very naturally by the crown chakra.

Indeed, I've been prone to make astral journeys since my late teens (when I experienced two spontaneous exits), and I've steered and controlled them while meditating since I was twenty-one, with my self-conscious astral body exiting directly through the awakened crown chakra. Any very high state of consciousness will provoke such extension of my spirit and reaching out to the higher spirit dimension. Yet I had learned a lot about these astral travels through a tough experience of continuously meditating while starving for months in a row in India. At that time (of my first eighteenth-month travel), I was getting in astral for an hour or so about twice a day, whether willingly while meditating or unwillingly any time—like the day I got into such an OBE trance in the middle of a step while walking along the beach; I was simultaneously conscious of my hyperdimension trip and of my (stupid) immobile posture with one foot ahead, on the shore. I sustained this near continuous meditation and food deprivation for about four months, where I would get a small banana with a tiny roundish white bread every three or four days but luckily one or two *chai*, the Indian milk tea, each day. Until one day, I was impeded from exiting through the crown chakra by what appeared like a large hand forcing my energy-body back in. At which point I understood that continually exiting my body and roaming in the astral dimension was depriving my body of energy and aggravating the effect of starvation, thus becoming quite dangerous for me (I had lost some forty pounds in a few months and had only skin on my bones). I then grasped that I had to find another way to expand my consciousness to the higher dimension—as this was my essential mode of knowing and exploring. And I did discover another way: one could, while having part of one's consciousness centered within the crown chakra and keeping watch (the Vigilant), stretch the Self-consciousness (the Voyant) to a faraway locus or higher realm, or even expand one's semantic field all over a landscape, or else get into harmonizing and fusioning with a group of minds as in a Telhar field mode (even if I didn't used the latter term at the time, I had already invented the terms "*harmonic field*" and *semantic field* which I later shortened to *syg-field*). And I immediately switched to this new modus operandi, exploring even further the immaterial reality while replenishing my body with prana energy.

To get back to the Santo Daime Church, as I was raising my consciousness to the higher-frequency realm (with my energy-body), I realized I was blocked under the high roof and unable to traverse it. Let me explain here that this process—of both traveling toward a higher or remote place and traversing whatever roof and walls are on the way—is usually spontaneous and doesn't even require my attention, as I usually find myself instantly conscious and aware wherever my intent wants to be or is focused.

Astonished to face a barrier I couldn't pass, I got back to being centered in my body sitting on the chair and aware of my surroundings, in order to study the roof and find out what was blocking me.

And what I saw was an incredibly dense mesh formed by electrical wires dotted with tiny colored light bulbs of the kind we use to decorate a Christmas tree. These wires were hanging all over the beams and across the roof framing, thus making a mandala of crisscrossing wires, like a spiderweb, putting out tiny sparks of all colors.

It was utterly strange and unheard of for me, that a simple intent of moving upward in space, roof or no roof, would not be immediately effective. So I closed my eyes again, discarded the disturbing freezing sensations, straightened my back on the so-uncomfortable wooden chair, and focused on studying this bewildering energy-structure blocking my energy-body.

What I was now seeing (eyes closed) in my heightened consciousness, was the field of electric energy itself; it seemed like the 60 hertz of electricity running in the numerous wires had created a uniform field at the height of the roof, which was, at the midpoint of the beams, about twenty feet high. This field had the appearance of a regular grid of undulating lines running in parallel and crisscrossed perpendicularly by another set of parallel undulating lines. (Note that when "seeing" the grid, eyes closed, I was no longer perceiving the matter dimension of the beamed roof and the wires.)

My hyperconscious vision had just zoomed right into the organizational level of electrons, at the particle scale and frequency—and probably at the low hyperdimensional waves scale, as we'll see.

Whether it was just electrical or had magnetic components was of course irrelevant in my state of consciousness—I was just "seeing" a field that was a barrier to my spirit, and this from the (hyper) dimension of my Self vision, triggered by the high state.

The patch of electrical grid I was seeing may not have been, by itself, superposed to the material space (and whole mandala) of the roof, yet, as systems theory goes, it was essentially connected to that whole grid of lights that had created it; what I mean by that is a perturbation or a modification at any point within the roof grid could easily affect the whole grid.

A Parenthesis on Psychic Vision Versus Our Current Scientific Paradigm

Brazil's electrical grid (just as that of the United States) has a frequency of 60 hertz, meaning that it pulsates sixty times a second, and this gives us a wavelength of 4,750 kilometers (that is, 3,000 miles per cycle).* So that, obviously, the crisscrossing grid of parallel waves I was seeing in the middle of the roof couldn't in any way be related to the actual wavelengths of the electrical current. We'll discuss this question after I relate what

*As countries' electrical grids worldwide have a frequency (f) of either 50 Hz or 60 Hz, the wavelength (λ) is about 6,000 km for 50 Hz and 4,750 km for 60 Hz (that is, 3,000 miles per cycle); this, according to the formula λ = c/f or [300*10^6 m/s] / 60 Hz. Brazil, the United States, and Canada have a 60 Hz residential grid, while Europe is on 50 Hz.

happened to me the very way I saw it and understood it at the time.

Meanwhile, I ask you, my readers, to keep in mind two things: for one, our scientific knowledge at the present is quite limited compared to what it will be in fifty or a hundred years in the future; proof is, it is so much more advanced than it was fifty or one hundred years ago! Second, the hyperdimensional clairvoyance is able to perceive another level of reality—one that could be a chunk of what's missing now in our scientific knowledge. Think of Kekulé, the great chemist, who "saw" the octagonal structure of benzene as he had the vision of an Ouroboros—the serpent that bites its tail, thus forming a perfect circle—in his fire while dozing in front of it, and this is how he discovered its true hexagonal atomic structure. But Kekulé was also able, more than one time, to "see" and penetrate the very scale of atoms and molecules, and he saw them dancing around, including that time when he saw the structure of benzene. And he had not taken ayahuasca! (We will come back to Kekulé in a short while.) So I ask you to keep an open mind and avoid rejecting beforehand my experience because it *apparently* doesn't match our current knowledge.

The Vision of the Electrical Grid

To resume, what I was seeing was a grid made of two sets of parallel undulating and pulsating waves, which crisscrossed quasi-perpendicularly. Strangely, as I was intending to draw my ayahuasca perception of the grid for this book, I realized that it had precisely the form of "a field of particles with alternating focus" that I had drawn in 2012–2015 for my ISS theory book, thus eight to eleven years earlier, (see fig. 10.9, p. 268). Thus I unconsciously linked what I perceived in Brazil with what I understood later to be an HD level (and as I'm interpreting it here).

This Brazilian grid definitely had the features of a field; that is, a structured and uniform, or evenly spread, configuration of vibrating energy lines. (We'll analyze it in depth in chapter 10.)

The nodes at which these waves intersected orthogonally (nodes known to be at a half wavelength, and where the wave amplitude or motion is zero) were, in my vision, spaced about five inches apart, and I was focused on a patch of the grid that comprised about five or six of these nodes both in width and in length, and on all the waves connecting these nodes. This patch didn't have a defined outside boundary; I saw the waves kept extending farther, on all sides. The patch of the grid I was seeing at the level of the roof had an *apparent* size of about a yard in width and length.

I was seeing this whole field literally pulsating, the waves moving up and down dynamically and rhythmically at a very precise speed (which I assumed was the electrical one at sixty times per second). Altogether I understood how this field created a dense, flat barrier. I pondered the problem, while trying to sense deeper into the field, with its dynamics and pulse, by focusing more on it.

"How then can I cross it?" I asked myself, because, if one thing was sure, it was that I was going to access fully the dimension of my higher Self during this ayahuasca experience. There was nothing more essential that I had to do while in a heightened state, nothing of more value for me. Anything else—even the harmonic-telepathic field with the initiates and other attendees—was of no import or was even limiting me if I couldn't connect simultaneously to my higher Self. For sure I was going to pass; but *how*?

I was intensely observing the vibrating grid, from a global or higher-dimensional perspective that felt like I was bent *over* it. It's still quite strange since my astral body was below the roof and my body twenty feet below it. As I was seeing this whole spiderweb oscillate in between nodes (the crossing points) with a definite rhythm, the part of my spirit that is deeply attuned to rhythm took over. As we saw, I'm an ardent freestyle drummer. I'm very fond of drumming, in a shaman and yogic way; that is, using it to get in a heightened state and be in direct connection with my Self, and then to create a Telhar field; and I have played with lots of drummers and musicians in many different cultural contexts.

It occurred to me that what I was seeing was a 3D representation of a rhythmic field—I mean, a rhythm spread in space, or rather configured within a mandala of sorts. And now, all of a sudden, I knew how to control it: I just had to harmonize my mind with the frequency, while doing that from a much higher frequency in the harmonics.

So I instantly raised the frequency of my spirit to a harmonic of this (EM) field but at a much higher frequency range. It was like, when improvising in a jam session with several drummers, it's possible to play a much quicker rhythm that, nevertheless, falls in sync perfectly with the main beat of the slower rhythm. For example, if the drummers are following a four-beat rhythm, one can set oneself on a complex twelve-beat rhythm (4 × 3) and, despite being three times faster, one remains in perfect sync with the group. Now, however, I was seeing the rhythmic field as curved segments (vibrating up and down as strings) connecting nodes in a flattened grid landscape.

So I harmonized my main beat with the beat of all the vibrating strings simultaneously (in my landscape patch), and in a powerful and lightning-speed move, I took hold of all nodes at once, imposing my higher rhythm on the grid, and instantly, I found myself on the other side of the roof! Free to roam the spirit world, the dreamtime dimension of this Brazilian culture and more.

THE HIGHER-DIMENSIONALITY OF SOUND AND MUSIC: THE RHYTHM LANDSCAPE

I want to draw some parallels here with other anomalous experiences I had with sound and music, especially one in which, in a highly altered state, I had seen such a *rhythm landscape*. It happened during a jam session with other musicians. I was improvising on a large drumskin, and started tapping with one thumb alone on the round skin in a four-beat rhythm, precisely at the four corners of an imaginary square contained in the round skin. I tapped them one by one with my hand turning around the skin (and then adding quicker beats in between these four nodes). As I was utterly fascinated by this new possibility of linking a geometric form to a rhythm, the square (or rather the four corners near the rim) now appeared as a real energy figure on the drum skin, like an illuminated square landscape; so I directed myself to make a more perfect rhythm by hitting the drum more and more precisely on the square's corners, one by one, and indeed, it worked. So there was, in the four-beat square rhythm, the same kind of flattened rhythmic landscape (with the whole drumskin vibrating after each tapping, which is what produces the sound).

And of course, while reevoking this long-past experience from my memory, I cannot miss its convergence with my ISS theory, in which *Rhythm-HD* is one of the three interlaced braids of the hyperdimension, corresponding to hypertime—that is, a time-field or, in brief, a time spread in space, as a rhythm landscape.

There is, indeed, a higher dimensionality to sound (as frequency) that we may infer just by how it interacts with *form*—like a square or a round—in contrast to how a single guitar string vibrates when pinched one time. And form, in my ISS theory, is another braid of the triune hyperdimension, called *Center-Circle-HD*, the hyperspace. (As for the third and most crucial braid, we have met it already in *Syg-HD*, the cosmic consciousness layer in which our Selfs dwell.)

We do have a whole science and expertise dealing with sound frequencies and musical instruments; for example, what *length* and *width* will give a guitar string the specific frequency of a given note (like C or D); and how the sound of vibrating strings is amplified by the *shape* of their resonance case, such as with violins and guitars.

However, I believe we still have a lot to understand about how frequencies interact with specific geometric surfaces, or *cymatics*. This relationship was first discovered around 1630 by Galileo Galilei; then, in 1680, Robert Hooke evidenced nodal patterns while running a violin bow along a glass plate covered with flour. Then the German physicist and musician Ernst Chladni experimented with bowing on a square

Fig. 7.3. Chladni vibration patterns on a sand-covered plate. Illustration taken from *Elementary Lessons on Sound* by W. H. Stone, Macmillan and Co., London, 1879

plate sprinkled with fine sand and sorted out various modes of vibration according to the plate's geometry, as well as the original frequency that sets the glass plate vibrating in resonance. Furthermore, if the plate is fixed at its center, the patterns created will always be centered and symmetrical geometries. In fig. 7.3, the separate regions are vibrating in opposite directions and are delimited by nodal lines of zero vibration; in other words, the sand or powder collects along the lines where the surface is stationary—notably at the points where the two fingers hold the plate (or where a finger would press on a guitar string).

In fig. 7.4, we can see how an isosceles triangle produces a spectacular six-point star or base-3 mandala, which points to each apex and to the middle of the sides.

Now, a very interesting set of experiments was done by the Experimental Nonlinear Physics Group in the Department of Physics at the University of Toronto, Canada (presented on the group's website under a link to "Chladni patterns in vibrated plates"). They used,

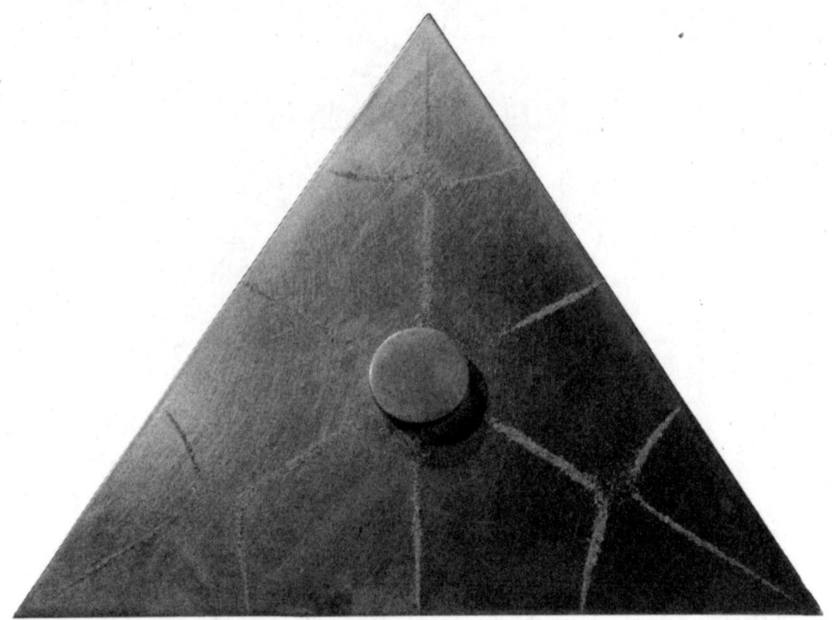

Fig. 7.4. Chladni six-point-star pattern on a triangular plate
Photo by Matemateca (IME/USP)/Rodrigo Tetsuo ArgentonDMGualtieri

among other shapes, a square plate of aluminum (28 inches on a side, driven from its center and attached to a shaker), and tested a range of frequencies (in hertz), as shown in fig. 7.5. The square shape produced base-4 mandalas of increasing complexity and density with the frequency rising and clearly presenting the multiple 8.

In view of Chladni's patterns, it's quite possible that my idea of tapping the drum in a square fashion was triggered in the first place by the anomalous perception of the square form that vibrations take naturally when a round-rimmed drum skin is tapped on the four corners of a virtual square; and then while I kept banging precisely on these corners, the supraconscious vision of the illuminated square became clearer as the vibration pattern was reinforced.

I have also been able to perceive sound waves moving through space on a few occasions, like the waves coming out of a home speaker, and how they were wildly perturbed when I accidentally knocked on that speaker. In another instance, my crossing a large movie theater room while passing

Fig. 7.5. Chladni base-4 mandalas of increasing complexity with the frequency rising; from top to bottom: *a.* 1225.0 Hz, *b.* 3678.1 Hz, *c.* 5875.5 Hz

Photos by Stephen Morris

in front of its two huge speakers (left and right of the giant screen) modified audibly the sound of the music, distorting it as it came out of a first speaker, then after a dozen more steps, of the second speaker.

Zooming In on the Scale of Atoms and Molecules

There is a lot of information we may also infer from this ayahuasca experience regarding how we may perceive (superconsciously) the scale of atoms and molecules. But first let us understand in more depth what we know about Kekulé's experience in that respect.

August Kekulé, one of the most prominent chemists of the nineteenth century, revolutionized organic chemistry by his theory of chemical structure. He was the first one to show (in 1857) the links (or valence) between carbon atoms, and the order in which they were bonded in a molecule. Kekulé was prone in his reveries (often in front of his fire) to observe the dance of atoms and molecules.

This is how, one day, he "saw" the structure of the benzene molecule as a ring—precisely as a snake biting its tail, as in the renowned archetype of the Ouroboros (see fig. 7.6). And not only was he able to

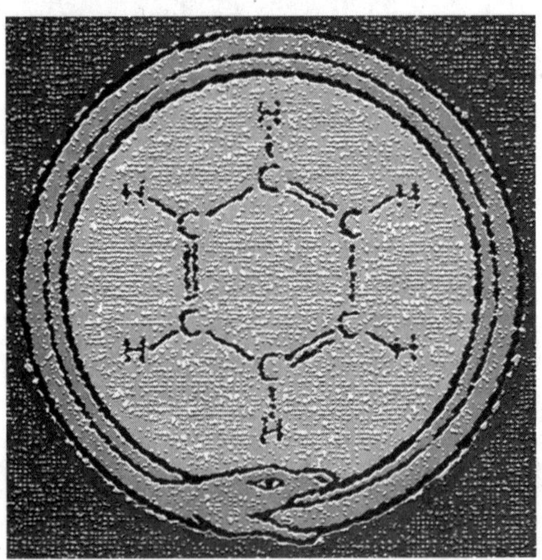

Fig. 7.6. Kekulé's daydream vision of the structure of benzene as an Ouroboros
Photo by Haltopub; retouched by Chris H. Hardy

figure (in 1864) the ring-shape of the six atoms of carbon within the benzene molecule (each linked to a hydrogen atom), but their alternate single and double bonds. It was in a speech he gave in 1890 that Kekulé recounted this memorable vision, as well as an earlier one of the dance of atoms and molecules while he was daydreaming on the upper deck of a horse-drawn omnibus crossing the city of London. That first vision of the dance of atoms led him to conceive his theory of chemical structure.

The interesting point in Kekulé's visions of the atomic scale of matter is that they were an exact representation of reality at that scale, whose validity was asserted when the six-atom ring of benzene was later proven by X-ray crystallography.

Archimedes and the Eureka! Moment

When Kekulé saw in his reverie the atomic scale and the structure and dynamics of molecules, he had a eureka moment, or epiphany, due to his deep knowledge of the domain he was constantly studying. In the same way, the renowned Greek polymath Archimedes had such a moment circa 250 BCE while at a public bath—when he understood that the volume of water displaced by his body sinking into the bath equaled the volume of his body immersed in the water. Running home naked, he kept shouting *eureka!* ("I have found it!" in Greek). He then wrote his treatise on hydrostatics called *On Floating Bodies* (see fig. 7.7).

The eminent mathematician Henri Poincaré had a number of such epiphanies; namely one while boarding a bus and posing the foot on the step, and he analyzed this process of intuitive discovery in mathematics in his book *Science and Method*. He proposed that the unconscious or "*subconscious ego*" was intelligent and precise enough to discover new mathematical equations. He relates:

> *For fifteen days I strove to prove that there could not be any functions like those I have since called Fuchsian functions. (. . .) One evening,*

Fig. 7.7. Archimedes's eureka moment. A sixteenth-century woodcut

> *contrary to my custom, I drank black coffee and could not sleep. Ideas rose in crowds; I felt them collide until pairs interlocked, so to speak, making a stable combination. By the next morning I had established the existence of a class of Fuchsian functions, (. . .) I had only to write out the results, which took but a few hours.* (Poincaré 1952)

Astral Travels, Out-of-Body Experiences, and Sleep

The unconscious connections and interactions between our ego-consciousness (in waking life), our traveling I-consciousness (delocalized in our astral body), and our higher Self (in the consciousness HD) are generally an easy, free-flowing, and positive process, as natural as sleeping; it happens mostly during our dreaming state (thus unconsciously), although many people have had conscious experiences of astral travels and OBEs.

Astral travel (or *ecsomatic,* "out-body" in its Greek root) is a term used in cultural anthropology, as well as in spiritual and esoterica literature. It describes the out-of-body travel of the ancient shamans in many cultures on earth (such as in animist and shamanic ones in Africa). Indeed, it's my informed opinion that the religions of the forces of nature—with sun, earth, fire, storm gods or goddesses—were the primeval religions everywhere on Earth. As the best expert in shamanism, Mircea Eliade, described it in his book, the astral voyage of the shamans in a trance up to the highest seventh sky (for purpose of seeing the future, for healing, or for finding a lost soul) was one feature common to all these shamanic cultures (see Eliade 2004). And no doubt this "sky" was none other than our hyperdimension where dwell our Selfs, the immortal guides, ascended masters, as well as the souls of the deceased, as I showed in *Living Souls*. Furthermore, astral travel with the energy-body is one of the siddhis (psi or mind-powers) attested in most great religions of the East, namely, in Buddhism, Taoism, and Hinduism (see plate 19).

OBE, or out-of-body experience, on the other hand, is a recent term willing to be more neutral in studying reports of such feats, which generally are spontaneous and much less sophisticated than the shaman's controlled travel for a set purpose. As the statistics show, more and more people have had such OBE experience, and when they happen during a lucid dream, they can be both conscious and controlled (see LaBerge and Rheingold 1990).

As is often the case, negative experiences (such as being blocked by the electricity grid) are more prone to being registered consciously. It's like we are not aware of the steps we take while walking, because it's automatic . . . unless we have a thorn in the foot.

My understanding is that all of us are naturally exiting and rising out of our bodies during sleep and visiting people and places within and through the HD, but we are not aware of it unless some obstacle such as a pyramid scale-model impedes us from doing so (as we'll see in chapter 10). And in high states, we similarly rise with our astral body to travel through the HD and connect with our HD Self extremely easily, unless some strange barriers impede us from doing so.

ENERGY-BODY, ELECTROMAGNETIC FIELDS, AND THE HYPERDIMENSION

Let's now leap to a more holistic scale to bring together all that we learned through the diverse anomalous experiences dealing with energy and frequency anomalies. And first of all, let's analyze deeper the information revealed by the ayahuasca fight with the electrical grid, in terms of the Self, astral body, and (hyper) physics.

After years of advancing the ISST cosmology, I became convinced that our current knowledge about electromagnetic waves, and therefore electricity, is limited to the extent that we don't understand yet how the hyperdimension is connected to, and interfering with, these waves and fields.

An experiment done in 1959 by Yakir Aharonov and David Bohm, showed with evidence that there is more to the electromagnetic fields than just the B and E fields as we know them at the present and proved that there is a hyperdimensional component to them. The experiment implied a superconducting torus, in which both the magnetic field B and electric field E were hermetically shielded, thus leaving the internal region totally field-free. When a beam of electrons was fired orthogonally through the torus's central void circle, the electrons' electronic state (their wave functions) was modified, although it couldn't be a direct effect of the electromagnetic field hermetically contained inside the torus. Thus the *Aharonov-Bohm Effect* reveals clearly a higher dimensional component of the EM field (within the torus) interacting with the orthogonal electron beam.

In fact, as in a 2020 paper, I'm now articulating that, in quantum waves, the waves themselves must have a higher dimensionality than the particles they are linked to (in our ayahuasca case, the negative electrons driving the direction of charges, positive or negative, in the electrical circuit); and I'm proposing that the pilot waves postulated by David Bohm, already deemed nonlocal (thus contravening EM laws), are in fact hyperdimensional (see Bohm 1980, Bohm and Hiley 1993). In this case, the weird wave-behaviors exposed by quantum mechanics (such as entanglement, nonlocality, superposition of waves, or retrocausality) would in fact be hyperdimensional behaviors (Hardy 2020, "Quantum Coherence").

Due to their previous years of study, both Kekulé and Poincaré, when they had a eureka moment, knew immediately they had found *the* solution, even before they did the (left-brain) calculations to ascertain it, and despite their vision bringing no empirical proof; and it was only years later that it was finally proven right and/or a scientific advancement.

In my own case of peering into the particles and waves scale, I did get some degree of proof during the experience itself, even if only an empirical one, in the sense that I fought against a barrier and was able to find a way to pass through it. But in any case, let's take my experience at face value for the sake of discussion, and let's see where that leads us.

The questions we may ponder are:

- What component of the EM field could block my energy-body?
- What part of my spirit was able to see and visualize the electrical grid in minute detail and yet from a more global perspective?

Let's ponder another case, that of Robert Monroe who, in his book *Journeys out of the Body*, describes how his astral body (and attached I-consciousness) was often forcefully attracted and pulled by any electrical tower standing in its path, and being so stuck to it that it took his best efforts to get free from its attraction. Similar to mine, this case displays (1) a very negative interaction between the energy-body and electric/EM energy, and (2) the need for a kind of fight in order to disengage.

Could Monroe's account and my account be two different outlooks or perspectives on the same phenomenon? But then, why have I met this problem only a single time in my life, despite my numerous intentional astral journeys?

The comparison doesn't feel right, and we instead have to accept

Monroe's experience and mine as original and valid on their own grounds:

- Monroe's astral body was attracted and trapped by electrical towers—and there must have been some of those in the vicinity of his home (to account for the high occurrence of his problem during astral travels).
- In the Santo Daime church, the dense electrical wire mesh at the roof, together with its geometric architecture, created a strong enough force field to block my astral body—*without a specific attraction to it.*

If our personal spirit, our Self, dwells in a hyperdimension of consciousness, with frequencies immensely higher than the highest-frequency EM waves (i.e., gamma and cosmic rays), it is implausible that it would be constrained by any E/EM field; the reason being that, from the Self's perspective, the space between electrons would be gigantic. Therefore, no electric current or field, no system of particles or atoms, and no EM field (at the electron scale) can ever constitute a barrier to an HD structure/field.

Moreover, in most hyperdimensional models (derived from Kaluza's theory), and in ISST as well, the HD is coiled within all the particles, at (or below) Planck scale, and thus electrons have an HD core at the sub-Planckian (sub-quantum) scale. We have to conceive these HD cores as highly active and creating HD fields connecting them together, which are superposed to the EM fields of matter particles.

Let me make a quick retrospective. It was in 1919 that the physicist Theodor Kaluza conceived of a brilliant way to rewrite Einstein's equations by introducing a 5th dimension—that is, a 4th dimension of space, or hyperspace. To his surprise, he could derive from it both the EM field equations of Maxwell and Einstein's field equations for gravity. In 1926, his theory was further elaborated by the renowned

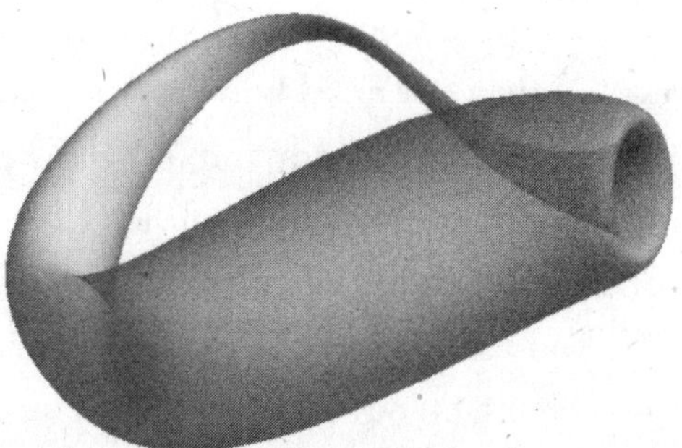

Fig. 7.8. A Klein bottle
Photo by Wridgers

mathematician Oskar Klein, whom we readily associate with his famous Klein bottle and other stupendous topological objects and mathematics (see fig. 7.8). The Klein bottle is a four-dimensional one-surface object, in which the inside becomes the outside and vice versa.

Klein brought to Kaluza's theory the concept that the 5th dimension had a physical reality, and was *curled up in a tiny circle*, the *radius* of which was at the Planck scale (i.e., with a Planck length of 10^{-33} centimeters). The 5th dimension is thus called compact. Now, when Klein linked the radius of the 5th dimension to Planck constant, the equations of quantum mechanics were also derived. And thus the four fundamental forces (EM, weak force, strong force, and gravity) could now be slowly unified; as it stands, gravity still poses some problems as the only force acting below Planck scale; that is, before the first quantum, and thus before matter (particles, atoms) and spacetime were born.

In ISST, the hyperdimension is not contained at Planck scale, but instead occupies the immensity from the origin up to Planck scale; it deploys in a spiral fashion—an infinite spiral staircase (ISS)—as a quasi-infinite spectrum of states, of decreasing frequencies and rising wavelengths up to Planck scale.

At our human personal scale, the hyperdimension exists at several scales. (1) Given that any system has its own syg-field (made of HD syg-energy), we thus have the syg-fields of neurons, organs, somatic and physiological systems; (2) our body has its global syg-field—the body consciousness; (3) then our mind-body-psyche system has its global syg-field—composed of the energy-body and our HD Self. Thus, human beings have an individual link to the bulk of the HD, which is the deep reality underlying our whole universe, and in which our immortal souls, the Selfs, dwell. (4) And finally, we have the hyperdimension of collective consciousness, in which all our personal Selfs dwell (the One-plural field, the Tao, brahman, Shakti).

Thus, in ISST, all matter-systems and bio-systems at all scales (from the particles to the whole brain-body), have at their core a syg-field (an ISS-spiral) branched on the HD bulk; and this provides the multifaceted links between our HD-Self (mind) and our body—the links that were missing in the previous paradigms. In this framework, our *energy-body is a low-HD vehicle* of our Self. With the interesting phenomenon of the "vibrating chakras" in the next chapter, we'll see that these high-frequency links create Self-ego resonances.

In order to be blocked by an EM field, the energy-body has to have at least a part (a component of itself) that stands at about the very same spectrum of frequencies, or scale, as that of the blocking structure/field. And, vice versa, the blocking field must have the same spectrum of frequencies as the energy-body.

In the scientific research on the biofield (the aura), with state-of-the-art detection of EM energies and fields, a magnetic aura has been mapped surrounding the body (Bagnall 1975). Margaret Moga has demonstrated that oscillations of the healer's magnetic field occur during Healing Touch biofield therapy, of a low-frequency type (0–40 Hz) as measured with Hall-type gaussmeters (Moga 2014).

The autonomous part of the energy-body, able to travel and fly, in contrast, is a hyperdimensional energy as it can pass through matter such as walls (unlike EM energies). It belongs to the low frequency of the HD syg-energy spectrum, and thus *it can only be blocked by low-HD frequencies.* But if that's so, this ayahuasca experience would mean no less than this: *a (low) hyperdimensional energy-field had been created out of an electrical/EM field, and/or by a certain form* linked to this field—that is, a HD field had been produced in 4D objects (the geometrical roof and its mesh of electrical wires).

This, in itself, is consistent with ISST's postulates that all matter structures/fields have an HD syg-field, and that EM fields have a yet-uncharted HD component (acting as their pilot wave); but there's more to it in terms of HD-fields created by specific geometrical forms (as we'll explore later in chapter 10).

8
CHAKRAS VIBRATING WITH OUR HD SELF

Let's turn now to another repeated experience of mine involving a hyperdimensional energy that activates my chakras during sleep. In the following suite of strange occurrences, my "vibrating chakras" put my whole body in vibration during deep sleep and, as I wake up and become aware of it, I'm able to experience and survey it for five to ten minutes more. I have called these the *vibrating chakras experiences* (VCEs), which show that our Self may regularly send replenishing HD energy to our energy-body.

I started to notice this phenomenon in my late twenties when it would wake me up from my night sleep or naps. As far as I was able to be aware of it, it went on for about seven years, spanning the course of two love relationships of about three years each and into the beginning of my marital relationship. Since it occurred in three different cities and buildings, the least we can infer is that it rules out any type of physical or electromagnetic cause or vibration source coming from either the building or the environment.

VIBRATING CHAKRAS EXPERIENCES IN PARIS

Now let me first clarify that, starting with my late teens meditation practice and then with spiritual masters in different spiritual traditions and countries, I had gained a great sensitivity to the energy of chakras and had learned a lot about the types of fields they could create. In fact, after three years of constant meditation and the awakening of the heart and then the forehead chakra (learning directly from my higher Self), I achieved the awakening of the crown chakra right on my arrival at the Sufi ashram (*rhonerah*) at the beginning of my first eighteen-month journey to the East; concomitant with it, I started experiencing intentional astral travels during meditation, when my energy-body (and I-consciousness) would exit my body through this crown chakra (more in chapter 9).

Thereafter I remained steadily centered at this crown chakra during my entire travel in India and well into the beginning of my second long journey, which I started by crossing Africa (thus about two years altogether), although I still reach this state easily in meditation. In practical terms, it meant I was able to know at which higher chakra my psychic energy was centered, and to sense and see the specific field a chakra was creating. For example, I could perceive the specific energy-structure that one person meditating (myself or somebody else) created during transcendent states, as well as the larger energy structures formed during collective states of harmony—the telepathic-harmonic fields or Telhar fields that I have recounted and analyzed in *The Sacred Network*. It also meant I was able to center at will all my ki energy in one specific chakra and create such fields (chakra-specific). Through the years, I devised techniques for creating fields with various purposes such as protection, self-defense, healing, and the like, that I used to teach in my workshops (and described in "*La pensée Agissante*").

On with my story.

My Flat, Northern Suburbs of Paris

The first time I became aware of the phenomenon was a shock for me. I was living in a fourth-floor flat in a northern suburb of Paris with Pat, the guitarist, and our bedroom, rather large and in which I had also my writing space and table, had a large wood-framed window to the north, opening on a low-traffic intersection and a vast empty area. It was a nineteenth-century stone building, five stories, with a wooden staircase and wooden floors in the flats. In brief: there was no concrete reinforced with metal frames anywhere around.

I woke up in the early morning (at an unusual time for me), on the large bed I was sharing with Pat, my side being that of the room and the window, while my companion was sleeping along the wall. The bed had a low bedstead, a rectangular wood casing set directly, without legs, on the wooden floor. The room was never totally obscured, because of some street lights, leaving it in penumbra all night long; but that morning, the light of day was there already.

On waking up I became aware of my whole body vibrating, a phenomenon so strange and extraordinary that I held my breath to analyze it and avoided any movement apart from shifting my eyes left and right. Then I immediately focused all my attention on the strange vibration—a reaction I would have when confronted by any strange or anomalous event.

Yes, my body was indeed vibrating in a steady way, from head to toe, the vibration extremely fine and regular, totally unperturbed by my sudden awareness of it.

On my left, Pat was deep in sleep but his face had a surprisingly different appearance (but that's another story, just reflecting that I was in a heightened-consciousness state).

Trying to understand more about this vibration, I saw that his body was also vibrating, and that, indeed, the whole wood casing of the bed was also vibrating: I could see the very fine vibratory movements of the casing against the background. How was that possible?

Let me explain here that since adolescence, I've been prone to having extremely clear perceptions of the etheric dimension of reality during the hypnagogic state on waking up; that is, the state between sleep and wakefulness. I came to understand that this state allows us to retain the heightened consciousness that we reach when connecting to our Self during our sleep and dreams. Thus it allows for a perception of the hyperdimensional reality, notably syg-energy structures and phenomena. On several instances I was able to see straight, thin, laser-like rays emanating from my heart or forehead chakras and linking me to a sacred object in the room or even shooting toward the stars. (I recounted these experiences in *The Sacred Network*, chapter 6.) When we have the chance of perceiving something of this syg-energy reality on waking up, refraining from making any movement apart from moving our eyes permits us to prolong this out-of-the-ordinary perception for a good five minutes or more. In this heightened state, we are able to see the etheric dimension and the unusual phenomena and energy-structures pertaining to it and to the hyperdimension.

This is why, when I became aware of my own body vibrating, this *first* vibrating body experience of mine, I was able to analyze and refine my observation for maybe four or five minutes.

Then I got up carefully and noiselessly and sat at my desk to think about it. From my experience of the energy-body, I knew that the chakras are sometimes vibrating at a very high frequency. So high in fact, for the forehead and crown chakras, that no movement or vibration of the body ever occurs. In a high samadhi state, the crown chakra emits a very specific field, that of a torus rotating at blinding velocity around and slightly above the chakra itself (as I have drawn it in fig. 7.2). The torus's structure is produced by HD strings (the sygons) that turn at a very high velocity, counterclockwise, around yet above the crown chakra, which clearly acts as the center of the dynamic torus structure and even the larger field generated around the head, the torus being only the inner circle of this head aura (look back again at plate 2). As I am able to understand it now, the hyperspeed and structure of this torus belongs to the hyperdimension; and the ability to see the rotation of the torus itself clearly denotes a heightened consciousness.

It is the only instance (as of now) in which I was able to see the entire body (mine and Pat's) and even the bed casing submitted and taken into the same vibrating energy. It was astounding.

As I mentioned, on three occasions I had witnessed rays emanating from my head chakra and shooting toward the stars by the open window (*The Sacred Network*, 119–20). In these three instances—in which I was able, each time, to note exactly where the half-pencil-width whitish ray was passing (on its 45-degree upward angle) just below the upper wooden frame of the window aligned with my mattress set on a wooden floor in Igny—there was no vibration, either of my body or of the ray itself. And as I was so precisely looking at the frame to memorize where it passed, I would have noticed such a vibration if it had existed.

What I'm able to conclude now (with more experience and especially with the knowledge of the HD) is that a vibration that can be transmitted to a bed and two bodies lying motionless on it definitely does *not* belong to the immensely more rapid syg-energy spectrum of the crown chakra.

Rather, it denotes a lower hyperfrequency—that of the forehead or the medium chakras—the heart, navel, or hara. What is sure, though, is that only a chakra can be put into vibration like this, and what does it is an energy from a higher source connecting and getting in sync with it. Only then is it transmitted to the body, then the mattress and the bed casing.

But to dive deeper on the subject of the immaterial energy related to our energy-body, let's realize that we have, with the seven chakras (eight if you count the East Asian hara), a scale of syg-energy frequencies, from the highest at the crown to the lowest (yet not the least powerful) at the base of the vertebral column, where the energy of the Goddess Kundalini—the Shakti—is supposed to rest in a coiled state until it is awakened and starts to ascend through the kundalini channel. Thus, human beings have access to eight immaterial frequency levels, and the same is true for animals, according to Hinduism, as I saw a whole Hindu book with colored illustrations of chakras in various animals. So, if we consider this fact, we can only wonder how many levels exist in the hyperdimension! Clearly, my own categorization of three levels—body, energy-body, and Self—is rather minimalist, but at least it's neither complicated nor confusing.

If there were other instances around that time in which I felt my body vibrating on awakening, they were not so noticeable as to remember them.

House in the Woods in Igny, South of Paris

The next period that saw a drastic increase in both the phenomenon and its frequent repetition was about four years later. I was living at the time with Paul in my family country house in Igny, south of Paris. Since Paul was a classical flutist diving into Gregorian music, I now had a partner to visit old churches and abbeys. One of my explorations into the etheric layer of Earth was to meditate in sacred buildings (in all countries I visited) and sense their energetic structure deployed like geometrical arcs from the top of the steeple or dome. Paul loved to play flute in the stunning acoustics of these stone mandalas, and his musical monologues were entrancing.

During that period, I was more prone to wake up and sense my body vibrating when I had taken only a short nap of thirty to sixty minutes. But that doesn't mean the phenomenon was not occurring as well during my night sleep (as in the first occurrence I mentioned). Moreover, when taking a nap, I would be alone in the bed and my workroom (thus more focused), and for years I had used these naps as a way to void my mind and to collect my energy before a long night of writing.

As these VCEs were now more frequent, I started noticing that there was, each time, a specific chakra from which the vibrations were emitted and which was inducing my whole body to vibrate in sync with "the wave," so to speak.

Generally, it was the heart or the forehead chakra. In the stone house in Igny, my mattress was directly set on a wool carpet along the window on the wooden floor, and I had no bed frame that could be put in vibration.

The vibrations were so clearly sensible—as an inward, eyes closed sensation—that I became more and more intrigued, and started conceiving that there should be a way to study them objectively, and I had a friend I thought would be the right person to help me with that.

Since my return from Ivory Coast (where I had finally split up with Pat), I had written and published my first book, then had launched a second one, a book of interviews of leading scientists and scholars who were integrating consciousness into their new scientific theories.

I had also started a long search for a doctoral thesis director who would accept that my subject be parapsychology—a dire obstacle course, given that they all wanted their doctoral students to work on their own research domain—this on top of parapsychology being total nonsense in their eyes.

For my book, I was thus interviewing the foremost scientists in France, in several fields. And early on I had met Hervé Moskovakis, a young polymath extremely well connected to many of these scientists, and who was going to become, with his girlfriend and future wife, Annie, among my best friends and colleagues in my new scientific endeavor. The four of us were regularly spending evenings passionately discussing at their place or mine. Hervé was, at the time, building a Kirlian machine to study the energy-body, and we soon launched a research association and started organizing conferences.

So, of course I turned to him and asked him how we could register these vibrations and study them closely. And being the bright brain he was, he had soon conceived an apparatus.

The positive aspect of years of meditation—a good dozen by that time—was that I mostly slept on my back, the body well balanced, and would often wake up in the same position, especially for short naps. That made the registering part easier.

Hervé's first apparatus was a coil made of a thick metallic wire that was first curled into a large round base, then would make a few spiraling turns upward (quite well spaced out), and finally curved back to the perfect center of the coil, where a thinner metallic thread was shooting straight upward about five inches, like a needle. I was to install the coil on my chest, precisely on the plexus (heart chakra), and its spiral and long needle were going to increase the tenuous vibrating movements of my body, rendering them larger and easier to perceive at the top of the needle. Finally, a still camera would record the movements of the coil, larger at its needle tip.

It worked and we thus managed to see that yes, my chest was indeed vibrating at a much quicker rhythm than my heartbeat. But the device was not sensitive enough to clearly sort it out. Hervé soon devised a second apparatus that, this time, involved a stress gauge used for detecting tiny tensions or stress in solids. The gauge sent its recorded vibrations to a polygraph, where a needle was tracing them on a paper graph.

After a few trials and tinkering with the experimental design, we were now able to study the graphs and, sure enough, we found a second type of pulsation, much more rapid than that of the heart—itself very recognizable because it is so large and regular—and superposed on it.

VIBRATING CHAKRAS EXPERIENCES IN PRINCETON

I finally found a doctoral thesis director who accepted that I would write a thesis on scientific psi research—parapsychology. And, no wonder, Remy Chauvin, an ethology and sociology professor at Sorbonne, was one of the most brilliant visionary scientists I had interviewed!

Now that I was administratively enrolled in a doctoral thesis with him, I decided I was going to tour all the laboratories and researchers dedicated to parapsychology in the United States, as a way to get a grasp of the domain. I embarked right away on what was to become two and a half months of travel (it was summertime), with a serendipitous open-mileage ticket for students. I headed first, following Chauvin's research connections, to J. B. Rhine's Lab in Durham, North Carolina, where I was given a list of these researchers and provided with all I needed to make appointments. Then I started my visits, first on the East Coast, then on the West Coast. On returning from the West Coast, I was called for a second visit to the PRL lab in Princeton, New Jersey, whose director, Chuck Honorton, then proposed that I come and work as a research assistant. I was thrilled.

Back in France, I set myself to completing the book I had started writing with the biologist Etienne Guillé—who had developed a new theory about the vibrations of cells and alchemical metals in the DNA provoking mutations in it. It took me another eight months. Meanwhile, my relationship with Paul had deteriorated, mostly due to my new shift of focus. My mind was on this new avenue of psi research, full of promise. We split when I left for the United States the next summer.

I experienced a new series of vibrating chakras while working in the lab in Princeton, and after I had, a couple of months later, started dating one researcher, M.

On arrival at the lab, I had discovered with enthusiasm the recently marketed Apple IIE computer and had begun to learn programming in Basic; I was so thrilled by it that right away I got to developing a program of Tarot divination that could be used for research and was presented as a game (the blueprint of the program later sold to the Minitel company). It was great fun, but doing that for hours in a row each day was greatly stressing my body. Sometimes I needed a short twenty-to-thirty-minute nap—and there was a couch in the large experiment room that featured two computers, on which M was generally working.

I had told him about my strange sensations. As it happened, this small couch bed was set along the wall, about two yards behind the desk and computer on which M was working, with his back to me. And I was now able, on awakening and sensing the vibration, to call out to M softly, and then talk to him in low tones, without disrupting the vibration. I would ask him if he could see my body vibrating (he couldn't) or if he could check the frequency on his watch. And I would then mark the beat so that he could measure the seconds. That, of course, led us nowhere apart from reinforcing my own conviction that it was, indeed, an observable phenomenon, distinct from the heartbeat, that could have been the object of a serious investigation.

At PRL, we were one among only two labs in the United States already devising computerized psi experiments, for hardly a year on the Apple IIE, and both labs were in Princeton. The other one, the PEAR (Princeton Engineering Anomalies Research) lab, was founded and directed by the dean of the School of Engineering and Applied Science at Princeton University, Bob Jahn, research director Brenda Dunne, and head researcher Roger Nelson; they were focused on mind-over-matter psi (psychokinesis or PK) and using all kinds of fascinating experimental setups, such as rare gases in hermetic vials. Both our labs developed micro-PK programs on the Apple IIE to study how the mind could alter the baseline of random distribution in perfectly random systems such as diodes; soon the random event/number generators (REG/RNGs) became computer cards inserted within our computers, and the results, as we saw, were highly significant (Radin and Nelson 1989).

In 1998, Roger Nelson, from PEAR, independently launched his Global Consciousness Project (GCP). Nelson arranged a grid of REGs disseminated in research centers worldwide that kept producing perfectly random numbers without any subject present, thus showing the distribution of randomness. These REGs all over the planet evidenced anomalies in their random behavior just hours or a couple of days before, as well as after, major collective events.* Nelson was thus able to demonstrate that collective events of maximum import could bias the distribution of randomness. For example, a Paris Climate Agreement-related mass meditation on December 12, 2015, had yielded such a deviation from the baseline of randomness that it reached (by itself) a significant probability value of p = 0.155. The sixteen-year GCP database (to December 2015), comprising 513 collective events, shows a 7.3-Z score (i.e., a mind-blowing probability of p = 1.3^–13). Nelson states: "the odds against chance of this mean shift over a database this size are about *a hundred billion to one*" (my emphasis). All of

*See the Global Consciousness Project (GCP) website, "Meaningful Correlations in Random Data," and the discussion on global results on GCP's "Main Results" web page.

this was proving the inescapable reality of the collective unconscious and its constant effect on our world. (Let's note that CERN's level of proof to deem the Higgs boson a discovery is 5-sigma (i.e., odds of one in 3.5 million; however, this is reached in singular trials, not by large numbers of them.)

As Stephan Schwartz (2015) argues, six psi-experiments' protocols actually reach a 6-sigma level of proof: "Under rigorous double or triple blind, randomized and tightly controlled conditions, each of these six has independently produced six sigma results. Six sigma is one in a billion." The six protocols Schwartz lists are mind-over-matter (as micro-PK), the Global Consciousness Project, as well as remote viewing, ganzfeld-telepathy, presentiment, and precognition-retrocognition.

The psi research conducted in our similarly trailblazing PRL lab was mostly focused on studying telepathy via ganzfeld (a state of relaxation simulating the hypnagogic state).

The canonic psi phenomena were, and are still, very delimited in terms of types: telepathy, precognition, PK, and clairvoyance (or remote viewing). The latter was the specialty of the Stanford Research Institute lab in Stanford, California, the foremost physics and computer sciences lab in the United States (see Targ and Puthoff 2005). Telepathy in dreams had been a groundbreaking study by Ullman and Krippner (1973). There was also research on OBEs carried out by professor Charles Tart (1969) at the University of California, Davis, who had launched the new research domain of altered states of consciousness. His "subjects" in his experiments were reporting that they used to hover over their sleeping body under the ceiling.

One day, at an informal wine-sharing gathering, I was chatting with the secretary of our lab and another psi researcher. As the topic was on OBEs and they were very excited about it, I came up with recounting my first fully conscious exit while meditating in my Sufi master's ashram (in fact, I exited slowly by my just-opened crown chakra). I started describing how I was so enchanted to be liberated from the weight of the body, that I got into dancing in this weightless space (some fifteen to twenty feet above the ashram garden), and then felt an impulse to go and visit my quester friend (Christian) in the monastery in France, and instantly I saw I was flying down in a large spiral that started far above the roof and was aiming at the door of the building . . . That's when first the secretary abruptly excused herself and left, and then, hardly a few words of mine later, the researcher mumbled an excuse and left also. I found myself standing alone with my glass of wine and really wondering how they could be so excited by people hovering under the ceiling but be totally shocked and disbelieving if one had the idea of flying a bit further.

As I learned months later, the lab had, on being set up two years earlier, bought some equipment to investigate physiological responses to the unconscious reception of psi information—polygraphs and sets of electrodes—and never used it. Just the perfect sophisticated equipment to study my vibrating chakras . . . if only the research paradigm had allowed it!

Despite being still in the habit of taking a one-hour nap before setting myself up for my night of writing, I haven't woken up with this strange vibrating sensation since Princeton. It's also sad that, after a half dozen changes of homes, I have lost the precious graphs recorded with Hervé.

So what is my take on this strange and yet persistent and quite robust phenomenon? I believe that spiritually healthy individuals regularly exit their bodies at night and reconnect with their source or Self; hence the common dreams about flying and visiting places, or discussing with faraway friends or even deceased relatives.

Our Self is our consciousness on a higher-vibrational plane—the hyperdimension, with its superluminous syg-energy. When we reconnect with our source during meditation or sleep, we receive a load of information and get in sync with our higher-dimensional being. And this reception of hyperfrequencies is essentially attuned to our higher chakras and our energy-body. But these HD frequencies cover a large band, and this must be why, on a specific connection, a specific chakra will be more attuned and in sync with the quality of the syg-energy being received/exchanged. And that chakra will be put in resonance with the incoming flow of syg-energy/information. The body, being without tension during sleep, will then also have a tendency to resonate as a whole with the vibrating chakra.

All in all, proving that these vibrations exist (as distinct from bodily rhythms such as the heartbeat), and that they are issued from a chakra (itself resonating) and able to put the whole body in sync with them, would not only prove the existence of the chakras and that of the energy-body but also show that we are connected to other dimensions of reality from which these vibrations originated.

9
THE "SUPERPOSED LANDSCAPE" PHENOMENON

Let's now turn to some rare yet exceptional visions I had about layered levels of reality—clearly evidencing the HD.

I had several anomalous perceptions that showed me with great clarity that the dimension of our Selfs, aka the HD, sometimes appears like a second floor, or a whole other landscape, superposed at about a story's height above our heads, in what I can term a "superposed landscape phenomenon."

These visionary perceptions fall into two categories.

In the first category, the higher landscape per se, I perceive an interaction between two superposed planes of reality—for example, deceased people visiting our material 4D world—or, even more astounding, I see living persons or groups on two vertically superposed layers: they are in their physical bodies (interacting normally at a social level), yet they appear simultaneously in an immaterial higher "landscape" as their own Self (or higher soul). Sometimes I see my own Self there above, interacting with them in a way that differs from the physico-social events below, thus revealing that the higher HD world has its own order and organization. Instances of this are *An Indian guru and his group on two dimensions* and *The deceased attending his burial from an immaterial mezzanine*, which I'll describe.

In brief, it shows that while living our lives on Earth, we also dwell—continuously and simultaneously—in the hyperdimension of Selfs, as a fully conscious individuality. Now, what I don't know for sure is if the superposed landscape phenomenon reveals a tighter superposition or conjunction of the two reality-layers happening solely during specific momentous events and peak experiences, or if it is a permanent feature of the HD that we can perceive only in these peak states. In fact, I sense that this superposition exists permanently but in a much more remote fashion, and that in certain circumstances, the layers are tightly linked.

In the second category, I sometimes perceive that perfect material volumes—generally charged sacred objects—do project several reflections of their form upward in the hyperdimension, as if the HD had a finely layered texture, as in the *reflections of altar objects* instance, below. (I was able to model this layered HD texture using my ISS theory, in a 2020 paper. See Hardy 2020, "Quantum Coherence.") Of course, the fact that I see the first two or three reflections (up to two feet vertically) lets me suppose it keeps going higher.

Just to get some perspective on our own complex being, let's remember that, as we have seen in chapter 7, we live on at least three different levels:

1. *The body* and 4D matter level, which comprises EM energies and fields inside our bodies, some of which traverse the skin and constitute the first layers of our aura (such as the electric aura and the magnetic aura).
2. *The energy-body* (and its energy-centers, the chakras) is created and infused by the syg-energy of the HD, yet at a low-(hyper) frequency of this HD scale. The activated energy-body creates whole-body auras, brightly colored, depending on the chakra(s) creating them. Additionally, as I have analyzed in depth in *The Sacred Network*, the awakened chakras create very specific

fields (around themselves) that are luminous and dynamical (chapter 6). Turning wheels, for example, are mainly seen/felt around the heart chakra (at the solar plexus). And indeed, in Sanskrit, the word *chakra* means "wheel" and they are referred to as lotuses. Moreover, I've often seen a torus turning at immense speed above and around the crown chakra (at the top of the head) of people during meditation, myself included. This syg-energy radiating from the chakras can also, in the specific state of shared consciousness within a group (or Telhar field), create a larger spinning torus connecting the crown chakras of four meditators sitting in a circle (*The Sacred Network*, chapter 3. "A Telhar Field . . . Manali." pp. 65–68).

Within this energy-body, the astral body is that part of the energy-body able to exit from our body and perform OBEs and voluntary and controlled astral travels. This astral body (also a low frequency-band of the hyperdimensional syg-energy) allows us to access and roam through the HD, and to reconnect with our HD Self—or even merge with our Self in states of fusion or samadhis.

3. And finally *the Self,* our immortal spirit dwelling permanently in the HD beyond space and time, and with whom we (our I-consciousness, and presumably our astral body) merge after our bodily death. Of course, we are constantly connected to our Self, but depending on the actions and behaviors of our ego, and its worldview, the link to our true source is more or less strong or loose, because this connection has to be reinforced willingly by the ego, as a path of self-development, knowledge, and wisdom.

INSTANCES OF "SUPERPOSED LANDSCAPE"

As mentioned, I had two experiences of a superposed landscape phenomenon in which I was seeing people standing and behaving in the quintessential, spiritual layer above; and in only one of these was I seeing myself there on this second, immaterial level above, interacting and discussing in a lively manner with them. In several other instances, as I was either in deep meditation or in OBE (in my energy-body), I was discovering another "whole other landscape" atop the one we inhabit. But since these last instances lack any reference to social events, they do not bring us as much information as the former two, and therefore I'll skip them.

An Indian Guru and His Group on Two Dimensions

Remember the episode of the guru giving a speech in Delhi (chapter 2), who heard my silent telepathic call for help and spotted me, despite the fact I was seated about twelve yards away, sideways from his line of sight and among two dozen of his Western followers? Then he had, in hardly two minutes before he started talking, poured a powerful syg-energy in me that rose from my feet upward and freed my own syg-field from a noxious entity's grip.

Now, his intense energy, added to that of my true Self, pulled me into a superconscious state and made my chakras vibrate at much higher frequencies and intensity, and that in turn enhanced my perception of the syg-hyperdimension—the consciousness-HD, the dimension of our Selfs. And I had two powerful visions or rather perceptions of the HD-layer:

At the very instant the guru pronounced the first word of his speech, two human-size papier-mâché statues of Krishna and Ganesh (the gods of Love and Wisdom, respectively), set on each side of the podium, became lighted like candle flames (despite the venue being in full daylight). That in itself was not a rare perception for me; I had seen statues and sacred objects light up and vibrate as if they were inhabited by an alive spirit, at very specific moments of prayers or rituals. One had been an ordinary footed glass used as a chalice, whose aura suddenly was illuminated and sparkled at the very moment the Celtic Orthodox monk pronounced the words of consecration during mass in Brittany. And as I could perceive in my extensive travels, all religious temples and sacred statues have a spiritual aura, an alive spirit, and especially in India, their lighting up during prayer was a frequent sight for me.

Let's remember that all beings, natural systems, and objects have a hyperdimensional field of consciousness, a syg-field, constituted of syg-energy. Concerning sacred sites, temples, and statues (generally built on ley line crossings, whatever the religion), part of their syg-energy stems from their connection to the immense collective syg-field of the deity/entity they represent, that dwells in the HD (beyond space and time). Another part is derived from the planetary consciousness (Earth's syg-field, Gaia) mixed with the field lines of the geomagnetic field of Earth (with its energy heightened at the crossing of ley lines). Moreover, the syg-energy fields created by sites, statues, and sacred objects are also charged by the syg-energy of devotees/followers, and thus ancient temples preserve the specific print of their everlasting syg-energy (in their stones and wood).

To get back to the guru's crowded public address, what was truly novel and exceptional was that I was now perceiving two dimensions of existence, of being. Above the material dimension we are used to, in which I was far away on the guru's right side and looking at his close disciples on the wooden podium, there was another stage set on another transparent quasi ground—that was about ten to twelve feet above their heads. And on that immaterial plane, I was on the podium with the guru, the Mataji, and the sadhus. My I-consciousness was still centered in my brain/body on the chair, and I was seeing my energy-body farther up on the second stage. The group we formed up there was standing and discussing, all of us gathered in the middle of the immaterial podium, yet in my conscious mind I was not able to hear our conversation. The guru's and his group's spatial configuration on the HD-stage was thus different from the one on the matter-plane—with the guru up front, ready to start talking, the Mataji just behind him, and two rows of venerable, white-bearded sadhus and pundits, seated at the back on some carpets.

To dive deeper, the immaterial and higher "ground," a sort of podium itself, was quite strange. It seemed to be totally transparent or even inexistent as far as my psi perception (still embodied) went—like, it didn't impede the view from anything behind/above it. Yet all the persons in their energy-body up there were definitely standing and walking on a flat surface. In contrast, the persons were more substantial, despite being ethereal; to be more precise, it's like they were glowing from the inside. All the colors of their clothing—traditionally saffron, white, and orange for devotees—had harmonized, yet luminous, tones.

The Deceased Attending His Burial from an Immaterial Mezzanine

The second such perception of an immaterial plane, with the two dimensions of reality superposed on each other, happened at the burial of my brother-in-law, Guy, a dozen years back. My boyfriend Pat (with whom I made, in my late twenties, a tour of West Africa) had passed his adolescence in Ivory Coast and was the best friend of Guy, at the time a musician managing a music club with his younger brother Bernard in their mother's restaurant in Korhogo and also playing in Abidjan, Ivory Coast. It is at this time that my sister, who had spent a year as a physician in a hospital in Diré, Mali, and who was in the summer replacing a physician in Abidjan, met him; both were already living together in France while I was touring Africa.

During this trip with Pat, I had gotten acquainted with Guy's brother, two sisters living in Abidjan, and their mother, but hadn't encountered the father, who had become estranged from his wife and children a long time ago.

In the early 2010s, Guy died of cancer, and he had lost Bernard four years earlier. The intimate funeral ceremony took place in a small village church in Provence.

The choir, where the altar and the priest stood, featured a high lectern and was flanked on both sides by a row of five or six chairs, thus perpendicular to the main rows of about eight chairs each filling the church's nave. My sister Colette and the older generation were seated on the left side; Guy's niece and nephew (whom I had just met for the first time) were together with Colette and Guy's son and daughter on the right side of the choir, while I was sitting on the first row of the nave chairs, on its right side.

During the ceremony, and while we were standing in prayer, I became aware of a strong presence *above* the bodies of the African-rooted side of the family. I focused my peripheral vision (that I know sees the semantic dimension better), and now I perceived clearly a small group standing there, as if on a second (transparent) floor of the church.

I was totally dumbfounded to see them there in ethereal bodies, yet finely dressed up in black. They were in two rows, and in the front one—exactly above the younger generation on the right row—were standing in deep concentration Guy himself, his brother Bernard, and, astonishingly, their father. About a yard behind them stood Guy's mother, and a girl in her late adolescence who I felt was her daughter.

They had the same attitude as the people attending the mass: standing serious, rigid, and focused on the priest. They didn't seem to sense that I was seeing them, or at least they didn't react in any way to it and none of them looked my way. Their features were so clear that I could have drawn a portrait of the father, whom I had never seen even in a photo.

I knew that Guy's mother had died too, and I recognized her by her imposing size, but I couldn't figure who the young woman was.

Guy, beyond being a musician, was a sensitive—he had some psi capacities; namely, a rare empathy. Many a time over the years we had played music together with Pat and other musician friends. And I knew from my travels that most Africans are able, routinely, to see and to interact with their deceased parents and kin. So that, after the ceremony, when only the close family circle remained in the cemetery, I went to see Guy's niece and nephew who were, as it happened, discussing together near the gate. I described to them what I had witnessed, and then voiced my astonishment at the adolescent girl's presence. I asked in earnest:

"Did Guy have a third sister that I didn't know of, and who has already died?"

The niece, dumbfounded, responded:

"Yes, indeed. She died when a baby, a few months old, and this is why nobody speaks about her."

So we see quite staggering similarities between Guy's burial case and the Indian guru one. Namely, a second-floor effect, on which surface ethereal spirits (HD Selfs) can stand and walk as if on hard matter. This transparent quasi ground (which let my eyes see the whole group of people, from front to back, whereas a high material podium would not allow it) was about ten to twelve feet above the heads of the standing guru and Mataji, and in the burial case, the church being so small, it was just about three or four feet above the children of Guy when standing.

In these two instances, the nature of the social event called for the Selfs to be strongly involved in it (e.g., their own burial) or else to support their own incarnated individualities (thus transfusing a high spiritual energy from their Self to their ego).

Let's now sort through the dissimilarities. In the guru instance, my own Self was also on this superposed landscape, interacting with the Selfs of the guru and his inner circle. Whereas in the burial case, I just had a vision of the immortal Selfs of the deceased family members.

Let me note also that in one case, the veracity of the HD vision was corroborated by the firsthand information about the third sister's existence. And in the other case, it was vindicated by the fact that I was freed by the guru from the invasive entity, and then I had enough power to free my friend from its clutches.

Lastly, I want to mention that it was on my first intentional astral travel (at twenty-one), while sitting in deep meditation in the Sufi rhonerah (ashram), that I experienced this superposed landscape for the first time. When my energy-body (and I-consciousness) exited through my crown chakra for the first time intentionally, while meditating, I felt so liberated from the weight of gravity and the material world, that

I started dancing in the ether, above my body. But the exit itself was a strange and slow motion, during which I had the sensation of passing just my eyes through a sort of immaterial ceiling, and now seeing a totally novel landscape of sheer beauty that enchanted me so much that it pulled my nose out and, now breathing in this pranic air, my whole etheric head; and then suddenly all of myself was out there, a dozen feet above my meditating body, a free and liberated spirit in a new landscape or world, expressing my pure joy by dancing. Still in this explosion of joy, I suddenly remembered a promise my soul-brother Christian and I had made to each other, that the first one of us reaching a controlled astral travel would visit the other one; and with that thought I was already initiating a slow spiraling landing above the Celtic Orthodox monastery in Brittany where he was now living. Within the next second I was going to land at the building entrance, when I suddenly sensed my heart, so far away in my physical body, getting in a frantic tachycardia and pulling me back; and the next instant my I-consciousness was back within my body.

In that instance, the impression of a new ground with a new landscape had been, as far as I could interpret it later, just passing through my skull by the crown chakra.

REFLECTIONS OF ALTAR OBJECTS IN A LAYERED HYPERDIMENSION

I've seen sacred objects being reflected vertically as a series of purer and purer forms—possibly reaching to their archetypal form and essence. As I intuited it, this is the hyperdimensional reality (of all beings, systems, and things) being superposed to the matter and 4D reality. The most exceptional vision involved my writing room altar.

Since my late teens, I have been in the habit of writing practically every night, and I've had an altar in front of my desk or at the center of the room. Throughout my life, I always managed to have a workroom for myself alone—in reality, a writing and meditating room; and I write on a low table, sitting cross-legged as an Oriental scholar, as I find this posture excellent for maintaining my concentration and for keeping one's back and neck straight, and thus the kundalini energy in a flow. This way of life—the writing during the night, a short five-hour sleep starting at dawn, and the secluded writing room—have been crucial for my keeping, along the years and decades, a strong and unwavering focus on my own thinking, writing, and meditating path. This included nurturing a steady connection to my higher Self, while being involved in loving and marital relationships, business dealings, and whatever else in the day and evening time. (This is how I've never stopped writing and researching and kept the flame of creativity going.)

My writing room always features a mattress on the carpeted floor that's needed either for meditating cross-legged, for various exercises, or even for naps and occasional sleeping. It also comprises a hi-fi music system, because whatever I do, writing or thinking or being on the phone, I have a constant musical background, with specific frequencies fitting different modes and activities. And it is completed by a thermos of tea and a small Moroccan tea glass. Voilà! Now you know all or nearly so about my writing place—a place I deem no less than sacred, hence the altar in my line of sight!

All this to explain that, when I get into a peak state while sitting at my table, writing, thinking, or even meditating there, I've a view of the whole altar softly lighted by its central candle and by a desk lamp dimmed with an orange cloth. (I assessed long ago that such an orange tone significantly boosts my creativity.) The altar being another large low table, the nearest sacred objects are about a yard from my head, and the farthest ones about a yard and a half.

And so it happened that one night, in a heightened state of consciousness, I had an exceptional vision of the main sacred objects that were on my altar (at the time). I remember them well—a round, multifaceted crystal at the center in front of the candlestick, set on a Chinese stand;

a natural crystal (about five inches high) shaped as a nonsymmetrical obelisk; a smaller, obelisk-shaped crystal; and a glass reproduction of Teotihuacan's Pyramid of the Sun. Also, some other objects were not reflected, such as a Tibetan *dorje*.

I was seeing a vertical superposition of their reflections on three layers upward, with about two inches between them. These mirroring images were getting smaller and less contrasted the higher they got, and the third layer of resonance upward was fading a bit. It was so remarkable that I made a drawing of the vision on the spot; but unfortunately, I have been unable to find it. On the drawing I did recently (see fig. 9.1), I tried to convey my experience of seeing these layers of the quintessential deep reality; that is, the hyperdimension. I got the impression that the reflections kept projecting farther on, ad infinitum. The whole perceptible group of reflections was narrowing from the table upward, slightly pointing toward the infinite as a vanishing point (as would appear in a perspective). The whole space of the vision was rising above the altar table about twenty-eight inches.

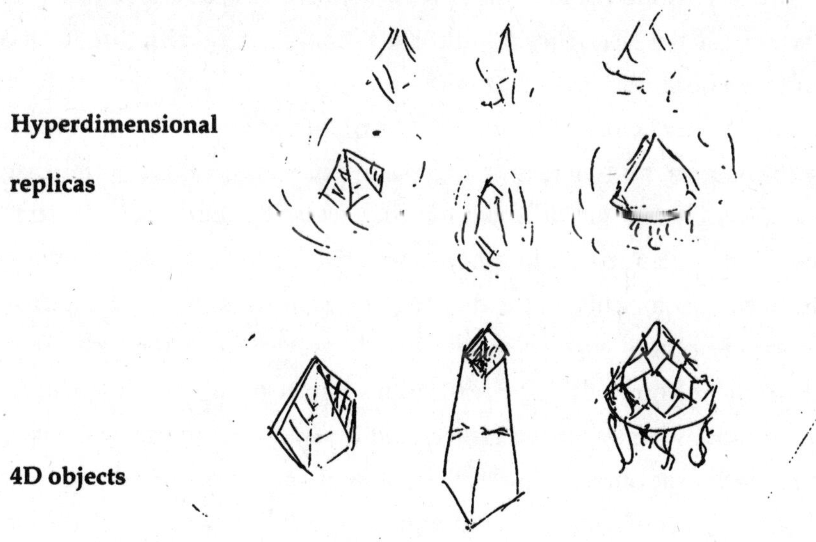

Fig. 9.1. The subtle resonance of my altar stones in the hyperdimension's layers
Artwork by Chris H. Hardy

This true vision signified with great clarity that the hyperdimension is made of layers; that is, it has a discrete structure. As we saw in ISST, all systems and objects have a syg-field (as their HD layer). Thus, I cannot escape the idea that what I saw as reflections in the HD could be in fact the syg-field of these altar objects, despite the unexpected conundrum of their being endlessly mirrored, and this, I infer, all the way up to their archetypal source.

This is possibly how (and why) sacred forms and places trigger resonances in the HD with the archetypes they represent, either by their symbolic forms or their embedded ideas.

In my ISS theory, these layers of the hyperdimension are predicated on the structure itself of the Infinite Spiral Staircase (ISS) at the origin of the universe. The ISS is a *golden spiral* staircase; that is, it is formed by a suite of quarter circles (the steps) that unfold as an algorithm of phi, following the Fibonacci sequence. This means that each of its steps has a specific hyperfrequency note (and a correlated wavelength). ISST hypothesizes that these hyperfrequency steps also instantiate specific archetypal ideas and forms, processes, life-force, and organization. Networks of syg-frequencies could thus "code" for specific life-forms, events, or concepts.

The ISS at the origin would thus birth our universe-bubble, seeding it with the matrixes (syg-fields) of all beings, intelligences, and forms that have existed in our parent universes; these matrixes are reevoked, reembodied, and optimized, while new ones are created by us—one among many civilizations who are the dwellers of this universe. Thus the eternal ongoing creation is pursued and it uses, as creative tools, the archetypes and pearls of knowledge and realizations issued from past experiences. With creativity, and while we evolve as a human species together with the animal and plant ones, we'll steer variations of ancient beings/ideas/forms or boost their transmutation, and moreover, we'll create new ones. This is our collective work of art, the alchemical grand opus, of all of us, the consciousnesses dwelling in our universe-bubble, and it is also our very onus and responsibility to do so in a harmonious and spiritual way.

This opus—what we'll have been able to create, live, and produce—will be, let's be aware of it, the heritage we'll give and transmit to our descendants, the inhabitants of the future universe-bubbles we'll birth. And this heritage of ours will contain all the bonus we will have achieved, but also the inevitable malus issued from our worst drives.

Lastly, let me clarify a point. It is far from uncommon for me to have visionary states of great acuity, such as seeing the auras of sacred places or sacred objects. As I mentioned, I can *see* the energy of the hyperdimension (the syg-energy) and the force fields and rays it creates or belongs to, since my sudden awakening at eighteen.

And because of that, I must stress that I know (with 100 percent confidence) that my "visions" are exact perceptions of the hyperdimension and its syg-energy dynamics and structures. Not only is it as much of a real perception for me as the 4D reality (*would you doubt seeing your hand holding the pen you are writing with?*), but my confidence also rests on the fact that a great number of these visions have been proven correct or corroborated as to the information they brought, in various ways. They could be validated by later information, by similar events or visions showing the same rare facet of reality or by events happening simultaneously. Another affirmation of their value, in my eyes at least, is when they can be predicted by, or inferred from, the ISS theory.

In this specific case of sacred objects showing immaterial layered reflections, the indirect corroboration comes from: (1) the congruent phenomenon of the superposed landscape; (2) several similar visions; (3) it is intrinsically coherent with our standard theory in quantum physics positing a discrete quantum substrate; (4) it is predicated on the ISS theory's discrete and Fibonacci-based ISS hyperdimension at the origin.

TWO-WAY COMMUNICATION WITH THE HD IN PEAK STATES

Let's now focus on the two-way communication that takes place between our conscious ego and our hyperdimensional Self. As far as

I have experienced it, it implies a back and forth of syg-energy—the highest immaterial and spiritual energy of consciousness filling the hyperdimension.

The Flight of the Pi *Drawing*

The Flight of the Pi (L'envolée du Pi) is the drawing I spontaneously did on November 17, 2012, to express an insight I had at that moment. It conveys how, when we have peak experiences, we are indeed communicating with our HD Self; and moreover, symbols and sacred forms, as well as high places, are creating resonances with their perfect archetypal forms in the HD (see fig. 9.2). This insight arose from my musing on some previous peak experiences, notably at the Pi gate temple in India, and in the sacred site of Meteora in Greece.

In the *Flight of the Pi* insight, my perspective is from the earthly plane—namely, the fact that, in peak states, we may perceive how sacred places and architectures trigger resonances in the HD; for example, how the Pi gate, as a potent stone sculpture prodding meditation (in the temple), is itself, as a form *and* a symbol, ringing resonances up in the HD all the way to its root-symbol—the archetypal Pi. This perception shows how the HD intrudes into the 4D reality—through the "holes in the reality" or antennae to the HD, the horizontal ribbon of vortexes labeled on the left, mid-height.

Thus, sacred buildings and high places in the Sacred Network create (above them) spiraling energy vortexes connecting them to their HD archetypes, that we may grasp as holes or windows in our 4D reality during peak states, opening on the hyperdimension.

On the Earth Level (4D Spacetime World, Bottom Half)

- *Bottom right*: the Pi gate temple (Porte Pi). The peak state that I experienced at this temple, predicted by a vision in the fire (chapter 3 and 5).
- *Bottom left*: Meteora, Greece. This marks a memorable peak state one afternoon in Meteora, among the giant rock formations

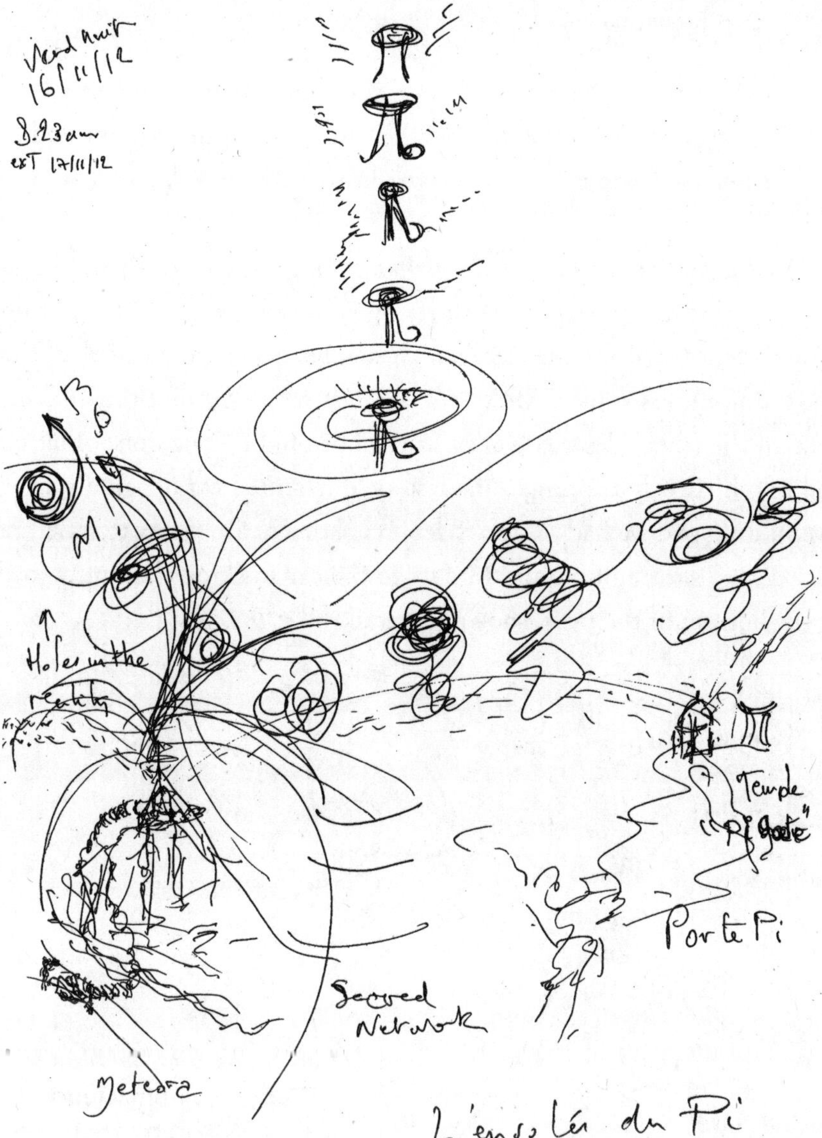

Fig. 9.2. *The Flight of the Pi* (L'envolée du Pi); drawing by Chris H. Hardy, dated night of November 16, 2012 (real time November 17, 8:30 a.m.). An insight on past peak experiences of communicating with the HD.

Bottom left: Meteora, Greece. *Mid-bottom:* the Sacred Network; that is, highly charged places and monuments in the sacred grid of Earth. *Bottom right:* the Pi gate temple (Porte Pi) in India. *Left, mid-height:* "Holes in the reality." This caption refers to the whole wavy ribbon of spiraling energy vortexes as "holes" opening between the 4D and HD dimensions, perceived during peak states. *Top:* layered resonances of the pi symbol (and sacred buildings) into the hyperdimension.

Artwork by Chris H. Hardy

> (see plate 20). My ex, M, being of Greek-American ancestry, had strong experiences there when he was younger and had wanted to come back there, to that very striking sacred place.

In the early afternoon, we had had a long time of meditation and some spectacular experience with the huge rocks—not only their stunning presence, making the place a high site, but also their particular echo and harmonic resonance. Afterward, as we were driving on a tiny snaking road in the (then) deserted valley, at the bottom of a tall stone pillar on top of which was standing a monastery, our rented car's engine started overheating and we had to stop to let it cool down. On the bottom-left of fig. 9.2, is a sketch of me and M next to the car stuck on the empty road at the bottom of the peak, shown in detail in fig. 9.3.

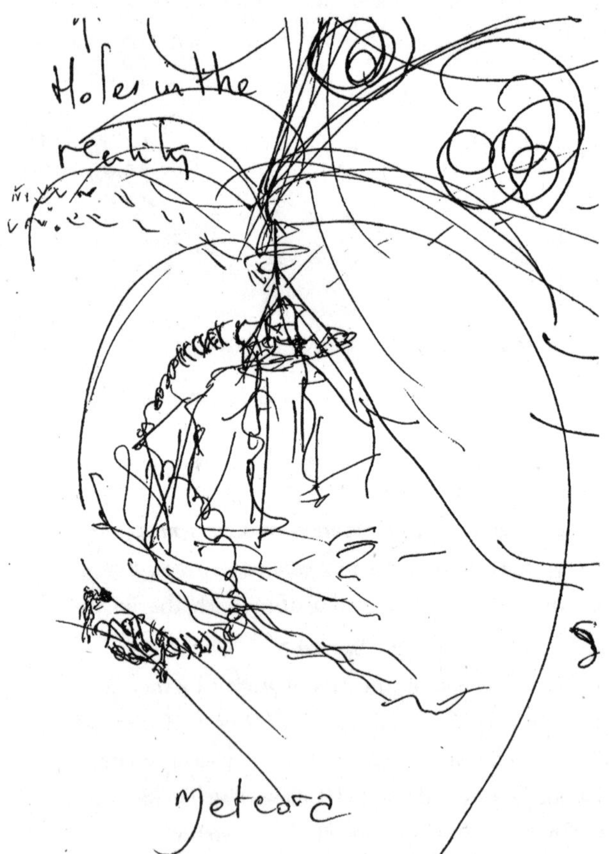

Fig. 9.3. *The Flight of the Pi.* Detail of Meteora
Drawing by Chris H. Hardy

While M (on the left) stands in front of the car's open hood, upset and seething, I'm at the rear (on the right) and having another peak state. What happened is that, while standing there and contemplating this stunning landscape and despite the monastery (what we could perceive of it) looking like a tiny stone building so high up there on this tall peak, I sensed the mind of an invisible monk and was in telepathic contact with him. This is what I represented as a ribbon of wave lines spiraling upward in a S shape, from my head all the way up to the monastery. The monastery (the pointed roof) is itself creating a "hole in the reality"—that is, it is a direct antenna to the HD, first as an architecture in a sacred site, and also given that highly spiritual monks were living there for centuries and had thus charged and illuminated the place.

- *Mid-bottom:* "The Sacred Network." This refers to high places and sacred temples and buildings—especially those built on the sacred proportion *phi*, the golden number, such as cathedrals and churches (see Ghyka 2016). (My namesake book recounts many peak experiences with this grid.)

Intermediary Level: Holes in the Reality (Mid-Height)

This caption (on the left) refers to the whole horizontal and undulating ribbon of such "holes" represented as dynamic spirals or vortices. These holes, created mentally in peak states or by the sacred network, are gateways or antennae for two-way contacts with the HD and notably with our own Self.

On the HD Level (Top)

In the upper part of the drawing, the first symbol excited or put in resonance by the earthly experience/site is the Egyptian *Eye of Ra* (see fig. 9.4), which expresses the all-knowing spiritual and intuitive intelligence of the Self, or divine dimension.

As the resonance-wave unfolds into higher levels, it triggers a more essential and holistic form, that of the pi sign as a gate; indeed, the

Fig. 9.4 Eye of Ra, Egypt
Photo by Kompak

Eye of Ra already has one right leg (or curved pillar) under the eye, which in itself contains the roof of the pi. Finally, the flow of resonances illuminates a perfect pi sign in the HD.

I had this new insight (nearly two decades later) right after I had written the core of my hyperdimensional cosmology theory (about 150 pages) in a record eighteen days, ending on the night of November 14, late in the morning—thus two nights earlier. (This also shows how the discovery of the hyperdimension afforded me new insights about earlier spiritual and psi experiences.)

The Two-Way Syg-Energy Exchange with the HD

In the *Flight of the Pi* drawing, my insight has been from our own earthly perspective—namely, how we get in touch with the HD and our Self, and how we trigger resonances in the HD. But how does the HD respond and send us meaningful syg-energy?

Interestingly, I was just shown how resonances work from the HD perspective: while writing this segment on the Pi gate drawing,

I had a striking experience—a vision in the fire that complemented my understanding of the Pi insight. I'm going to insert here the text I wrote on the spot (I just clarified and corrected it a bit), because it is a quite extraordinary example of how we are in deep communication, constantly so, with HD-beings (including our own Self). And it shows how they are indeed responding to us and adding their own murmurs into the weaving of our thoughts and conscious life. (We'll see another example of this with the wax sculpture in my candlestick in the next section.)

> *Tonight, 22 March 2021, as I had just inserted the drawing and its caption* The Flight of the Pi *(with the related text) and was still reflecting on its import in the book, I went down to sit a moment in front of my fireplace and mull over it further. I was still deep in my night's writing, despite the clock showing already past 5:00 a.m.*
>
> *So downstairs, there's only a dim orange light on the side of my chair, and the big logs I had fed the fire earlier have formed a bed of dark ashes on which sits one single log, mostly burnt-out black, yet self-consuming from the bottom, with a few large incandescent, golden-orange caverns in the wood. There are no flames anymore, just the bright caverns and a few sparks here and there. That's when I realize that there are, in the bed of ashes, sudden incandescences of bright orange light figuring eye-catching triangles or delta shapes (on the left side of the fire); then these give out two or three more triangular sparks. Now, on the slightly burnt top of the log (on the left), suddenly one perfect triangular shape brightens up and gives out variations of luminosity, as if active. And then on this same left band, at mid-height of the log, appear some tiny sparks and luminous variations as if responding to the talking top triangle; and all the while, the bottom triangular shape below one red cavern, in the ash bed, remains a brightly lit orange . . . As if there was an ongoing communication, centered on (or expressed by) a triangle symbol, between these three levels aligned in a vertical band.*

> *I suddenly realize that the fire is reproducing the* Flight of the Pi *drawing: (1) with the deep orange caverns and gray ashes representing the 4D world—just as on my drawing, the bottom horizontal band pointed our 4D world and the peak experiences I had at Meteora and at the Pi gate temple; and (2) the log itself represents two distinct layers of the HD, with the top one showing archetypal forms (triangles) and beings (the Selfs).*
>
> *And while I watch the display of sparks and alighted triangular forms in the fire, its meaning unfolds and I have a deeper insight—this vision presents me the reverse side of the Pi drawing; that is, how the Selfs inhabiting the HD see things and beings on Earth and communicate with them from their dimension.*

Let me point out here that, even for a fire-gazer like me who has had numerous visions and even communications with beings appearing in the fire, highly geometric or symmetric shapes such as the triangles and the pi shape remain extremely rare. Unfortunately, photos and videos of a fire are awfully disappointing because the light and especially the sparks are not reflected in a true way, and this is why drawings reflect my visions much more accurately.

So, to summarize:

When somebody has a peak experience in a sacred place, it excites their syg-field (higher consciousness and energy-body), making it shift to a higher frequency and getting lighted in bright colors, evoking the Self. This in turn triggers a string of resonances in archetypal forms in the intermediary layers. Let's figure that not only forms (triangles, pyramids, or obelisks) but also ideas and higher feelings do have archetypal roots or essences.

There is an ongoing communication between these three levels (the 4-D, the archetypal forms, and the Selfs) in a vertical band—displaying synchrony; that is, frequency harmonization and rhythmic resonance, as in a standing wave. This synchrony is not only issued from conceptual resonances, but also from *waves of form* (in hyperspace, the Center-Circle-HD).

Then, from the *high-HD layer* (the Selfs), a more perfect and archetypal concept/form is reemitted toward the person. This could explain how our guides, our deceased loved ones and great beings dwelling in the HD may become aware of us when we either experience a peak state of high spirituality, or even think about them, or pray for/to them. And how they may send us healing, soothing, or empowering syg-energy.

Pauli's "World Clock" Dream Sculpted in Wax in My Candelabra

The anomalous event that I'll now recount is another example of a two-way communication between our mind and the Selfs in the hyperdimension (including our own Self). When it happened, I was in a rare heightened state—a creative spree that lasted eighteen days (from October 28 to November 14, 2012), and during which I elaborated my *Infinite Spiral Staircase Theory* (later published as Hardy 2015).

Allow me to give you some context for understanding what happened and what it meant.

First, about my deep connection with Carl Jung and Pauli: I discovered Jung's books in my late teens, then he appeared as a mentor in a seminal dream in my twenties, and finally I experienced over the years anomalous short dialogues with his HD mind, which gave me pinpoint yet invaluable information and guidance concerning my theoretical work. As for Wolfgang Pauli, he had been both in analysis in Jung's Zurich institute, and Jung's friend and collaborator (notably on synchronicity research), providing him with most of the dream material he commented on in *Psychology and Alchemy*. As I mentioned earlier, I experienced an hour-long telepathic and visual discussion with him in 1996 that included some precise information I was able to corroborate later, as well as a prediction of a future new level of my SFT theory (*Living Souls*, 211–22). And up to now, I keep enjoying short but recurrent telepathic communications with Pauli just as with Jung. All in all,

I consider them both as friends, colleagues, and inspiring mentors.

Despite this physics framework and the fact that I presented (in the core model) several of Pauli's dreams on physics, I entertained no dialogue with him or Jung or any physicist for that matter, during this eighteen-day intense creative process during which I wrote what would become 220 book pages (that remained quasi-intact in the larger published book).

Yet something staggering happened, which expressed our deep interconnection in the realm of the Selfs, and probably his interest in my creative process.

A complex wax structure appeared in my large candleholder, resembling part of his own World Clock dream, which, interestingly was one I hadn't analyzed in the model.

This dream features two interlocked round clocks with thirty-two partitions (4 × 8)—one blue vertical and one four-colored and horizontal—sharing a unique (but void) center and first carried as a gold ring by a black eagle. The world clock has three rhythms: when the hand on the vertical clock has advanced thirty-two times (short rhythm), it moves the horizontal clock's hand 1/32 degree (middle rhythm). The completion of the 32 degrees on the horizontal clock, circled by the gold ring, is the great rhythm.

Pauli said he mulled over this dream for years and that this vision gave him "an impression of the most sublime harmony" because the three rhythms are interlocked in a base-4 fashion (the two orthogonal clocks). And obviously, given the name he gave it, he meant a harmony pervading or ordering the universe.

My large wax sculpture showed a hand of a clock, one-inch high and in the shape of a keyhole, set vertically at first on the rim of my candelabra (the cup itself is about 2.7 inches large and 0.8 inches deep, and supported by a tall and thin spiraling pole). Then, in a pool of half-melted wax in the cup of the candelabra, stands at center-left a somewhat conic mound of wax on which is set a funny and expressive head with eyes open (whom I dub "the Observer") and at center-right, a flame on the still-burning wick, both set like the two centers of an ellipsis. Moreover,

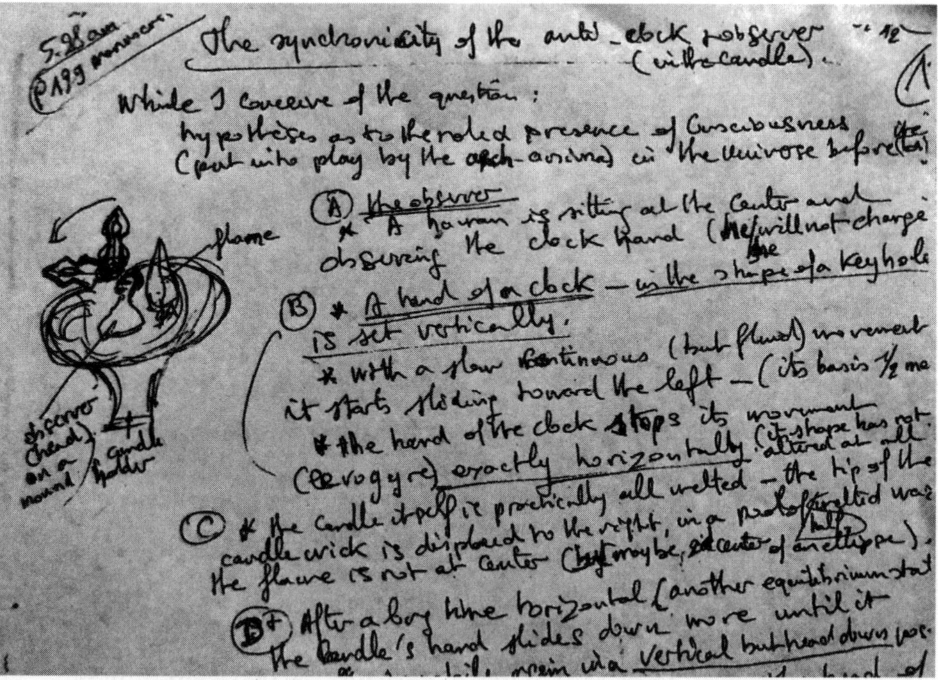

Fig. 9.5. Pauli's World Clock dream sculpted in wax in my candelabra and its ad hoc interpretation
Drawing by Chris H. Hardy

the tall sculpture evolved dynamically (with the remaining hard wax still melting) to show the vertical clock's hand move down slowly over fifteen to twenty minutes but, extraordinarily, in an anticlockwise way (leftward), which made me call it "the anticlock" (see fig. 9.5).

The vertical clock hand clearly set on the outside rim of a horizontal round is what made it so recognizable as Pauli's World Clock, with its (second) "center" being the mound-cum-face with observing eyes.

When it appeared suddenly, fully formed (or rather, when I became conscious of it), I scribbled the phenomenal event and the time on the margin of the page I was writing on, with a crude drawing to show the shape it took. And then, as I kept working, I added notes about where the clock hand was at what time, and the global shape it showed. Finally, I took a blank sheet of paper to draw the whole sculpture again and to make a quick interpretation of its symbolism. (I wasn't able to put my hands on them at the time I elaborated this text, and only now at the editing phase did I miraculously find the interpretation page with the drawing, shown above. This is a clear example of a psi phenomenon being much more elaborate, extraordinary, and meaningful in reality than the recollection that I—the (co)author—had of it.)

Here is about three-fifths of my interpretation page:

THE SYNCHRONICITY OF THE ANTICLOCK + OBSERVER (IN THE CANDLE)

While I conceive of the question: Hypotheses as to the role and presence of consciousness (put into play by the arch-anima) in the universe before the Big Bang.

A. *The Observer.* A human is sitting at the Center and observing the clock hand (he/she will not change at all).
B. A hand of a clock—in the shape of a keyhole—is set vertically.
   - with a slow continuous (but fluid) movement, it starts sliding toward the left.
   - the hand of the clock stops its movement (levogyre) *exactly horizontally* (its shape has not been altered at all).
C. The candle itself is practically all melted—the tip of the candle wick is displaced to the right, in a pool of half-melted wax. The flame is not at center (but may be [as the] second center of an ellipsis).
D. After a long time being horizontal (another equilibrium state), the hand slides down more until it stays immobile again in a *vertical but head down* position.
E. When the hand reaches below the horizon, the *head* of the observer suddenly falls (and disappears).

During all the time the clock was still "moving," I kept on writing and elaborating my theory in the very inspired mode I had that night and that would drive the process for another fortnight, with a quick glance to the candlestick every few minutes.

Despite being prone to having fantastic sculptures formed spontaneously out of melting candles or within the fire (as we have seen), in that specific instance I don't think the sculpture was produced by my own unconscious, because it was too specific and not really linked to the concepts I was developing that night.

So, how can I interpret what happened? Let's remember first that Pauli had, just like Jung, some psi capacities. His were mainly an astounding psychokinetic effect; in other words, a mind-over-matter gift that was mostly (as far as we know) unconsciously driven yet so spectacular that his scientific colleagues at the Institute for Advanced Study (where he was professor of theoretical physics from 1940 to 1946) in Princeton, New Jersey, had called it the "Pauli effect."

During our 1996 dialogue, an hour long, he had entertained me with his research in quantum physics after I had asked him why he didn't invent "the physics of synchronicity." Then I had asked for his advice about a problem I had at the time with my first theoretical framework (the Semantic Fields Theory) in cognitive and consciousness science. He had finally predicted to me that I was going to elaborate a whole new level of this theory at a later date. And here I was, creating it—a whole sixteen years later!

I can only infer, given our very special dialogue and his prediction back in 1996 that, from the hyperdimension where his mind dwells, he must have been curious about the creative process and where I would take it, and that he was kind of looking over my shoulder or, more precisely, watching me from his own signature clock in the candelabra, while letting me know that somehow he was in sync with it.

All in all, with Pauli's World Clock sculpture in my candelabra, we see another aspect of this two-way communication with the HD during peak states: that of a very personalized synchrony and relationship, a clear spiritual bonding between, on the one hand, the Self of an ascended spirit (Pauli), and on the other hand, the Self of a living person in sync with their own incarnated mind during a heightened state.

The closeness and individualized communication and harmony with the dimension of the Spirit, the possibility of an ego-Self harmonization, is something that most institutionalized religions apart from the Eastern ones have discarded or even demonized. And in this epoch of novel spiritual and psi capacities on the rise worldwide, we certainly will discover new facets of our deep link with the hyperdimension of the Selfs.

10
HYPERDIMENSION, SACRED VOLUMES, AND EARTH'S GRIDS

We'll now ponder another case of a barrier to the astral body, this time by a simple wooden pyramidal shape. This anomalous experience will show us that a strong hyperdimensional energy-field is created in 4D objects whenever they embed the perfect proportions of a (sacred) geometry and/or volume.

IMPRISONED BY A WOODEN PYRAMID

I had just read a book on the strange properties of a pyramidal structure replicating the exact measurements of the Great Pyramid in Egypt (the Pyramid of Cheops, the tallest of the three in Giza) (see fig. 10.1). The authors (whose names I have forgotten) detailed some experiments they had made using a tabletop scale model; namely a square base and four slanted edges made of tiny wooden battens. For example, various vegetables or fruits set under the 3D form would not decay but only dry up. The authors had written a lengthy development on how the pharaohs of Egypt could have used these astonishing properties for the conservation of their mummified bodies, and they also quickly mentioned some effect on mental states.

What they recounted about the four-sided pyramid with Cheops

Fig. 10.1. The Great Pyramid of Giza in March 2005
Photo by Nina Aldin Thune

proportions got me excited enough to try an experiment on myself and build such a model. (I still remember my experiment vividly, even the exact size and shape of the pyramid towering above my mattress and the square edges overlapping it on the floor.) Since I was a natural sensitive and also a meditator, I was expecting to sense something about the pyramid shape's properties, either by meditating or sleeping under it.

As they had provided the exact proportion of the base and height, I went to a large supply store where I bought eight long and thin wooden battens, with a square width—this skeleton of a pyramid was to be large enough for me to sit in meditation under it or sleep inside it. And then I sawed and bevel-edged the sides of the base and that of the upward structure. Finally, I used a thin twine (made of natural fibers) to tie together the four slanted edges at the apex and the four edges of the base, since they were too thin and fragile to use nails.

I had assembled the pyramid right in my writing room in Igny, where I used to sleep also, in such a way that it would surround my mattress set on a wool carpet covering the floor. This room, which had a wooden floor, was in a stone-walled house under a traditional slate roof. Even my mattress was a traditional woolen one! Everything was thus nonmetallic and natural. And now I was ready to experiment with the pyramid that same evening.

I started by meditating under the pyramid for my usual length of time (around forty to sixty minutes), sitting on my mattress with my head right under its pointed apex, but I felt no noticeable effect. And thus I looked forward to sleeping underneath it that night. And that's when things got really strange.

I woke up in the middle of the night, still shaken from a horrendous nightmare. I was imprisoned in a large square field surrounded by tall barbed-wire fences that had watchtowers with armed guards at each corner—just like a concentration camp.

I was trying, again and again, to walk toward the fences to get out and free myself, but each time I was repelled by the fences as if they produced a strong repulsive force. I was not hurt or injured by the energy of the fences but I was being violently pulled backward. The psychological stress, the anguish at being thus trapped and imprisoned, and the impossibility of freeing myself was excruciating. On waking up, I was still awfully distressed, but then the meaning of the nightmare, which was evident for a seasoned astral traveler like me, made me burst into laughter. Indeed, the pyramid shape was very powerful; it had blocked my astral body from traveling as usual during my sleep! And hence the repeated attempts at trying to cross the energy-field of the sides of the pyramid—and the evocation and imagery of a barbed wire and electrical fence imprisoning me. Just as I inferred in chapter 7 that the octagonal roof and mesh of electrical wire created a low-frequency hyperdimensional syg-field, here also it is evident that only such a low-HD field could have the property of blocking my low-HD energy-body.

Waves of Form: The Science of Sacred Volumes

In this ad hoc pyramid experiment, we see a wooden 3D geometrical structure with the (somewhat) exact proportions of the Cheops pyramid creating an unknown type of force field impeding the energy-body from passing through it.

It's unclear how such a property could be used in the afterlife existence of the kings and queens in Egypt. At death, the *ka*, or life-force, remains in the body (then embalmed as a mummy), whereas the soul or *ba* (represented as a bird with the dead person's face) exits the body and travels through an intermediary realm toward the immortal realm or Duat, kingdom of Osiris (see fig. 10.2). In the Duat, the worthy ba (somehow integrated to its heart and ka) will be transformed into an *akh* (a light-spirit with power), a consciously acting, enlightened, and ascended spirit. However, the *Book of the Dead* depicts the ba regularly returning to his/her mummy and able to visit and act in the material world of the living. So, if the pyramid was efficient in the preservation of mummies and possibly the confinement of the ka (the energy-body) inside it, I'm unsure how the ba (the astral body) could visit it within a pyramid, unless this transmuted spirit of light (ba-akh) belongs to a high-frequency of the syg spectrum, which it should as an ascended spirit.

The interesting point about constructing this pyramid shape in my Igny house on a high hill within Verrières forest (connected only to the

Fig. 10.2. The soul or ba, as the deceased-headed bird, exiting the dead mummified body. Papyrus of Ani, Luxor, c. 1250 BCE.

electrical grid and phone lines) is that this force field cannot in any way be associated with an EM field since there was not a speck of metal that would conduct electricity or act as a magnet in this house, and no antennae around it. We then have to conclude that the pyramid's force field is a non-EM energy—and could be of a hyperspatial type; that is, created by a perfect *sacred volume*. And by "sacred volume," I mean one founded on specific proportions, such as *pi* or *phi*, as this science was handed down to us from ancient Greece, notably Pythagoras and Plato, and then refined by the cathedral builders in Europe.

There were in France (since at least the mid-twentieth century) a few scientists researching what they called *ondes de forme* or "form-waves"—that is, waves of forms, created by 2D or 3D forms/structures. (It has nothing to do with "wave-form," which means the form/properties of the wave itself.) There were fringe studies about mysterious rays created by specific angles as well as 3D volumes, and the four-sided pyramid was one of them.

Just think about how the science of musical instruments in pre-scientific cultures everywhere on earth has evolved quasi-naturally, using rules of thumb and heuristic trials, in order to find the most suitable shapes and quality of resonating materials (wood, gourd, calabash, bamboo) in order to get the best acoustics and sound box for a violin, guitar, sitar, or flute.

And think about the fact that, similarly, the shape and volumes of stone churches and abbeys in France were not only based on the golden proportion, *phi*, but were also conceived for their acoustics. And indeed the musical resonance of a wall-sized organ or that of a choir singing Gregorian chants is breathtaking in some well-known monuments such as Mont-Saint-Michel Abbey, or Thoronet Abbey.

Let's note that Plato had a model of the five sacred solids (tetrahedron, cube, octahedron, dodecahedron, icosahedron—respectively 4, 6, 8, 12, and 20 identical faces) as the fundamental bricks of life, expressing the five elements. Many ancient Greek philosophers studied them, with some, such as Proclus, crediting Pythagoras with their discovery. Then

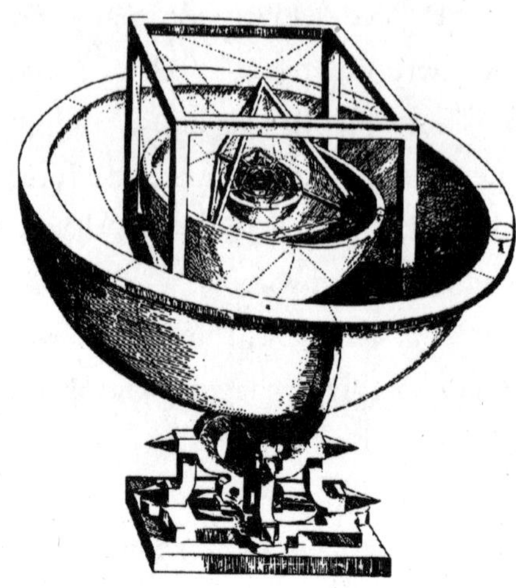

Fig. 10.3. Platonic sacred volumes in Kepler's solar system model. From his treatise *Mysterium Cosmographicum* (Tübingen 1596, Tabula III)

the Platonic solids were adopted by the astronomer Johannes Kepler as essential structures of the solar system (see fig. 10.3).

Let's remember that Pythagoras had studied the ancient sacred sciences in Egypt for more than twenty years, and many of his philosophical concepts, math, and geometry originated there.

If, according to these scholars, the perfect proportions and sacred volumes played a central role in the making of our solar system, then they also did so in the unfolding of our universe, and it means that they probably existed at the origin. And it follows that they are archetypes of sorts, exactly as both Jung and Pauli thought they were (see Jung 1960 *Structure and Dynamics*; Pauli and Jung 2014). Pauli, for example, thought that numbers were part of the deep reality that had the attributes of both energy-matter and psyche. In ISST, it is the golden spiral at the origin (the infinite spiral staircase or ISS based on both *phi* and *pi*) that launches the unfolding of our universe in the hyperdimension. Thus, we have both a sacred form (the golden spiral) and sacred proportions (the phi-based development of this spiral)—with the ISS launching the first sygons (HD strings) carrying this hyperdimensional quasi-infinite suite of hyperfrequencies. In ISST then, both the forms (Center-HD, hyperspace) and the numbers (frequencies or

Rhythm-HD, hypertime) exist as archetypes in the hyperdimension at the origin (the golden spiral).

Hyperdimensional Energy-Fields Created by Perfect Geodesics and Sacred Volumes

From this pyramid experience, we can infer that these sacred volumes are archetypes carrying a potent meaning, and that an essential part of their reality and properties is hyperdimensional. Whereas other objects (nongeometric, nonsacred) will all have a hyperdimensional syg-field, just like all beings and systems at all scales, the very special syg-field of sacred volumes will resonate all the way to the core of the HD at the origin, in the highest hyperfrequencies.

As we have seen in chapter 9, sacred objects, even natural crystals that are not perfectly geometric, do create scale-reflections of themselves (volumes and form) in the HD, composed of HD syg-energy. Given the discrete and layered structure of the HD that I predicate, ascending in the hyperfrequencies toward the ISS at the origin, these scale-reflections have higher and higher hyperfrequencies.

The human energy-body, in other words, stands at the lowest end of the hyperfrequencies domain, whereas the golden spiral at the origin and the Selfs are at its highest end.

Sacred Octagonal Temple and Ayahuasca Experience

Let me weigh the influence of a sacred temple on a community.

Normally, a perfect geometrical structure/volume (such as the eight-point-star beamed roof topping the octagonal temple) does create an HD field in hyperspace (Center-Circle-HD). All such temples based on sacred geometry, as I have explained in *The Sacred Network,* should have a spiritualizing influence; that is, raising the consciousness-state of the people gathered within or near it; ideally they should enhance the connection ego-Self of participants (through the HD), thus creating an evolving *collective syg-field,* in which the values, intents, and ethics of this community bond them together in a dynamic way.

This is how the cathedrals and their spires work as an antenna to the sacred or divine realm of Selfs and spiritual guides. Many a time I have thus meditated exactly under the exact center of the churches' domes, and I was drawn to elevate my consciousness and energy-body through the roof. This is how I discovered and explored the curved geometries of the sacred lines jetting at their tip like a water fountain. Of course, all churches and temples embed arches and domes; that is, curved geometries nested within squares, rectangles, and octagons.

Then what makes the difference with a four-sided pyramid or the roof in Brazil, which blocked the energy-body? For one, the four-sided pyramid has no embedded curves. And second, the roof in Brazil had a conducive 8-base mandala, but it was polluted by a mesh of 60-Hz electricity.

I do remember that, when I finally succeeded in leaving the building alone and had lounged down in the garden with my back on the grass, I entered a mystical connection with the stars that I had hardly ever seen so bright and huge in my life. But soon an aide came and harassed me until I went back inside with her; thus there was a clear-cut avoidance of any personal connection not only to one's own Self, but also to the vibrant cosmos. As an ethnopsychologist, I'm not sure this is the best way to become a highly spiritual, benevolent, and liberated person, a state that, in order to blossom, would need a harmonization and fusion with the Self (intently and progressively achieved). In terms of spiritual communities, I prefer a free and dynamical group of spiritually open individuals, creative and network-synergic.

Collective Syg-Fields and Egregores

This concept of collective syg-field is a more complex and theory-founded elaboration of an ancient Enochian and esoteric concept: that of an *egregore*, whose Latin root *aggrego*, meaning "I group together," gave us "to aggregate." An egregore is thus an aggregated-psyche created by a group of believers. We thus have the egregores of esoteric societies such as the Templars or the Freemasons. The egregore referred to an immaterial collective construct, embedding a system of ideas (but without self-awareness or capacity to act). It was thought to be mostly indestructible, and it was said that the Freemasons reappropriated the egregore of the Templars when that order was dissolved and many members died.

Viewing them as syg-fields would add that the field is multidimensional, with:

- *A spirit on the HD level:* a constellation of similarly minded Selfs, their values and shared beliefs, ideas, worldview; their architectural and symbolic knowledge, their spiritual lore.
- *A material 4D level:* first, the body-psyche of all participants (behaviors, activities, relational styles); and second, the material structures of the community (sacred sites, temples, libraries, artworks, natural resources) and their communal rituals and activities.

The collective syg-field exhibits collective intelligence, yet within the constraints of the group's beliefs, laws, and worldview. It is a collective psyche that is alive, self-conscious, and evolving with its members' free evolution. In contrast, the egregore is only a fixed collection of ideas and values, and a spiritual force depository, yet unchanging.

The collective syg-field thus includes also the members' behaviors, which are derived partly from their values, social code, and philosophical or creed beliefs, and partly from the psychological profiles of the leader(s) and most influential persons.

The leader could have a schizophrenic psyche enabling them to act and do the opposite of their stated values. For example, a priest preaching Christ's ideal love for innocent children, and nevertheless being a pedophile harming the children he should protect and negatively affecting their entire life: this would then alter the syg-field of this faith group or community, as some adults at least are silently complicit.

Thus the concept of syg-field allows to analyze, given a group, sect, or creed, the degree of individual fealty (versus freedom) of its members, their mental flexibility and inventiveness (versus dogmatism, bigotry, corrosive attachment to past traditions), their strength and shortcomings, and finally, the level of threat and risk this group may pose, as well as the possible range of oppressive, violent, or criminal behaviors it could produce.

PERCEPTION OF A GRID IN THE SKY IN BRITTANY AND NASIK

On two occasions in my life, both times in very spiritual places, I detected, while walking, a clear boundary on the ground where my own state of consciousness would suddenly and drastically shift in and out of a collective state of shared consciousness. In Brittany, I realized that what had been a too-bothersome constant telepathic field among the monks, into which my mind was drawn, had a precise boundary on a small path toward the fields, at which my mind was suddenly back to its own intimacy, or, on the return, drawn to share it again (something I verified every day). In the sacred town of Nasik (near Mumbai) a year and a half later, I discovered on the road down to the temples that at a precise point my mind was suddenly swept into a wondrous state of harmony and shared consciousness of a spiritual nature, and on the way back, I would lose it and be alone in my mind again; this, each and every day I was there. Both times, within the spatial limit of the telepathic-harmonic field (or Telhar field), I could see very clearly a kind of grid high up in the sky that presented grayish, near-straight lines crisscrossing orthogonally, forming fat rectangles.

In both instances, all people within the field were in deep telepathic or harmonic attunement within a collective mind (or syg-field). To my utter amazement, these two fields showed identical energetic features: a clear delineation in space marked by a precise boundary on the ground (thus in spacetime environment), as well as a grid in the sky, forming a dome above the place (obviously hyperdimensional).

Let me recount these experiences, the Brittany one being the most precise regarding the grid.

At twenty years old, I visited with my boyfriend and brother quester

Christian a small community of monks of the Celtic Orthodox order in Brittany, and experienced for the first time a field of collective consciousness that was telepathic in essence. At the psychological level, I could feel the minds of the monks constantly present in my own mind. This was very disturbing to me, because I had the impression that it robbed me of my intimacy with myself, something essential for the writer and poet I was already. And to regain my inner state, I felt I had to go some distance from the monastery; while walking in the fields, I found a perfect flat rock on which to sit and spend hours each day, reading, writing, and meditating. This experience would have been nothing but anecdotal evidence of group telepathy were it not for two wholly unexplainable observations linked to space.

The first observation was my discovery of a precise spot on the small path to the fields, beyond which, quite abruptly, I realized that I was alone with my thoughts again. I couldn't believe it and played with this "limit"—going within and beyond it—until I was utterly convinced that a single step brought me inside the telepathic field (sensing the others' minds crowding mine), while retracting that step brought me outside of it again. In the following days, the limit didn't change (I had made a kind of signpost on the vegetation), and the mental shift was just as abrupt and drastic. It became evident that the persistent telepathic sharing somehow occurred within a precisely delimited space and that within these limits, it was quite inescapable. At the time, I came to call it a telepathic field because, just like electromagnetic fields, it had a coherency within itself and a spatial component: the telepathic field was extended in space within a precise boundary. I also presumed this telepathic field delimited a circle around the monastery and adjoining dolmen and church of about 250 to 300 yards in diameter.

A second unexplained observation in Brittany was a grayish grid that was neatly visible in the clear summer sky above the monastery and was stable day after day. It was composed of long, grey lines (against the pale blue sky) crossing at near right angles so that they formed a grid of fat rectangles, imperceptibly curved, as if the geodesic grid was quite large. Each elongated square was about one and a half times the apparent diameter of the moon. It appeared as though a geodesic dome existed over the monastery and the nearby tiny church, which was very sacred as it was built next to a huge dolmen—a two-yard-wide, roundish megalithic table. The grid was a steady sight from within the monastery's yard, day after day, and at the time it was rather unsettling to me but, unlike with the spatial boundary, I didn't make the connection between it and the telepathic field.

A year later, I was on an eighteen-month journey in India and visited the holy town of Nasik, where I was swept into a very harmonious yet powerful field of shared consciousness (yet devoid of disturbing thoughts) while visiting the sacred core of town, filled with dozens of temples on and near the river. Just as with the Brittany field, the Nasik Telhar field had a precise boundary in space. At this very spot (at a turn of the road and facing a chai shop), while climbing down toward the river each day, I experienced a shift to a higher state of consciousness and was swept into a collective Telhar field, and on returning, I turned back suddenly to my individual self. What's more, I could also see very clearly the grayish grid on the blue sky.

A grid of thinly elongated squares, visible against the sky, was thus the upper dome above these two sacred places, whose base had a precise limit on the ground. An essential point for us is that both places were sacred and—this is now my assumption—the specific Telhar fields existing there were creating a large half sphere—three hundred yards in diameter in Brittany and much larger and elongated along the sacred river in Nasik—whose dome was the HD-energy grid.

Another crucial point is that we have, in these two instances, the three braids of the ISST hyperdimension: (1) the Telhar field born out of the harmony and synchrony of minds in a sacred place (Syg-HD); (2) the quasi-spatial form of a dome and its precise boundary at the base (Center-HD, hyperspace); and (3) the frequency and wavelengths of the crisscrossing HD lines constituting the sky-grid (Rhythm-HD, hypertime).

The sky-grid is perforce hyperdimensional because (1) it is a feature of a consciousness field, and (2) it is unrelated to any technological antenna or energy source (that didn't exist in the late sixties either in the Brittany countryside or in the city of Nasik). With its orthogonal crisscrossing lines, it has some similitude with the HD field I saw in Brazil's Santo Daime church and Pauli's Deep Reality grid. It has both similitudes and dissimilarities with the Hartmann and Curry grids, which we'll now explore.

Earth's Grids and the Geomagnetic Field

The unusual hyperdimensional field structure superposed to the 60-Hz field created on the roof that I saw in Brazil (with its two orthogonal sets of undulating waves crisscrossing at multiple nodes) could have, beyond the densely tangled wires, *been produced or at least affected by the global form of the perfect eight-point-star-shaped octagonal beamed roof* delineated and enclosed by the walls of the room, which was built as a tall octagonal volume espousing the roof mandala. But first, how did it fit the usual EM fields configuration?

Electric and Magnetic Field Lines

The straight waves I saw did not display the usual curvature of the magnetic field lines (B) flowing from the north pole (N) toward the south pole (S) around a dipole bar magnet (see fig. 10.4).

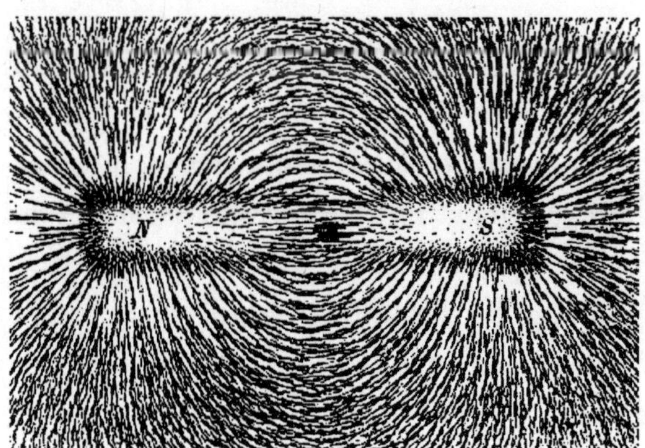

Fig. 10.4. Magnetic field lines around a bar magnet, represented by iron filings sprinkled on paper placed above it
Photo by Newton Henry Black

It didn't fit a static electrical field either, in which the lines (E) are similarly curved (see fig. 10.5). In both the electric and magnetic fields, the current is always flowing in a curved way from the positive pole while attracted to the negative pole and the curved lines never cross each other.

What about electric currents then? When electric charges are in motion—that is, changing with time (e.g., in electric currents) in an electric field—a magnetic field is produced, resulting in an electromagnetic field. Accordingly, as there were lots of electric currents moving through the mesh of wires around and across the roof beams, there was necessarily a large, roof-size electromagnetic field being produced, yet, let's remember that normally the curved lines don't crisscross.

Geomagnetic Grid, Hartmann and Curry Grids

Strangely, this field structure of orthogonal energy lines is also how several geobiologists have mapped minute grids at the surface of earth. The Hartmann (H) grid (described by the German physician Ernst Hartmann around 1950) is a grid of rectangles with small sides oriented north–south (6.5 feet, 2 meters) and long sides oriented east–west, thus following the Earth's parallels (mean length: 8.2 feet, 2.5 meters). The rectangles' long sides are smaller toward the poles and longest at the equator.

The Curry (C) grid (also ascertained around 1950 by another German doctor, Manfred Curry) is oriented at 45 degrees to the north and thus runs diagonally to the Hartmann grid. It is a grid of squares whose mean sides are about 14.7 feet (4.5 meters) and decreasing toward the poles. These grids don't seem to carry an EM energy and they operate at a few yards scale, thus differentiating them from ley lines of a much larger wavelength—the geomagnetic field lines or telluric lines circling around Earth's polar axis.*

*For a detailed analysis of the geomagnetic grid and the sacred lines (leys) connecting sacred sites and monuments, see my study and phenomenological data in *The Sacred Network* (Hardy 2011).

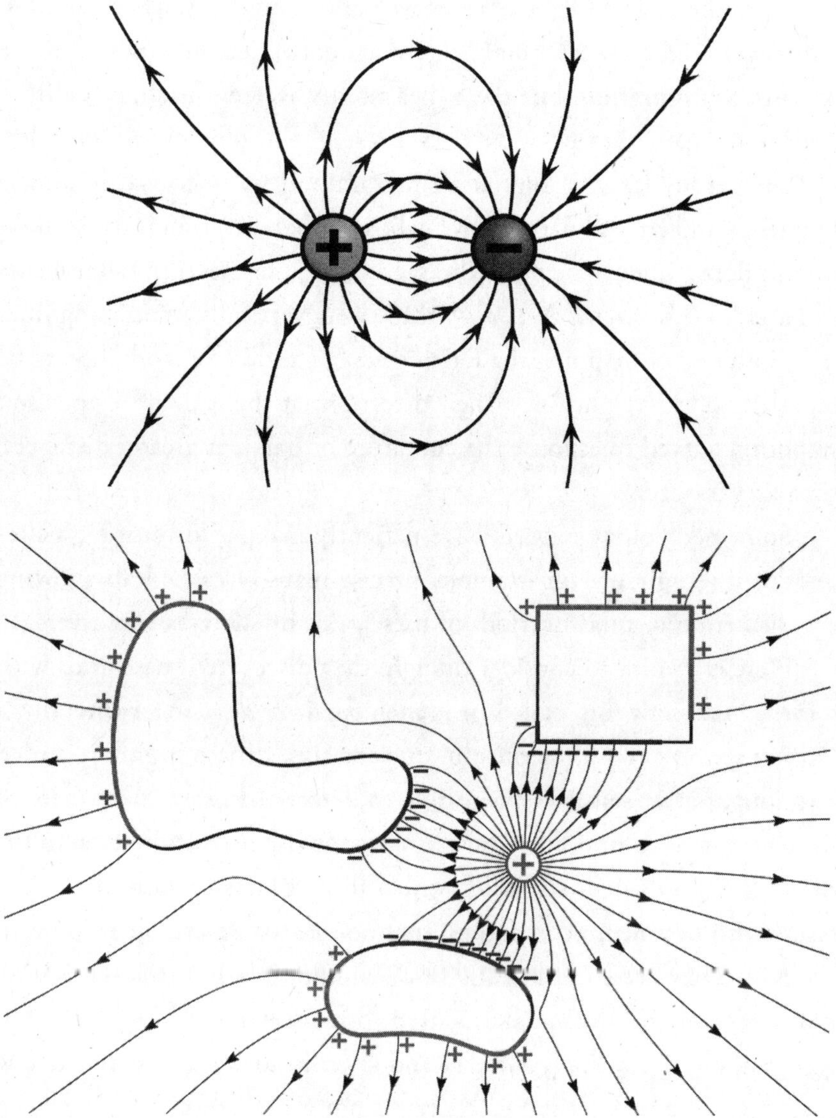

Fig. 10.5. Electric (E) fields.
Top: E field surrounding a positive (+) and a negative (-) charge
Photo by Geek3

Bottom: The electric field (lines with arrows) of a charge (+) induces surface charges areas—positive (+) and negative (-)—on metal objects due to electrostatic induction
Photo by Chetvorno

Thus the H and C grids both have parallel quasi-straight lines crisscrossing at right angles, the C one diagonally; geobiologists all agree on this configuration, but their measured wavelengths slightly differ. Let's note again that no wave is ever straight in physics and even less so in hyperphysics, and that at a finer grain, it will necessarily show a frequency and an undulating wave, whose global direction is the straight line. Indeed, when I mapped the sacred lines connecting monuments in Paris (in *The Sacred Network*), these were vertically undulating lines that, in terms of mapping the Earth grid and sacred network, had to be represented as straight lines (their direction) at the scale of regions, yet smoothly curved to espouse the curvature of Earth at greater distances, such as a country.

Some geobiology experts have patiently mapped diverse high sites and ley lines, giving, for example, precise maps of cathedrals showing the distortion or modifications of these grids by subterranean rivers.

Here is a point to consider though: they discovered these grids with a forked dowser's rod, called in French *baguette de sourcier* (literally, a "spring-seeker's rod"), because in ancient times these highly regarded and sought-after sensitives were able to detect the exact spot where to dig a well so as to find subterranean water or else petroleum, even in the driest lands—a talent so well-founded in real facts (behold their contracts with petroleum companies) that no one would ever question it in the past. They used a forked rod or a pendulum, *because* the waves were not detectable by any apparatus used to register EM waves and fields. In short, it's highly likely these H and C grids do *not* belong to the EM spectrum, and hence their discovery is not a proven scientific fact *yet*. In contrast, the geomagnetic grid is part of an essential science about the enveloping magnetosphere protecting Earth from solar flares and cosmic radiation.

Thus, we have to assume that if these H and C grids are not spacetime EM waves, they are necessarily hyperdimensional waves. Furthermore, geobiologists mapped these grids within sacred architectural sites, where the lines, however thin (in the centimeter range) were strong and possibly influenced by the architecture; they must have been also modified by the widely larger curved sacred lines (about two to three inches for the minutest ones) and their usual crossings over sacred monuments. Let's look at the latter, as I've studied them in detail.

The Sacred Network Lines Turning Around Earth

I have been able to perceive often and with great clarity the lines of the sacred network interconnecting sacred buildings, and even standing stones, while meditating under the domes of churches or on-site. They are large, curved lines undulating above, and then under, the Earth's surface—thus going upward (a half wavelength) then downward under the surface (a half wavelength), on and on. The sacred monuments

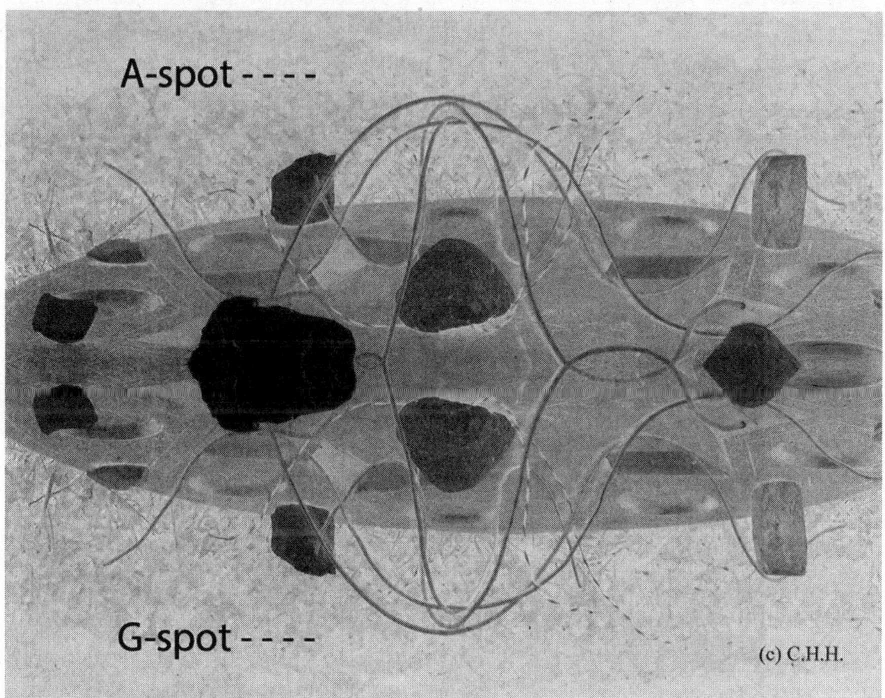

Fig. 10.6. Crossing of four cosmo-telluric lines undulating vertically. Ascending spot: crossing above ground (spiritualizing); grounding spot: crossing below ground (healing)
Concept and digital artwork by Chris H. Hardy (*The Sacred Network*, plate 2)

or standing stones were erected precisely at their crossings, to utilize their *ascending* and spiritualizing energy (A-spot) or their *grounding* and healing effect (G-spot), with the stones or monuments lifting the crossing's height to above their tops (see fig. 10.6).

The largest lines have a half wavelength of about five hundred yards in open terrain, three or four feet in width, and they turn around the planet. In *The Sacred Network*, I've analyzed in detail how these vertical arcs intersect in a star fashion, always with an even number of lines (which is obvious since they keep running through the crossings). Thus, there is a stark discrepancy between the large-scale curved sacred lines and the straight H and C grids ostensibly working at a much smaller scale—I made that very clear in that book. However, there seems to be more to these H and C grids than I understood at the time, as we'll see now.

A CHECKERBOARD HYPERDIMENSION PERVADING SPACETIME

All this leads me to reevaluate the barrier I fought against during the ayahuasca experience. If it wasn't the roof's curved EM field, what then did I "see" as crisscrossing straight waves in my superconscious state?

In fact, these two orthogonal sets of parallel straight waves reflect quite accurately the dream image of quantum physicist Wolfgang Pauli that alerted him about the existence of a deep reality, deeper than the quantum mechanical level of organization. (My study of Pauli's dreams has convinced me that he was truly connected to the HD and that his "visions" were as accurate as Kekulé's ones.) In Pauli's dream, the "deeper reality" level is itself represented by these intersecting sets of straight lines running diagonally, through or above which runs a single undulating line.

Let's keep in mind, though, that *a grid of finely undulating lines would be schematized by straight lines*, as in Pauli's drawing. Thus, the single large undulating line (in Pauli's drawing) is possibly a higher-dimensional wave created by the basic grid, itself already HD at its lowest frequencies . . . or else it could be the even higher level of HD pilot waves, which the hyperdimensional Selfs are able to steer purposely. Thus, could my heightened mind's intent on controlling the roof-grid be such a higher-scale wave? Because, in my perception of the waves' rhythm, I was able to zoom in and then adjust to their frequency (the low-HD frequency waves superposed to the electricity grid), which means that my superconscious mind was at a much higher frequency. And how was this rhythm interlaced with HD waves?

Form (Center-HD) and Frequencies (Rhythm-HD) Interlaced

So let me make sense, as we stand now, of the frequency patterns linked to these different layers and scales.

All in all, there seems to be a mysterious interaction and intersection of form and frequencies that plays between spacetime and the HD. In ISST's HD layer, form is hyperspace (Center-HD) and frequencies are hypertime (Rhythm-HD), and both HD braids are enmeshed; that is, influencing each other. Moreover, they are also entwined with a third braid, Syg-HD, which gives them a crucial consciousness component. So let me list what we have gathered so far:

- Sacred objects, as well as landscapes, show one or more hyperdimensional layered reflections (vertical and upward), as in the altar objects and the superposed landscape.
- The Hartmann and Curry grids, being non-EM, are perforce hyperdimensional.
- In spacetime, form is modulating the frequency (length of strings, patterns of sound waves in rhythm landscapes and cymatics).
- There is a higher dimensionality to sound (as frequency) revealed by the way it interacts with form—such as a square or a round—in cymatics.
- There seems to be a higher dimensionality (of an HD type) to EM fields (ISST research; Hardy 2024).
- ISST posits that in quantum waves, the waves themselves (the

> superposed states in the wavefunction) have a higher, HD, dimensionality than the particles (e.g., electrons in the E circuit) to which they are linked; ISST projects that the wave components are in fact hyperdimensional pilot waves (Hardy 2020 (PSTJ)). (Or to put it another way, that the pilot waves modeled by Louis de Broglie and David Bohm are in fact hyperdimensional.)

Pauli's Deep Reality is represented by two sets of lines intersecting diagonally (just as on the Hartmann grid), on which runs a loose undulating line (see fig. 10.7).

This large undulating line could be the HD pilot wave I postulate and that, entwined with Syg-HD, would express the power and influence of the Selfs (cosmic consciousness) on the spacetime world (such as the power of intent, healing, PK, etc.)

My persistent perception of the grid on the sky in Brittany and Nasik, while I detected the limit of a Telhar field on the ground (both verified several times), presented grayish quasi straight lines crisscrossing

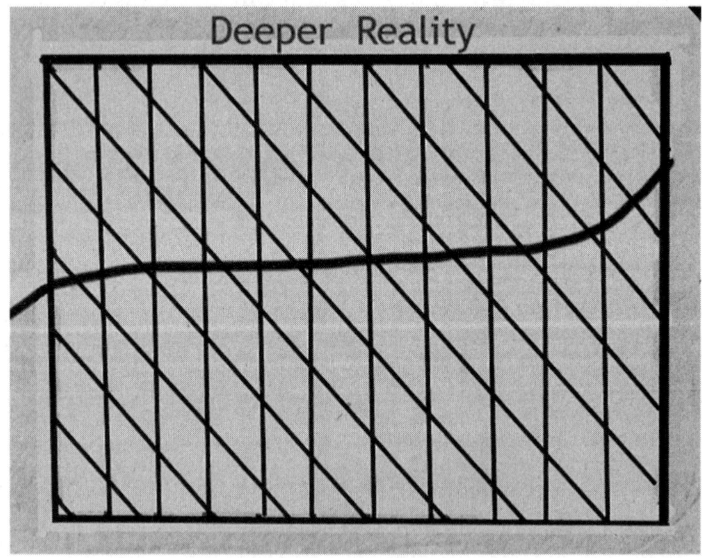

Fig. 10.7. Pauli's Deep Reality dream.
In Pauli and Jung, 2014: Letter 62, May 27, 1953.
Digitized by Chris H. Hardy

orthogonally, forming slightly elongated squares. But for an observer under the zenith (or near to it), the geodesics of a half sphere dome made of such a checkerboard would present more elongated rectangles on the sides, compared to quasi squares at the zenith (in terms of perception). The stupendous Roman mosaic in fig. 10.8 shows how a geodesic dome is constructed, this one with two centers (an ellipse as its cornerstone). It gives us an explanation for how the large, curved sacred lines creating the Telhar fields domes can, by their interference and crisscrossing, create such a checkerboard grid high in space, delimiting quasi squares with slightly curved lines. It is extremely informative since the Brittany sky-grid must have had two centers: the monastery and the dolmen.

Now block with your hand two-thirds of the image on the right and imagine you stand under a dome like the one-third on the left; at the center, you'll see quasi squares (just as I saw them in the sky-grids), yet

Fig. 10.8. Two-center geodesic Roman mosaic floor, second century CE, Getty Museum
Photo courtesy of Carolyn Whitson, from her website Pilgrim to the Past

on the sides (top and bottom of the image) they will appear as elongated rectangles.

In both occurrences (Brittany and Nasik), we have the three entwined braids of the ISST hyperdimension: the Telhar field born out of the harmony and synchrony of minds in a sacred place (Syg-HD, hyperconsciousness); the quasi-spatial form of a half sphere—the overwhelming dome and its round limit at the base (Center-HD, hyperspace); and the frequency and wavelengths of the HD lines constituting the sky-grid (Rhythm-HD, hypertime). And without false humility, for me, this counts as a significant corroboration of the core nature of the HD as three entwined braids. (Similarly, space and time are indissolubly interlaced in our physical world, as Albert Einstein postulated in his General Relativity theory, which was later vindicated by loads of facts.)

Hyper-Consciousness (Syg-HD) Entwined with Form (Center-HD) and Frequencies (Rhythm-HD)

However, my line of thoughts about the checkerboard sky-grids suddenly branched to another type of checkerboard, this one at the scale of particles—that I postulated in *Cosmic DNA at the Origin* (244–46)—and that has the interesting characteristic of being a switchboard between the hyperdimension and spacetime (at the particles/waves scale), yet operates also at the level of a person's syg-field. (I have to introduce a few terms, but I'm going to do it sparingly. Bear with me. Of course, this goes without saying, this is all ISST, a postulated theory, not mainstream stuff.)

We know already about the universe consisting of two domains:

- *QST or quantum-space-time*; i.e., 4D-matter, spacetime, and the EM spectrum, down to the quantum scale of particles (themselves following spacetime laws; for example, the light-speed limit).
- *CSR-HD*, the *Center-Syg-Rhythm* triune hyperdimension, with its three entwined braids: Center-HD, hyperspace; Syg-HD, hyperconsciousness; and Rhythm-HD, hypertime.

Thus, reality consists of two superposed domains (or manifolds) that have to interact with each other for the world to exist and function. I proposed that the switchboard was within the particles themselves (whose core is a compact, curled, triune 5th D), in the sense that each particle would have two possible states, one focused on (and linked to) spacetime and the other on the HD. Thus a particle is either in CSR-focus *or* in QST-focus, and it will constantly shift from one state to the other, at blurring speed (for more detail, see Hardy 2015, chapter 7, 240–44).

- *When CSR-focused*, the wave-particle is open and interconnected with the Syg-HD (all connected HD syg-fields and Selfs); and the higher its *semantic intensity*, the stronger its influence on connected systems. Moreover, the syg-field of a person, at a larger scale, operates the same way and also switches focus. And this is the reason we can interconnect with our HD-Self and experience a range of spiritual and psi capacities, from intuitions, precognitive dreams, synchronicities, and insights up to the highest states of fusion ego-Self in meditation and peak states.
- *When QST-focused*, the particle bathes in the fields of interactions of matter and energy particles (EM fields, strong or weak forces, etc.). It is then subjected to causal and in-forming forces.

How, then, does a field of particles operate?

Stationary waves and many other types of EM fields pervade our 4D world—one being all over the planet as a grid: the geomagnetic field. Thus the real world is replete with patterns of interferences between EM waves belonging to the same system or to different EM fields. So that any wave-particle (aka string-particle) has to be integrated in a field of crisscrossing wave-particle systems.

A befitting representation would thus be a checkerboard of interfering waves/particles (see fig. 10.9), where each square represents one wave-particle. Each particle is a superposed system with two alternating

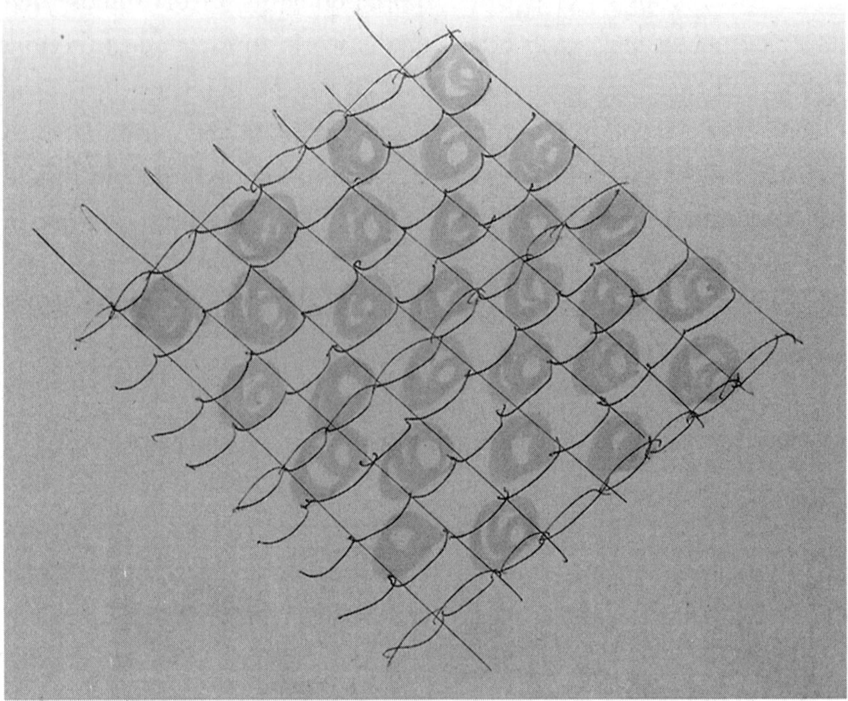

Fig. 10.9. Checkerboard representation of a field of particles with alternating focus: CSR-focus (grey) and QST-focus (blank)
Concept and artwork by Chris H. Hardy (*Cosmic DNA at the Origin*, 246)

focus-states (grey/CSR, blank/QST), with the square it occupies shifting ceaselessly from grey to blank.

Since, in this framework, all wave-particles in the universe are switching ceaselessly but alternatively in space (all the blank squares become grey at the same split-instant and vice versa), the checkerboard reality itself remains stable on the physical layer, because at any point in time, only half of its particles are focused on the hyperdimension.

The Hyperdimensional Checkerboard at Different Scales

We now reach a holistic understanding of the hyperdimensional energy—made of sygons, the HD strings (virtual particles) of syg-energy—as it pierces through spacetime at different scales:

- The sky-grid, perforce HD, enclosing in a half sphere specific Telhar fields harmonizing people between them and with the sacred places, these dome-like Telhar fields featuring a ground-level circumference ranging from about three hundred yards wide (in Brittany) to possibly one mile long (in Nasik).
- Pauli's deep reality (aka HD) structure (under the large sinusoidal wave).
- The H and/or C grids, at the sacred monuments and high sites scale.
- The checkerboard of crisscrossing waves created at the octagonal roof level, entwining EM (60-Hz) fields and the HD.
- The checkerboard of a field of particles/HD-strings alternating from CSR-focus to QST-focus, with all their connections, as the double-edged boundary between quantum and HD-fields. (This is congruent with all quantum fields being modeled as surfaces as well as with Jack Sarfatti's modeling of the quantum void as a dual membrane, a complex flat surface. See Sarfatti 2006.)
- The checkerboard of our personal syg-field, with its HD-strings, the sygons, thus connected to either the 4D or the HD reality of consciousness; this giving us the capacity to choose to connect and expand our consciousness to either of them at any moment.

A Holistic View of the Hyperdimensional Sky-Grid

Can we make sense of this rich yet variegated information about the HD in a way that expresses its holistic and unified reality, as well as its integration with our matter reality?

I think that the *two-focus checkerboard* is *the* core organization of the unified 4D+HD reality (beyond being a fecund model), given that it appears as a core system in peak states known as reaching beyond spacetime. Furthermore, the checkerboard is also an omnipresent symbol and archetype of gigantic proportions of the interlaced black-and-white reality—represented as a tiled checkered floor in Freemasonry, alchemy, architecture, and art, as well as strategy (chess) and war games.

In a Quora discussion titled "Why do Masonic lodges have checkered floors?" I found this stunning answer: "They believe that in order to find balance, both light and darkness are part of the same whole. The balance of that duality [is] made whole through the ratio of Phi 1.618 also known as the golden mean." (*Phi* is also called the golden number; see Ghyka 2016.) Now, that's interesting, given that any golden spiral (such as the cosmic ISS at the origin) evolves, due to *phi*, with a new quarter *circle* within a *square* whose radius grows on the logarithm of *phi*. In a golden spiral, we have thus an interlacing of the circle with the square—another set of basic dualities, such as black and white.

Another key element of a coherent and unified 4D+HD reality lies in the *sky-grids encompassing a Telhar field*. Namely, a sacred place/building supports an HD Telhar field of shared consciousness, contained within a half sphere standing on the ground, and whose outer and upper boundary is a geodesic HD-grid of quasi squares, delineated by slightly curved HD waves (often represented as straight for simplification). Its base and limit on the ground is also precisely marked and triggers an abrupt shift in consciousness in and out of the Telhar field. This Telhar field buttresses a harmony of minds within the field, with telepathic and synchrony properties having a spiritualizing influence on people. Through their sacred geometry and the Telhar field they help create, these sacred places and temples offer a direct connection to the highest hyperfrequencies of the HD—the archetypal and divine realm.

At a more global, planetary scale, large *sacred lines* undulate vertically at the surface of earth, attracted and raised by all summits (of mountains, for example), pointed spires, or tips of domes; they are geomagnetic (GM) lines that are charged by cosmic and hyperdimensional syg-energy when above ground, and charged by, and resonating to, earth energy when underground. *These sacred lines thus instantiate the higher dimensionality of EM/GM waves and fields and particularly those of the geomagnetic field.*

This is why temples and standing stones were erected precisely under their crossings by the sages of old who knew their spiritualizing and elevating or healing effect on people. Crossings have an ascending energy, a spiritualizing/elevating influence when happening above ground; and they have a grounding influence and enhance healing when happening below ground—with major temples such as cathedrals with their crypts or Greek temples with their dream-healing caves (*asclepieion*) having both at once.

I've recounted in *The Sacred Network* my own natural seeing-cum-sensing of these lines (without any dowser's rod), and I've no doubt that the megalithic people who erected dolmens and menhirs could also simply see them as well as the antenna and anchoring role of huge trees, pointed stones and pillars, and mountain peaks. In my view, they transmitted the tradition of the leys and crossing points to a line of seers and initiates, and it eventually made its way to the Druids, then the Templars and Freemasonry in the West, with similar traditions transmitted in *all* other major cultures (such as that of the dragon ley lines in Chinese and Taoist-derived feng shui, the Dreamtime lines or paths of the Australian Aborigines, and the cult of sacred trees and megaliths in all shamanic cultures).

And this is why a core principle of sacred architecture and geomancy is that all monuments must be not only set under crossings but moreover oriented according to these undulating sacred lines turning around the world, with their spiritualizing and inspiring influence—and not according to the geometrical checkerboard grid, despite the fact that its HD-sygons at the core of matter-particles keep breathing in and out the hyperdimension. All ancient sacred buildings on Earth have been traditionally oriented toward the main sacred lines crossing at that place (I verified this in Paris and several regions of France). Thus, the main entrance of a temple always faces the main sacred line bringing in cosmic energy, and its global form and architecture will fit the specific crossing of lines; for example, a four-line crossing above ground (eight vectors, as in the A-spot on fig. 10.6 above) will be expressed by an octagonal tower with its central spire at the exact point of the crossing, as in the abbey of Notre-Dame d'Aigues-Vives (at Faverolles-sur-Cher, France).

Thus, at our human psychic level, our own Selfs are attuned to the hyperdimension in many different ways and are breathing in and out the vital and sacred prana energy (syg-energy) carried by the sacred lines, as well as leaving our own print and soul signature on them.

CONCLUSION

INTENDING A SOUL-HARMONIZED AND ECO-FRIENDLY PLANET

My hope with this book is to show that, indeed, the soft power of our soul and Self, and especially our collective intelligence as interconnected and harmonized Selfs, are not just an ideal vision but something we can make happen and achieve in our own lives, and by extension, they are our assets in this battle for our humanity and our planet.

We have to reach a shared-mind state—a telepathic-harmonic field, or Telhar field—at the scale of the planet.

In fact, if Telhar fields are experienced first at the group level, such as collective prayer or musical jam sessions, they are meant to become the collective state of consciousness of the whole of humanity as great scientists and sages have predicted.

We have to strive toward the Omega Point that Teilhard de Chardin has anticipated—a collective harmonization of the mind-sphere of humanity he called the *noosphere.* We have to steer the spiritual metamorphosis of humanity in sync with the planet that Carl Jung predicted.

Let us then work ceaselessly to co-create a stable harmonic-telepathic field at the planetary level. Despite mighty antagonistic winds, or rather because of them, we have to strive for a harmonized and pacified humanity, in deep accord with natural systems.

Let us keep our intent as a polestar always guiding us until we establish a lasting ban on war and total demilitarization of Earth and, even more crucially, the destruction of all nuclear stockpiles and weapons on Earth.

The *post-nuclear humanity* is an inescapable aim for us humans if we want, and if we are, to survive on this planet and other ones we'll inhabit. And I have no doubt we'll ultimately succeed in becoming, as many traditions have predicted, a harmonized and therefore sacred planet. And when we have achieved this, then the gate to the positive interconnection with other alien worlds will be open, and our integration into the galactic federation (whose probability of existence is overwhelming) will follow. And through this integration, an immense scope of accumulated galactic knowledge, and especially the revelation of our true history as a star-traveling human race, will be our inheritance.

BIBLIOGRAPHY

Avalon, Arthur [Woodroffe, Sir John]. *The Serpent Power.* Garden City, NY: Dover Publications, 1974.

Bagnall, Oscar. *The Origin and Properties of the Human Aura.* New York: Weiser, 1975.

Benor, Daniel. *Spiritual Healing: Scientific Validation of a Healing Revolution.* Bellmawr, NJ: Wholistic Healing, 2001.

Bohm, David. *Wholeness and the Implicate Order.* London: Routledge & Kegan Paul, 1980.

Bohm, David, and Basil J. Hiley. *The Undivided Universe: An Ontological Interpretation of Quantum Theory.* London: Routledge, 1993.

Bramly, Serge. *Macumba: The Teachings of Maria-José, Mother of the Gods.* San Francisco: City Lights Publishers, 2001.

Braude, Stephen E. *The Limits of Influence: Psychokinesis and the Philosophy of Science.* New York: Routledge & Kegan Paul, 1986.

Carr, Bernard. "Seeking a New Paradigm of Matter, Mind and Spirit." *Network Review*, Spring 2010.

———. *Universe or Multiverse.* Cambridge, UK: Cambridge Univ. Press, 2009.

Castaneda, Carlos. *The Fire from Within.* New York: Pocket Books, 1991.

———. *The Power of Silence.* New York: Pocket Books, 1991.

Coarer-Kalondan, Edmond, and Dana, Gwezenn. *Les Celtes et les extra-terrestres.* Paris: Marabout, 1973.

Combs, Allan, and Mark Holland. *Synchronicity: Science, Myth, and the Trickster.* New York: Marlowe, 1995.

Donnars, Jacques. *La transe, technique d'épanouissement.* Paris: L'homme et la connaissance, 1981.

Dossey, Larry. *Recovering the Soul: A Scientific and Spiritual Approach.* New York: Bantam New Age Books, 1989.

Eliade, Mircea. *Shamanism: Archaic Techniques of Ecstasy.* Bollingen Series, 24. Princeton, NJ: Princeton Univ. Press, 2004.

Evans-Wentz, W. Y. *Tibet's Great Yogi Milarepa.* New York: New Age Books, 2004.

———, ed. *Tibetan Yoga and Secret Doctrines: Seven Books of Wisdom of the Great Path, According to the Late Lama Kazi Dawa-Samdup's English Rendering.* New York: Oxford Univ. Press, Or. 1935/2000.

Ghyka, Matila. *The Golden Number.* Rochester, VT: Inner Traditions, 2016.

Hardy, Chris H. *Butterfly Logic: Experimental Planet Earth.* USA (online): CreateSpace IPP/Chris H. Hardy, 2016.

———. "Collective Consciousness & World-Soul: From Ancient Sages, to Jung, to a Hyperdimension of Selfs." *Journal of Consciousness Exploration & Research* 15, no. 3 (December 2024): 255–83.

———. *Cosmic DNA at the Origin: A Hyperdimension Before the Big Bang. The Infinite Spiral Staircase Theory.* USA (online): CreateSpace IPP/ Chris H. Hardy.

———. *DNA of the Gods: The Anunnaki Creation of Eve and the Alien Battle for Humanity.* Rochester, VT: Bear and Co., 2014.

———. "An Ego-Self Attunement Dynamics via a Retrocausal-Attractor Steering Self Awareness: A Hyperdimensional & Chaos Theory Framework. *Journal of Consciousness Exploration & Research* (JCER), 15, no. 1 (2024): 01–24.

———. *Living Souls in the Spirit Dimension: The Afterlife and Transdimensional Reality.* Rochester, VT: Inner Traditions, Bear & Co., 2020.

———. "Nonlocal Consciousness in the Universe: Panpsychism, Psi & Mind over Matter in a Hyperdimensional Physics." *Journal of Nonlocality* 5, no. 1 (June 2017): 1–21.

———. "Quantum Coherence, Telepathic Fields, Time-Travel & the Texture of Hyperdimension." *Prespacetime Journal* 11, no. 4 (August 2020): 369–92.

———. "A 'Retrocausal Attractor' Model of Visualization & Psychic Healing: Hyperdimensional Pilot Waves?" *Prespacetime Journal* (PSTJ) 12, no. 3 (August 2021): 300–24.

———. *The Sacred Network*. Rochester, VT: Inner Traditions, 2011.

———. "Synchronicity: Interconnection Through a Semantic Dimension." Paper presented at the Faculdades Integradas Second Psi Meeting, Curitiba, Brazil, April 21–26, 2004.

Hermes Trismegistus. *The Discourse on the Eighth and Ninth.* Translated by J. Brashler, P. A. Dirkse, and D. M. Parrott. In *Corpus Hermeticum*, available online at the Gnostic Society Library.

James, William. "Confidences of a Psychical Researcher." *American Magazine* 68 (1909): 589.

Jung, Carl Gustav. *Memories, Dreams, Reflections*. New York: Vintage, 1965.

———. *The Structure and Dynamics of the Psyche.* Vol. 8 of *The Collected Works of C. G. Jung*, edited by G. Adler and R. F. Hull. Bollingen Series. Princeton, NJ: Princeton University Press, 1960.

———. *Synchronicity: An Acausal Connecting Principle.* Vol. 8 of *The Collected Works of C. G. Jung*, edited by G. Adler and R. F. Hull. 20 vols. Princeton, NJ: Princeton University Press, 1960.

Jung, Carl G., and Wolfgang Pauli. *The Interpretation of Nature and the Psyche*. New York: Pantheon Books, 1955.

Krippner, Stanley, and P. Welch. *Spiritual Dimensions of Healing*. New York: Irvington, 1992.

LaBerge, Stephen, and Howard Rheingold. *Exploring the World of Lucid Dreaming*. New York: Ballantine Books, 1990.

Lovelock, James. *Gaia: A New Look at Life on Earth.* Oxford, UK: Oxford University. Press, 1979.

———. *The Ages of Gaia*. New York: Bantam, 1990.

McRae, Ronald. *Mind Wars: The True Story of Government Research into the Military Potential of Psychic Weapons.* New York: St. Martin's, 1984.

Mishlove, Jeffrey. *The Roots of Consciousness*. New York: Random House, 1975.

Moga, Margaret. "Magnetic Field Activity During Psychic Healing: A Preliminary Study with Healing Touch Practitioners." *Journal of Nonlocality* 3, no. 1 (2014): 1–23.

Monroe, Robert. *Journeys out of the Body*. New York: Broadway Books, 1992.

Morcol, Goktug, and Linda F. Dennard, eds. *New Sciences for Public Administration and Policy: Connections and Reflections*. Corpus Christi, TX: Chatelaine Press, 2000.

Nelson, Roger D., G. J. Bradish, Y. H. Dobyns, B. J. Dunne, and R. G. Jahn. "FieldREG Anomalies in Group Situations." *Journal of Scientific Exploration* 10, no. 1 (1996): 111–41.

Pauli, Wolfgang, and C. G. Jung. *Atom and Archetype. The Pauli/Jung Letters, 1932–1958*. Edited by C. A. Meier. Princeton, NJ: Princeton University Press, 2014.

Plato. *The Dialogues of Plato*. New York: Thoemmes Press, 1997.

Poincaré, Henry. *Science and Method*. New York: Dover Publications, 1952. Originally published in 1908 by Dover.

Potts, M. "Religious Levitation." *Psi Encyclopedia*. London: Society for Psychical Research website, March 9, 2015.

Radin, Dean. *The Conscious Universe*. New York: HarperOne, 2009.

———. *Entangled Minds*. New York: Paraview Pocket Books, 2006.

Radin, Dean, and Roger Nelson. "Evidence for Consciousness-Related Anomalies in Random Physical Systems." *Foundations of Physics*, 19, no. 12 (1989): 1499–514.

Ramacharaka, Yogi. *The Science of Psychic Healing*. Mumbai, India: D.B. Taraporevala Sons, 1997.

Rumi, Mevlana (Molana). *53 Secrets from the Tavern of Love*. Translated by A. Banani and A. A. Lee. Ashland, OR: White Cloud Press, 2014.

Sarfatti, J. *Super Cosmos: Through Struggles to the Stars*. (*Space-Time and Beyond III*). Bloomington, IN: Author House, 2006.

Schlitz, Marilyn. *Death Makes Life Possible: Revolutionary Insights on Living, Dying, and the Continuation of Consciousness*. Louisville, CO: Sounds True, 2015.

Schlitz, Marilyn, T. Amorok, and M. Micozzi. *Consciousness and Healing: Integral Approaches to Mind-Body Medicine*. London: Churchill Livingstone, 2004.

Schwartz, Stephan. *Opening to the Infinite*. Nemoseen Media, 2007.

———. "Six Protocols, Neuroscience, and Near Death: An Emerging Paradigm Incorporating Nonlocal Consciousness." *Explore* 11, no. 4 (July–Aug. 2015): 252–60.

Schwartz, Stephan, and Larry Dossey. "Nonlocality, Intention, and Observer

Effects in Healing Studies: Laying a Foundation for the Future." *Explore* 6, no. 5 (2010): 295–307.

Targ, Russell, and Harold Puthoff. *Mind-Reach: Scientists Look at Psychic Abilities.* Charlottesville, VA.: Hampton Roads, 2005.

Tart, Charles, ed. *Altered States of Consciousness: A Book of Readings.* New York: John Wiley and Sons, 1969.

Teilhard de Chardin, Pierre. *Phenomenon of Man.* New York: Harper & Row, 1965.

Tsogyal, Yeshe. *The Lotus-Born: The Life Story of Padmasambhava.* Boulder, CO: Rangjung Yeshe Publications, 2004.

Ullman, Montague, Stanley Krippner, and Alan Vaughan. *Dream Telepathy: Experiments in Nocturnal ESP.* New York: Macmillan, 1973.

Vivekananda, Swami. *Raja Yoga*. Kolkata, India: Advaita Ashrama, 1982.

von Bertalanffy, Ludwig. *General System Theory: Foundations, Development, Applications.* New York: G. Braziller, 1968.

Yogananda, Paramahansa. *Autobiography of a Yogi.* Los Angeles: Self-Realization Fellowship, Or. 1946/2014.

INDEX

Page numbers in *italics* indicate illustrations

acausal/lity, 178, 277
Advaita (Vedanta). See nonduality
afterlife, 248, 276
aikido, 33, 40–41, 47, 50, 56, 127
alchemy/ical, 14, 75, 214, 230, 239, 269
alien (E.T.), 56, 274, 276
ally/ies, v, 5, 12, 76–99, 108, 121, 128, 137
  dog, 79–82, 95, 99, 126, *129*
altar, viii, 41, *129*, 184, 220, 227–30, 263. *See also* sacred (object)
altered, 11, 100, 115, 159, 162, 185, 191, 216, 242, 279
angel, 9, 13, 26, 75
anima, 75–76, 242
animal (ally), v, 12, 78–99, 137
animus, 75–76
antler, vii, 85–90
Anunnaki, vii, 87–88, 276
archetype/pal, viii, 14, 90, 118, *133*, 136, 196, 227, 230, 232, 238–9, 250–51, 269–70, 278. *See also* dream
ascended (soul), 157, 199, 244, 248, 270
astral, 38, 50, 179, 182–3, 186, 190, 198–202, 221, 226–27, 245, 247–8. *See also* OBE
  a. travel/er, 43, 186, 198–99, 202, 207, 221, 226–27, 247
  a. body, 38, 50, 179, 182–83, 186, 190, 198–202, 221, 245, 247–48. *See also* energy-body
atman, 21, 59, 181–82. *See also* Self
aura, ix, 48, 64, 94, 104, 143, 150–1, 204, 209, 220, 222–23, 275, *pl. 2. See also* chakra, energy-body
ayahuasca, 183–85, 189–90, 196, 200, 204, 251, 262

ba (bird), ix, 122, 248
bio-PK, 42, 75, 130. *See also* healing
biosystem, 74

Bon/-po, 140, 144, 182
boundary, 190, 254–56, 269–70
brahman, 38, 59, 204. *See also* cosmic consciousness, Tao
Buddha/ism, 3, 5, 124, 182, 199

caduceus, vii, 89–90
candelabra, ix, 239–40, *241*, 243
cathedral, 249, 255, 252, 260, 271
Celt/ic, ix, 56, 84–87, *86*, 87, 90–91, 95–7, 222, 227, 255, *pl. 5*. *See also* Druid
Center-HD (hyperspace), 192, 239, 250–52, 256, 263, 266
Center-Syg-Rhythm. *See* CSR
Cernunnos, vii, ix, 84–91, *pl. 5*
chakra, 38–41, 47, 59, 87, 166–67, 181, 186, 220–21, 226–27
  vibrating c., 206–18
chaos (theory), 8, 145–46, 276
clairvoyance, 128, 178, 182, 189, 216. *See also* remote viewing
cognitive, 9, 36, 144, 166, 243, 289
collective intelligence, v, 1–12
collective syg-field, 223, 251–53. *See also* egregore, Telhar
collective unconscious, 2, 14, 37–38, 118, 126, 216
conscious (the), 35–36, 40, 75
cosmic consciousness, 10, 38, 46, 59, 63, 118, 132, 170, 179, 192, 264
cosmo-telluric line, *261*. *See also* ley, sacred line
CSR (Center-Syg-Rhythm HD), 266–69

dance/ing, 100, 102, 115, 117, 127, 141–42, 189, 196–97, 217, 227
deep reality, 9, 2, 8, 119, 130, 204, 229–30, 257, 262, 264, 269. *See also* Pauli
  d. dream, 9, *264*
deer, vii, 84–85, 87–88, *89*, 90
dervish, viii, x, 115, *116*, 117. *See also* Sufi
deva, 5
discrete (structure), 230–31, 251
divination, 127–28, 162–68, 171, 173, 214
dog. *See* ally
dolmen, 255–56, 265
dome, 211, 252, 254, 256, 261, 265–66, 269–70. *See also* geodesic
dorje (Tibetan), 229
dream. *See* archetypal, Pauli, precognitive
dreamtime, 182, 191, 271
Druid/ism, 91, 271
drum/ming, viii, 112, 140–44, *141*, 190, 192, 194

Earth's grid, vi, 12, 245–272
Earth's soul, 2, 11, 23, 59, 110. *See also* Gaia
ego (& Self), 11, 13–14, 31, 204, 226, 231, 276
  e. consciousness, 37, 50–51
ego-Self (fusion), 14, 51, 59, 149, 159, 244, 251, 267, 276
egregore, 252–53. *See also* collective syg-field

Egypt, viii, ix, 87–90, 102, *103*, 112, *236*, 245, 248, 250,
electrocution, 31, 40, 69–73
electromagnetic/ism, viii, 9, 12, 35, 38, 177, *178*, 200, 206, 255, 258. *See also* EM
EM, 38, 177, 179, 183, 191, 200–205, 220, 249, 257–58, 260, 262–63, 266–67, 269–70
empathy, 21, 66, 71, 76, 95, 111, 225
energy. *See* syg-energy
energy-body, 12, 14, 38–39, 64, 179–82, 186–87, 199–226, 238, 247–48, 251–2. *See also* astral, aura
Enki, 5, 84, 87–89, 91
entanglement, 201
esoteric societies, 252
experiment, 10, 24, 41–43, 129, 179, 193, 200, 214–16, 245–47
Eye of Ra, ix, 235–6, *236*

faster-than-light, 73, 119, 169, 183
Fibonacci, 230–31
Flight of the Pi, ix, 232–38, *233*, *234*
focus (CSR-f./QST-f.), ix, 189, 267–69, *268*
Freemason/ry, 252–53, 269, 271
fusion, 11, 13, 51, 83, 110, 117, 132, 138, 149, 159, 156–57, 221, 252, 267

Gaia, v, 5, 11, 13–30, 80, 99, 113, 223, 277
geodesic, ix, 255–56, 265, *265*. *See also* dome
geomagnetic field, 223, 257–58, 267, 270
geometry/ic, 123, 192–93, 202, 238, 245, 250–51, 270
golden number. *See* phi
golden spiral, 230, 250–51, 270
grid (on sky), 12, 264
  sky-g., 256, 265, 269

Hampi, vii–x, 84, 93–94, *93*, 98, 137, 140, *pl. 6*, *pl. 16*
harmony, 13, 59, 76, 109–10, 117, 207, 240, 244, 254, 256, 266, 270. *See also* Telhar
HD. *See* Center-HD, CSR, Rhythm-HD, Syg-HD
healing, 9, 14, 17, 42, 51, 90, 129, 182, 199, 204, 207, 239, *261*, 262, 264, 275, 277–79. *See also* bio-PK
  dream-healing cave, 271
Hermes, vii, 84, 87, 89–91, *90*, 132–36, *133*, 277, *pl. 8*
Hermetic, 14, 75, 150, 215
high place, 81, 94, 138, 232, 235
Hindu/ism, viii, 3, 57, 63, 84, 124, *125*, *141*, 181–82, 199, 210
horn, vii, ix, 21, 60, 87–88, *88*, 90, 92, *pl. 5*. *See also* Cernunnos, Pashupati
hyperconsciousness, 266
hyperdimension. *See* Center-HD, CSR, Rhythm-HD, Syg-HD
hyperfrequency, 210, 230
hyperspace/tial, 12, 38, 170, 177, 192, 202, 239, 250–51, 256, 263, 266

hypertime, 38, 170, 177, 192, 251, 256, 263, 266
hypnosis, 137

I-Ching, 4, 162, 165
I-consciousness, 43, 50, 56, 130, 179, 198, 201, 207, 221, 223, 226–67
Indus Valley, vii, i, 88–89, 91–92
invisible, 26, 43, 46, 149–52, 155, 172, 235
ISS/T, *Infinite Spiral Staircase* theory, 158–59, 179, 181, 183, 189, 192, 200, 202–4, 220, 230–31, 250–51, 356, 263–64, 266, 270

James, William, 118
Jung, Carl, /ian, 8, 9, 21, 37–38, 74–76, 118–19, 130, 146, 178, 182, 239–40, 243, 250, *264*, 273, 276–68, 289. *See also* archetype

Kaluza, Theodor, 177, 202
Karnak, viii, ix, 104, *104*, *105*
Kekulé, viii, 189, 196, *196*, 197, 201, 262
Khmer, 5
kundalini, 31, 36, 39–40, 46–47, 59, 87, 153, 181, 210, 228

layer/ed, 3, 39, 111, 118–19, 130, 192, 211, 221, 229
  HD l., 222, 230, 239, 263, 268
ley, 223, 258, 260, 271. *See also* sacred line
liberation (state of), 46, 59, 64
little deva, 5
Luxor, viii, ix, 102, 104–5, *248*, *pl. 7*, *pl. 9*

macro-PK, 43
magic/al, 11, 15, 21, 56, 78, 94, 109, 144
mahasiddha, 4. *See also* Padmasambhava
mandala, 184, 187–88, 191, 193, 252, 257
mantra, 7, 59–60
martial art, 33, 35, 39–40, 44, 56, 182
materialist, 3, 33, 36, 81
matter system, 14, 38–39, 51, 74, 119, 204. *See also* biosystem
megalith/ic, 256, 271. *See also* dolmen
Mercury, vii, viii, 89, *90*, 132, *133*. *See also* Hermes
Meteora, ix–x, 232, *233–34*, 238
micro-PK, 43, 215–16
Milarepa, 3, 276
mind-over-matter, 14, 39, 41, 120, 128, 138, 215–16, 243
moksha. *See* liberation
mosaic, ix, 265, *265*
music, 12, 102, 110, 117, 137, 141, 149, 166, 175, 191, 196, 211, 224–25, 228. *See also* Telhar
Myers, Frederic, 118

Naga, 5, 59, 128, *129*
  king/queen, vii, 5, *5*, 89, *129*

Nalanda, 124, 182
Nasik, 254–57, 264, 266, 269
nature spirit, 5, 32. *See also* little deva
near-death experience, 73
Nile, viii, x, 102–12, *103*, *109*, *pl. 10*
nonduality, 181. *See also* Upanishad
nonlocal/ity, 18, 178, 200–201, 276–78, 289

One (The). *See* The One
Oneness (State). *See* samadhi, The One
organization/al (concept), 120, 188, 219, 230, 262, 269
origin (of universe), 38, 57, 203, 230–31, 250–51, 268, 270, 276, 289
Ouroboros, viii, 189, 196, *196*
out-of-body experience (OBE), 43, 182, 186, 198–99, 216, 221–22

Padmasambhava, ix, 3, 4, 5, 279, *pl. 2*
panpsychism, 276
paradigm, 6, 8–9, 11, 14, 33, 36, 74, 188, 217, 275, 278
  cognitivist p., 8
  materialist, 3, 33, 36, 81
parapsychology, 9, 33, 145, 166, 183, 212–13
Pashupati/nath, vii, 84–85, *86*, 87–88, 91
  seal, vii, *86*, 87
  temple, vii, 84, *85*
Pauli, Wolfgang, ix, 75, 119, 130, 156, 239–244, *241*, 250, 257, 262, 264, *264*, 269, 277–78. *See also* deep reality
peak state, 73, 75, 220, 228, 231–32, *233*, 235, 239, 243, 267, 269
PEAR lab, 43, 215
phi (ratio), 230, 235, 249–50, 270
pi, 82–83, 99, 123–24, 137. *See also* Flight of the Pi, Pi gate
Pi gate, vii, viii, 79–84, *85*, 99, 122–26, *125, 126,* 128–29, 137–40, 232, *233–34*, 236, 238
Planck/ian (scale), 38–39, 202–203
  sub-P., 119, 202
Plato/nic, ix, 249–50, *250*, 278
Poincaré, Henri, 197–98, 201, 278
prana/ic, 90, 179, 181, 183, 187, 227, 272
precognition/ive, 9, 36, 122, 127–29, 136, 165, 171, 178, 216
  p. dream, 9, 26, 120, 130, 135–36, 267
predict/ion, 12, 84, 99, 119, 121–22, 128, 130, 135–36, 138, 140, 157, 231–32, 239, 243
proof, 9, 18, 118, 126, 178, 189, 201
  and sigma, 216
protector, 5, 84
psi research/er, 9, 24, 43, 156, 162, 171, 173, 178, 183, 213–14, 216
psychic energy, 1, 3, 36, 46, 150–51, 207
psychokinesis/tic (PK), 9, 33, 41, 51, 120, 127, 215, 243, 275. *See also* bio-PK, micro-PK, macro-PK

psychology/ist (science), 9, 33, 35, 37, 42, 118–19, 145–46, 149, 162, 252
Jungian p., 8–9, 21, 74–76, 239, 289
pyramid, ix–x, 102, 146, 147, 199, 229, 238, 245–49, *246*, 251–52, *pl. 17*
Pythagoras, 249–50

QST (quantum-spacetime), 266–67, *268*, 269. *See also* focus
Quantum Mechanics, 119, 201, 203

Ra (god), ix, 235, 236, *236*
ray (energy), 104, 150, 177–79, 197, 202, 209–10, 231, 249
remote viewing, 216. *See also* clairvoyance
resonance, viii, 75, 192–93, 204, 218, 229, *229*, 230, 232, *233*, 234–36, 238–39, 249
retrocausal/ity, 170, 201, 275–77
Rhine, J. B., 33, 42, 213
Rhythm-HD (hypertime), 192, 251, 256, 263, 266
Roman, ix, 265, *265*

sacred line, 271. *See also* ley
Sacred Network, 235, 260–62
Sacred Network (The), 51, 96, 207, 209–10, 220–21, 232–233, *233*, 251, 258, 260, *261*, 271, 277
sacred (object), 12, 209, 220, 222–23, 227–28, 231, 251, 263
site, 126, 232, 235
sacred volume, vi, ix, 12, 245–72, *250*. *See also* Plato, Pythagoras
sadhu, viii, ix, 46–47, 59, 63, 138, *139*, 223, *pl. 4*
Mataji s., 46–47, 65–66, 223
samadhi, 48, 209, 221
Self. *See* ego-Self
self-defense, v, 12, 31–77, 182, 207
self-development, 3, 11, 13, 183, 221
semantic field. *See* syg-field
Semantic Fields theory (SFT), 8, 144–5, 166, 183, 239, 243
serpent, 5, 88, 181, 189, 275. *See also* Naga, snake
SFT. *See* Semantic Fields theory
Shakti, 181, 204, 210
shaman/ic, 12, 16, 21, 79–82, 99–101, 137, 144, 146–48, 162, 182, 184, 190, 199, 271
Shiva, vii, 46, 58–59, *58*, *59*, 64, 82–91, *83*, *85*, *86*, 138, 181
siddhis, 3–4, 6, 199
snake, vii, 59, *59*, 87, 107, 196. *See also* Naga, Ouroboros, serpent
soul, ix, 1 2, 6, 9 11, 14, 21, 23, 25, 32, 64, 73–75, 77, 80, 95, 99, 110–11, 115, 153, 156, 192, 199, 219, 227, 248, *248*, 272, 273, 276. *See also ba*
spacetime. *See* QST
spiral. *See* golden, ISST
state of consciousness, 21, 100, 138, 158–59, 166, 185–86, 188, 228, 254, 256, 273
sub-Planck. *See* Planck
sub-quantum, 38, 119, 159, 177, 202

Sudan, 105, 107, 112
Sufi, 47, 112, 117, 207, 216, 226
and Dervish/es (whirling), viii, x, 115, *116*, 117, *pl. 6, pl. 13*
Sumer/ian, vii, 5, 84, 87, *88*, 89–91, 289
sun god, vii, viii, 87, *88*, *131*, 135
superconscious/ness, 5, 7, 22, 36–37, 41, 49, 50–51, 196, 222, 262–63
superposed landscape, v, 12, 64, 219–44, 263
supraluminous. *See* faster-than-light
syg-energy, 10, 12, 14, 18, 31, 37–41, 49–51, 56, 73, 90, 119, 158–59, 167, 169, 179–83, 203–4, 209–10, 217–18, 220–23, 231–32, 236–39, 251, 268, 270, 272
syg-field, 18–20, 22, 38, 181, 187, 203–5, 222–23, 230, 238, 247, 251–54, 266–69
Syg-HD, 38, 39, 119, 157, 170, 192, 256, 263–64, 266–67
sygon, 39, 209, 250, 268–69, 271
synchronicity/ies, 2, 10, 12, 21, 23, 25, 37, 75, 110, 129, 145–46, 148, 178, 183, 239, 242–43, 267, 275, 277
fields of, v, 12, 118–48
synchrony, 2, 14, 112, 238, 243, 256, 266, 270

tantra, 4, 181
tantrism/ic, 5, 186, 235
Tao/ism/ist, 4, 38, 84, 199, 204, 271. *See also* I-Ching
telepathy/ic, 9, 14, 18, 48, 65, 96, 134, 156, 158, 185, 190, 207, 222, 235, 239–40, 254–56, 270, 273, 276. *See also* Telhar
Telhar (field), 9, 14, 96, 185, 187, 190, 207, 221, 254, 256, 264–66, 269–70, 273
Templar, 252–53, 271
temple. *See* Pashupatinath, Pi gate
Teotihuacan, vii, x, 101, *101*, 147, 229, *pl. 17*. *See also* Tlaloc
texture, 220, 276
Thailand, vii, 41, 49, 52, *53*, 55, *89*, 176
The One/ness, 11, 117, 23, 181, 204
Tibet/an, 2, 4–5, 44, 63, 143–44, 182, 229, 276. *See also* Buddhism
Tlaloc, 101
Tlalocan (paradise), vii, 101, *101*
torque, 87
trance, 12, 100–102, 112, 115, 134, 141, 162, 182, 186, 199
tree (sacred), 271
Tuatha Dé Danann, 56, *pl.3*

unconscious (the), 35, 80, 118, 128, 130, 163, 197, 243. *See also* collective unconscious
unicorn/fish, vii, ix, 91, *91–92*, *pl. 5*
universe-bubble, 230–31
Upanishad, 153, 181

vision/ary, viii, 8, 12, 66, 82, 84, 110, 120, 122, 126, 128–89, 135, 188–90, 194, *196*, 196–97, 213, 219, 222, 226–32, 237–38, 240, 262

visualization, 1, 19, 22, 160–61, 167, 169–70, 277

vortex/es, 232, *233*

waves of forms, 249

wax (sculpture), viii–ix, 127–28, *129*, 237, 239–44

wheel, 29, 37, 50, 70, 107, 111, 121, 180, 221. *See also* chakra

World Clock (dream), ix, 239–44, *241*. *See also* Pauli

yoga, 13, 59, 142, 276, 279

Yogananda, 3, 279

yogi/c, vii, 2–4, 26, 36, 46–49, 58–59, *59*, 74, 87, 90, 99, 138, 162, 182, 190, 276, 278–89. *See also* Milarepa, Yogananda

ABOUT THE AUTHOR

Systems scientist, PhD in ethnopsychology, and former researcher at Psychophysical Research Laboratories in Princeton, New Jersey, Chris H. Hardy is both a seer and a scientist. After her bachelor's degree, she traveled extensively to the East, Middle East, and Africa to study the ancient paths of wisdom, developing an array of spiritual and psi talents that had blossomed at eighteen with her meditative practice. She then explored thought-provoking psi and mind potentials through systems theory, chaos theory, and Jungian psychology. Along the way, she developed her own cognitive and cosmology theories allowing for psi and transcendent states of consciousness, thus laying the foundation of a hyperdimension of consciousness in the universe (*Cosmic DNA at the Origin*, 2015). The author of more than ninety papers and nineteen books tackling nonlocal consciousness, she is an authority in scientific terms and as an author and lecturer.

Hardy also made an in-depth study of the Sumerian tablets, and their comparison with biblical and Gnostic texts led to two books: *DNA of the Gods* (2014) and *Wars of the Anunnaki* (2016); and she has authored two sci-fi books.

For more information about new book releases and research papers, visit:

Author's website:
https://chris-h-hardy.com

Scientific page:
https://independent.academia.edu/ChrisHHardy

BOOKS OF RELATED INTEREST

DNA of the Gods

The Anunnaki Creation of Eve and the Alien Battle for Humanity

by Chris H. Hardy, Ph.D.

In this book, Chris H. Hardy describes the genetic engineering of humanity by Anunnaki scientist Ninmah whose first female human creation, Tiamat/Eve, contained more alien DNA than the earlier male one, Adamu. She shows that the concepts of sin and the inferiority of women were born out of Enlil's attempts to enslave humanity, but that despite this ongoing history of conflict, we can begin to steer our own planetary destiny.

Wars of the Anunnaki

Nuclear Self-Destruction in Ancient Sumer

by Chris H. Hardy, Ph.D.

Drawing upon the work of Zecharia Sitchin, the Book of Genesis, Sumerian clay tablets, and archaeological evidence such as ancient radioactive skeletons, Chris H. Hardy reveals the ancient nuclear event that destroyed the Sumerian civilization and the power struggles of the "gods" that led up to it.

Living Souls in the Spirit Dimension

The Afterlife and Transdimensional Reality

by Chris H. Hardy, Ph.D.

In this exploration of consciousness, after-death communication, and near-death and out-of-body experiences, Chris H. Hardy reveals that all beings exist simultaneously in the material dimension and in the soul hyperdimension. She offers tested methods for accessing the soul dimension and explores what can be accomplished there, including communicating with those who exist beyond our own material world.